For God and Mammon

For God

Gunja SenGupta

and Mammon

Evangelicals and Entrepreneurs,

Masters and Slaves in

Territorial Kansas,

1854-1860

THE UNIVERSITY OF GEORGIA PRESS
Athens & London

© 1996 by the University of Georgia Press
Athens, Georgia 30602
All rights reserved
Designed by Walton Harris
Set in 11/14 Bodoni Book by Tseng Information Systems, Inc.
Printed and bound by Thomson-Shore, Inc.
The paper in this book meets the guidelines for
permanence and durability of the Committee on
Production Guidelines for Book Longevity of the
Council on Library Resources.

Printed in the United States of America

00 99 98 97 96 C 5 4 3 2 1

Library of Congress Cataloging in Publication Data

SenGupta, Gunja.
For God and Mammon : evangelicals and entrepreneurs,
masters and slaves in territorial Kansas, 1854–1860 /
Gunja SenGupta.
          p.   cm.
Includes bibliographical references and index.
ISBN 0-8203-1779-9 (alk. paper)
1. Kansas—History—1854–1861.   2. Antislavery move-
ments—Kansas.
I. Title.
F686.S46   1996
978.1'02—dc20   95-2804

British Library Cataloging in Publication Data available

Contents

Tables

Acknowledgments

I would not have dared venture into the intellectual exercise that grew into my 1991 dissertation at Tulane University, and subsequently this book, without the help of my professors, colleagues, friends, and family everywhere. I am indebted to Clifton H. Johnson for suggesting that I explore the role of the American Missionary Association in the antebellum Kansas conflict when I wandered into the Amistad Research Center in New Orleans eight years ago in search of a dissertation topic. To my dissertation adviser, Clarence L. Mohr, I will remain forever grateful for his invaluable guidance and encouragement at every stage of the manuscript's progress — and indeed my own development as a practitioner of American history. His magical knack for conjuring a meaningful argument out of my often nebulous, half-baked musings helped me crack many a thought-block in the past. To say that I owe him more than the suggestion of this book's subtitle, is a terrific understatement.

Larry N. Powell's stimulating graduate seminar on the Civil War and Reconstruction taught me a great deal of what I know about those subjects. His critique of my dissertation has influenced my thinking in important ways, as have Richard B. Latner's helpful comments. My other Tulane professors, especially Ralph Lee Woodward, Patrick J. Maney, Raymond A. Esthus, George Bernstein, and Colin MacLachlan, set high standards of scholarship for aspiring historians.

A grant from the Research Committee at East Texas State University funded a vital summer's research at the Kansas State Historical Society in Topeka. I thank the librarians, archivists, and their staffs at the Amistad Research Center, the Kansas State Historical Society, Washburn University at Topeka, the Western Historical Manuscript Collections at the University of Missouri, Kansas City, and the New York Public Library for their help with my research. The staff at the State Historical Society of Missouri at Columbia sifted through numerous manuscript collections to identify elusive historical figures whose fortunes I was attempting to reconstruct and arranged to transport those materials to Kansas City for my convenience. I also appreciate the prompt attention my requests received from the interlibrary loan offices at Tulane and East Texas State University.

I am indebted to William W. Freehling for his insightful suggestions for improving this book. Bill Cecil-Fronsman and Virgil Dean offered valuable critiques of the sections relating to the Christian abolitionists in Kansas. Karen Orchard and the entire staff at the University of Georgia Press have been wonderfully supportive of this project. I also thank John Hubbell and the Kent State University Press for permitting me to reproduce in chapters 2, 4, 5, and 6 of this book, portions of my article entitled " 'A Model New England State,' " published by *Civil War History* in its March 1993 issue, and Virgil Dean and the Kansas State Historical Society for allowing me to republish, in chapters 2, 4, and 5, segments of my article entitled "Servants for Freedom," which appeared in the autumn 1993 issue of *Kansas History*.

I am grateful to my friends and colleagues in East Texas, especially Frank Barchard for providing valuable practical lessons in the true meaning of those southern qualities my Yankee protagonists in Kansas rarely talked about: charm, graciousness, and hospitality. I am deeply indebted to Don Reynolds for his consistent encouragement of this project, including his suggestion of the book's main title. I also thank Harry Wade, Judy Ford, Ralph Goodwin, Robin Rudoff, and Joe Fred Cox for their enlightening conversations on American culture; Ty Cashion for his editorial comments on portions of this work; and Janice Connell for being there. Nandini Mookherjee and Nita Roy have served as my most patient sounding boards during moments of frustration, and Sunita Manian as my most incisive critic. Sabita Manian helped restore my flagging spirit during a crucial phase of the book's development. Jonie Varner and Elna Green have long been friends whose keen historical insights have often helped clarify my own thinking. Salim Darbar and Arna Seal provided great assistance during the early stages of this manuscript's preparation. Aloke Ghosh's unfailing love and loyalty, not to mention his computer expertise, saw me through every roadblock I encountered in the course of this project, whether intellectual, emotional, or technological. The exhortations of my parents and sister over the telephone from India propelled me toward the completion of this book sooner than I thought possible. My grandparents' enthusiasm for everything I do continues to keep me going. Without the love and moral support of all of them, I would not be a historian. It is to my family that I dedicate this book.

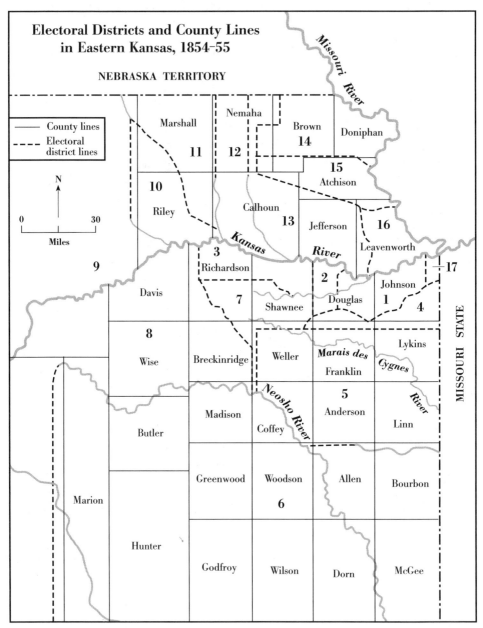

Map of Electoral Districts constituted in 1854 and county lines established in 1855, based on Map I, 1855, in collection of maps showing changes in counties and county boundaries in Kansas, 1855–60, Kansas State Historical Society Library, Topeka, Kansas, and published in Helen G. Gill, "The Establishment of Counties in Kansas," in *Kansas Historical Collections* 8 (1903–4): 449–72 and Russell K. Hickman, "The Reeder Administration Inaugurated," Part 1, *Kansas Historical Quarterly* 36 (autumn 1970): 314.

Electoral districts were created before the territorial legislature established county lines in 1855. Several county names and boundaries were subsequently changed.

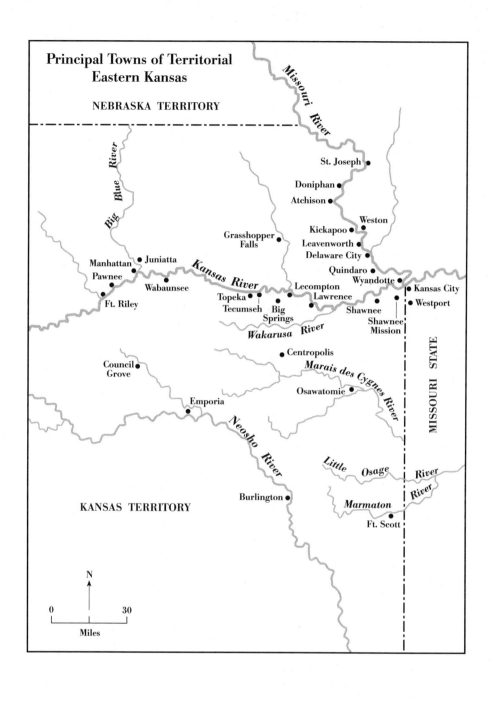

Principal Towns of Territorial Eastern Kansas

NEBRASKA TERRITORY

Missouri River

Big Blue River

St. Joseph

Doniphan

Atchison

Weston

Grasshopper Falls

Kickapoo

Leavenworth

Delaware City

Manhattan   Juniatta

Pawnee

Quindaro

Wyandotte

Kansas River

Wabaunsee

Lecompton

Kansas City

Ft. Riley

Topeka

Tecumseh   Big Springs

Lawrence

Westport

Shawnee

Wakarusa River

Shawnee Mission

Centropolis

MISSOURI STATE

Council Grove

Marais des Cygnes River

Osawatomie

Emporia

Neosho River

Little   Osage   River

Burlington

Marmaton   River

KANSAS TERRITORY

Ft. Scott

N

0   30

Miles

For God and Mammon

Introduction

In May 1854 the Kansas-Nebraska Act exploded on the U.S. political horizon, fueling a tide of emigration to Kansas Territory from all sections of Old America, ostensibly to settle the crucial question of slavery in the West on the principle of popular sovereignty. On July 17, 1854, a colony of New England emigrants left Boston for Kansas amid thunderous applause from cheering crowds that had lined the railway track for several blocks.[1] They were traveling under the auspices of a corporation later known as the New England Emigrant Aid Company (NEEAC), dedicated to securing freedom to Kansas and earning dividends for its bondholders through the organized emigration of free labor. This pioneer company of northeastern emigrants pitched its tents in the valley of the Kaw in August 1854, thus laying the foundation for the town of Lawrence, which went on to become the preeminent center of free-state activism in the territory.[2] Two months later, with much less fanfare than had accompanied the departure of the NEEAC contingent, Rev. Amos Finch, sent by the New York–based American Missionary Association (AMA) to advance the cause of abolitionism and racial justice on the frontier, made a quiet entry into Kansas and settled in Osawatomie, a free-state community at the source of the Osage River. Before long, the arrival of a cohort of clergymen sponsored by the moderately antislavery American Home Missionary Society (AHMS) added a somewhat conservative dimension to the evangelical assault on black bondage in territorial Kansas.[3]

Like the pioneers from the southern states and the Old Northwest who had preceded them, the NEEAC settlers and AHMS missionaries, as well as Reverend Finch, were no doubt prompted to emigrate in part by the desire to improve their personal fortunes. Nevertheless, there was a sincere ideological dimension to their mission in Kansas. For they were associated with organizations that represented, among them, the two major strains in American antislavery thought, namely, a color-blind religious-humanitarian impulse characterized by moral outrage at the slave's plight, and a concern for the economic welfare of white America based on the capitalist ideology of free labor. This book seeks to show how the compelling saga of Bleeding Kansas, refracted through the lens of this important coalition of northeastern evangelicals and entrepreneurs, broadened the appeal of antislavery politics in the free North on the eve of sectional conflict. At the same time, it attempts to reach behind free-state perceptions of the ruffianly Other to unravel the complex history of the South in Kansas: the ideology and experiences that animated and shaped the activism of its champions in the West; the contradictions between the strident optimism of proslavery rhetoric on the one hand and the precarious operation of the institution of slavery in the territory on the other. Yet however sharp the polarities of sectional discourse on human bondage, Yankee and Southerner in Kansas did not inhabit mutually exclusive, homogeneous worlds. A major concern of this book is to explore the northeastern free-staters' relationships with their western and southern free-soil allies and proslavery adversaries, in an attempt to draw attention not only to cleavages within the antislavery and the pro-Southern movements in Kansas but also to the shared interests and values among friends and foes of slavery that facilitated a surprising degree of intersectional cooperation both during and after the Kansas wars.

The free-state protagonists of this study represented a wide spectrum of opinion on human bondage, ranging from racially egalitarian Christian abolitionist absolutism on the one hand to free labor pragmatism on the other. Nevertheless, their diverse religious and secular critiques of slavery sprang ultimately from the optimistic notion of progress engendered by the evangelical and capitalist transformation of Northern society and linked with a "civilizing" mission to disseminate the values of that society among less advanced peoples, be they Southern slaveholders, Catholic immigrants, or western frontiersmen. Thus the northeastern opponents of slavery shared a common commitment to carry the torch of Yankee-style material, moral, and spiritual progress to the

West by planting free churches, schools, mills, towns, and other "tro-phies of free labor" on the untamed frontier, securing at the same time the future of America's republican experiment by guaranteeing to wage earners the opportunity of land ownership through diligent effort. The affirmation of Northern humanism, dynamism, and enterprise implicit in this broad definition of free-state goals legitimated antislavery politics in a way that Garrisonian abolitionism, with its indictment of American society as a fundamentally immoral institution, could never have done. Bleeding Kansas paved the path to the Civil War with compelling pub-lic images in the free states of civilization and savagery, freedom and dependence, North and South locked in mortal combat.[4]

Northeastern evangelicals and entrepreneurs in Kansas blended the liberal, individualist, yet nationalist language of progress with the imagery of power, liberty, and civic virtue resurrected from an earlier political tradition associated with the historic origins of the Ameri-can nation. Revolutionary republicanism, despite its eclipse from pub-lic discourse, had been woven into the fabric of antebellum North-ern culture through the institutional channels of schools and political parties.[5] In republican ideology, antislavery Kansans found a power-ful interpretative framework for making sense of territorial politics. From the free-state perspective, the Pierce Administration's endorse-ment of an illegitimate "mob-elected" proslavery legislature raised the real and alarming specter of "white slavery" reminiscent of eighteenth-century British tyranny. The resemblance between the subjugation of free-staters by a spurious legislature chosen and staffed by Missouri-ans foreign to Kansas soil at the behest of profligate slave masters in collusion with the national government on the one hand and the his-toric oppression of the revolutionary patriots by an unrepresentative British Parliament on the other was too striking to escape comment. Revolutionary language and imagery suffused the antislavery forces' conspiratorial references to the Slave Power's murderous plot against liberty, unraveling across the country from the plains of Kansas to the Senate chamber of a savagely brutalized dissenter. Washington's use of military force to disperse the free-state Topeka legislature invested sin-ister warnings about the fate of freedom in the nation with a credibility rooted in political memory of America's historical experience. The message was clear: New Englanders must salvage the republican experiment begun by their Pilgrim fathers—with "Beecher's Bibles" in the event that peaceful persuasion through free labor institutions failed. In this context, free-state blood spilled freely in liberty's defense became the very symbol of civic virtue, the epitome of self-sacrifice for the public, indeed national, good.[6]

A somewhat different, peculiarly Southern version of republicanism galvanized proslavery responses to the Yankee mission in Kansas. Republican apologists for slavery maintained that black bondage, by making race rather than money the mark of privilege, constituted the very basis of social and political democracy among white men in the South.[7] Southern republicanism upheld slavery as a guarantor of self-determination and personal independence essential to Southern honor. It often preached hostility to the encroachments of commercialism, becoming, in the words of historian Drew Gilpin Faust, "a political creed particularly appropriate to a South involved in a politics of cultural survival, defending itself against the onrush of modernity."[8]

To western Missouri's self-sufficient farmers, Yankee activities in Kansas, filtered through the prism of proslavery republicanism, assumed an ominous color. Many Missouri yeomen greeted the news of well-funded eastern ventures to "abolitionize" their neighborhood with much indignation, seeing it as an assault upon their independence and lifestyle by "foreigners." Their outrage was compounded by the impression that the tools of the Yankee abolitionist-capitalists in Kansas were a mob of "hired paupers" who were most unlikely to be repositories of republican virtue. For some of slavery's friends at least, the fight for Kansas transcended the dimensions of a narrow political crusade to become a defense of their most dearly prized values: independence and honor.[9] Clashing conceptions of republicanism, as much as the impelling power of Northern-style "progress," helped frame the terms of debate over slavery in territorial Kansas.

The contrapositions of political ideology, as well as the bloody responses they evoked in the West, however, obscured a more ambiguous reality. Key pro-Southern figures—no matter how "republican" their rhetoric—shared with their "abolitionist" foes a Whiggish concern for the economic future of their adopted home. Leading proslavery entrepreneurs, initially anxious to beat the Yankees at their own game through a combination of "fanaticism and money-making," ultimately abandoned fanaticism for money-making when the swelling tide of free-soilism made unconditional loyalty to slavery infinitely less worthwhile than the pursuit of Mammon. This book attempts to demonstrate how schisms within a competitive, business-minded proslavery leadership contained the seeds of commerce's triumph over political ideology in *some* proslavery circles. Prominent Mammon-worshipping critics of wage labor used some of the same tactics and appeals — fraudulent voting, appeals to anti-abolitionism, nativism, and racism — that were invoked against the "nigger thieves," to score points over their proslavery entrepreneurial rivals as well. In the end, for some Kansans, underlying commercial interests, not to mention a common commitment to white supremacy, provided ample grounds to bury the bowie knife and the Sharps rifle even before the slavery question had faded from the territory's political horizon, and facilitated a sectional truce at the expense of the Negro.[10]

This line of analysis must not be understood as a denial of fundamental differences between North and South in antebellum America. Whatever the degree to which such differences actually existed, the polarized public images conjured by Bleeding Kansas underscored the popular perception of North and South as mutually antagonistic civilizations.[11] Indeed, one of the principal objectives of this book is to trace the ideological roots of those images and explain their popular appeal, particularly in the free states, by showing how they resonated in the economic and cultural changes within antebellum Northern society. I do not suggest that the Civil War was anything but inevitable, or deny the real animosities that prompted the label Bleeding Kansas. Nor do I believe the free-state cause owed its victory in the territory principally to Mammon. I simply argue that the Kansas conflict was more multidimensional than a dichotomous portrayal of irreconcilable contending camps would imply. Moreover, to highlight the presence of common interests that eventually prevailed over moral and political convictions on chattel bondage in *some* proslavery circles, thereby *facilitating* rather than *causing* a rapprochement between several prominent former political adversaries is not to deny the fury of the Kansas tempest, but simply to

fascinating-
yes, we
wouldn't
be surprised at
the speed
of the
sectional
reunion

recognize its complexity. If the Kansas conflict presaged the Civil War, the sequel to it perhaps provides a clue to the impulses that prompted a relatively quick sectional reunion following Reconstruction in a nation torn, less than a generation before, by the bloodiest war in its history.

The rest of this prologue retraces, in as little detail as possible, the all-too-familiar path to the 1854 act that launched the Kansas civil war, and with it the Union, on the road to disruption.

The genesis of Bleeding Kansas lay, in part, in a fundamental mid-nineteenth-century shift in the terms of national political debate. Chattel bondage, that elemental mark of Southern identity, had usurped tariffs, banks, and federal spending on internal improvements as the dominant theme of political discourse, realigning partisan rivalry into sectional strife. America's Manifest Destiny to overspread and enlighten foreign realms had assumed dangerous sectional overtones. Many Southerners believed the expansion of slavery to be imperative to the survival of their civilization. The prospect of their "domestic" institution's confinement within its existing borders raised the specter of economic disaster, class conflict, and race war. The vindication of slave society—implicit in its extension into fresh lands—was, moreover, a point of Southern honor. By the end of the 1840s, however, a burgeoning politics of antislavery, rooted variously in moral and economic convictions, had targeted the virgin West as the battleground for freedom. The result was that Thomas Jefferson's metaphoric "firebell in the night" reached a bitter crescendo in national debate after debate over a host of vexatious issues ranging from slavery extension to the Mexican cessions of 1848, to Southern demands for an effective new fugitive slave law, throwing the second party system into deep disarray. In 1850 the American genius for compromise muted the din of sectional animosities briefly and superficially. Four years later, Jefferson's worst fears were realized when the "dangerous speck on the horizon" generated by debate over the Missouri Compromise of 1820 was propelled by the agreement's repeal to "burst like a tornado" upon a tenuous Union.[12]

The impulses behind the repeal of the Missouri Compromise are well known and need not be repeated at great length here. They proceeded in part from a dynamic people's never-ending quest for westward expansion and from a corollary interest in establishing communication links between Old America and the trans–Mississippi West by building a transcontinental railroad. Illinois Democrat Stephen A. Douglas, who presided over the Senate Committee on Territories, agreed that the nation's Manifest Destiny lay in bringing the whole continent under the progressive influence of white civilization. The organization of the territory west of Iowa and Missouri was also a necessary preliminary to the construction of a transcontinental railroad west from Chicago in Douglas's home state. Close as the senator was to the commercial interests of Illinois, he wanted to open up the Nebraska prairies, which afforded "a natural route to the Pacific" from his own state rather than allow rival claimants from New Orleans the right of way for the proposed railroad through the organized territory of New Mexico. The organization of Nebraska offered the additional bonus of advancing the Little Giant's own political fortunes as well as those of his party.

Douglas's continental vision, spelled out for a decade in bill after bill, died several deaths at the hands of Southern senators loath to organize Louisiana Purchase territory lying north of latitude 36°30' where slavery was forever prohibited by the Missouri Compromise. Southern acquiescence in Kansas-Nebraska required a concession to slave interests. Missouri's Democratic senator, David Rice Atchison, as the spokesman of the Missouri River valley's outnumbered slaveholders, was among the staunchest champions of those interests. Faced with an impending Senate race in 1855, the Missourian needed to build up political capital against a formidable prospective rival: the veteran St. Louis Democrat Thomas Hart Benton, who foreswore slavery agitation, for fear of disrupting not only the flow of white yeomen into the western plains, but the Union itself. After Southern senators thwarted Douglas's latest attempt to organize Nebraska in 1853, Atchison, in concert with a trio of his powerful F Street mess-mates in Washington—James M. Mason and Robert M. T. Hunter of Virginia, and Andrew P. Butler of South Carolina, chairs of the Senate Foreign Relations, Finance, and Judiciary Committees, respectively—offered the beleaguered Illinois Democrat a way out of the impasse. The men initiated a chain of cloakroom negotiations that culminated—with a decisive impetus from Kentucky Whig Archibald Dixon—in a bill that explicitly repealed the Missouri Compromise exclusion of slavery north of 36°30'. The final version of the Kansas-Nebraska Act, passed by Congress in May 1854, also organized the two territories of Nebraska and Kansas west of Iowa and Missouri and committed the question of slavery in those areas to the doctrine of popular sovereignty under which the settlers themselves would vote slavery "up or down."[13]

Douglas had hoped that his bill would "avoid the perils of . . . [sectional] agitation," by transferring the slavery issue from the political arena to "the arbitration of those who [were] immediately interested in, and alone responsible for, its consequences."[14] He was wrong. The repeal of the Missouri Compromise marked the beginning of the Union's end. As charges of a "criminal betrayal of sacred rights"—a "Slave Power conspiracy" against liberty and free labor—reverberated throughout the outraged North, the ailing second party system perished in the fallout from the explosive act. The sectional division of the Whig vote on the Kansas-Nebraska Act in Congress sealed the fate of the tottering Whig party. Nearly all Southern Democrats supported the bill. Although over half of all Northern Democrats voted in favor of the repeal, most of them failed to win reelection. This fact combined with the influx of Southern Whigs to give the "national" Democracy a distinctly Southern hue. Kansas-Nebraska completed the sectionalization of American politics by spurring the rise of various anti-Nebraska meetings that anticipated the emergence of a Northern antislavery Republican party.[15]

The wildfire of sectional antipathy ignited in the cloakrooms of Congress tore across the Republic, reportedly consuming effigies of Stephen Douglas together with much of the compromise sentiment the Little Giant represented, to nudge the prairies of Kansas Territory, where the spotlight of national attention now turned. There, a principal architect of the repeal, propelled by an uncertain political fate, was busy at work welding the potential and confirmed friends of black bondage on the Missouri River into a proslavery constituency large enough to sweep him back to the Senate either from Missouri, or failing that, from Kansas, which he would help bring into the Union as a slave state.[16] In this endeavor, David Atchison found faithful lieutenants in a pair of Weston, Missouri, law partners, the Virginia-born Democrat Benjamin Stringfellow and the Kentucky-born Whig Peter T. Abell.[17] These men, together with Stringfellow's physician brother, John, sought to weave the familiar ideological tools of planter hegemony into a proslavery appeal broad enough to bridge the chasm between Benton's constituents and those of Atchison, that is, between Missouri's non-slave-holding yeomen and its slave-owning planters. In this context, alarming news from the East — news that powerful Boston entrepreneurs had launched a heavily capitalized project to "abolitionize" Missouri's vicinity with the help of paid minions — became as effective a tool in rousing the republican sensibilities of that region's independent yeomen as in provoking the ire of its human property owners. Plenty of well-twisted hemp rope awaited the unfortunate arrivals from Yankeedom.

1

Appeal to the Census versus
Appeal to the Conscience

> We cross the prairies as of old
>   The Pilgrims crossed the sea,
> To make the West, as they the East,
>   The homestead of the Free.

—John Greenleaf Whittier

Kansas-bound pilgrims of liberty from the East were pioneers in more ways than one. They, among others of recent generations in the Western world, embodied a revolution in cultural consciousness that challenged centuries-old rationalizations for chattel bondage and simultaneously validated a new socioeconomic order emerging in the antebellum North. Fundamental cultural and economic changes within Northern society created a receptive climate for the arguments of nineteenth-century reformers who were driven by a variety of diverse impulses and experiences to join hands against an institution as old as human civilization itself. In this connection, historians have focused on the advent of two major, perhaps interrelated developments with far-reaching implications for the appearance of humanitarian awareness in general and antislavery in particular: the rise of industrial capitalism and, perhaps as a function of the discord generated by such profound economic transformation, the resurgence of evangelical Protestantism in North America.[1]

A vital strain of the abolitionist impulse stemmed from the religious revivals of the Second Great Awakening, which reached a peak in west-

ern New York in the 1820s under the able apostleship of Charles Grandison Finney. Finney preached a dynamic, romantic theology that forsook
the Calvinist concept of original sin for a faith in free will. Evangelical
Protestantism embraced an optimistic view of human nature based on
the notions of perfectionism and millenarianism. The demise of Calvinist fatalism and the shift to a gospel of disinterested benevolence
generated a missionary zeal to rid society of all sins, of which slavery
was the most grievous. Revivalism promoted the doctrine of spiritual in-
clusiveness, positing that master and slave, having undergone the same
conversion experience, were equal in God's sight. For one human being
to enslave another was, therefore, a gross violation of a "higher law" than
the nation's constitution. The new focus on personal agency in achieving
redemption, conviction in the perfectibility of society, and the faithful's
calling to realize it by working toward the societal expiation of all sins
combined to lay the evangelical foundation for immediatism in American antislavery thought. Its hopeful "vision of spiritual and personal
liberty" embodied in the progressive American Missionary Association
(AMA) and the more conservative American Home Missionary Society
(AHMS) helped define important elements of the free-state appeal in
Bleeding Kansas.[2]

Evangelical abolitionism, in its emphasis upon "an individualistic
ethic of personal self-government," was fully in accord with a system
of values concomitant with the rise of a new socioeconomic order in
the antebellum North. Historian Eric Foner has argued that in the
1820s and 1830s the federalist conception of an organic, hierarchical society gave way to a highly competitive, individualistic, market-
oriented North, thus providing an ideological framework conducive to
the development of an antislavery outlook. The language and aspirations
of an incipient, capitalist Northern society found their most articulate
expression in the Republican glorification of the middle class and economic independence. At the heart of an evolving Republican ideology
of free labor lay a conviction in the superiority of a dynamic, capitalist,
Northern society based on free labor over the stagnant slave society of
the South.[3]

Republican outlook exalted the dignity of labor, defined broadly as all
the "producing classes" —farmers, laborers, mechanics, and small busi-

nessmen. Yet with wage labor becoming a cornerstone of the emerging capitalist order, Republicanism also supplied a progressive rationale for such labor, traditionally despised as a mark of dependence destructive of republican virtue. It held out the prospect of upward mobility from wage-earning status to economic independence as the best incentive for diligent labor, and thus linked antislavery with laissez-faire—the ideal of a "free self-regulating market for labor."[4] Connected with the idea of social mobility was the ascription of personal success or failure to individual abilities rather than to impersonal social or economic forces. Republican ideology subscribed to the Protestant Ethic that glorified the qualities of "honesty, frugality, diligence, punctuality and sobriety" as essential to success in one's calling, but departed from that ethic in its focus on social mobility and economic growth in response to the dynamic, expansive transformation of antebellum Northern society. Implicit in its portrayal of Southern slave society as the mirror image of the progressive North was a severe and in the end politically compelling critique of chattel bondage in Northern eyes.[5]

Linked with the Republican critique of the South was the determination to secure America's western territories for freedom. The Republican portrait of Southern society in conjunction with the argument that free or inexpensive land in the West was essential for the maintenance of social mobility in the North helped ensure that the debate over the extension of slavery in the territories would be more than a narrow dispute over economic interests. The issue at stake was "whether the western social order would resemble that of the South or of the North," for the fate of millions of Americans hung on the nature of institutions being forged on the frontier.[6] For middle-class white Northerners, the ideological appeal of the battle for freedom in Kansas in the North stemmed in part from its recourse to the principles of free labor Republicanism. That ideology constituted the philosophical underpinnings of the New England Emigrant Aid Company (NEEAC)—an alliance that supplied a significant faction of the free-state political leadership in the territory.

The northeastern evangelicals and entrepreneurs in Kansas represented different degrees of radicalism on the antislavery spectrum, especially in their view of race relations. Nevertheless, their diverse religious and secular assaults upon black bondage stemmed from a shared faith in a version of what historian Howard Temperley called "an eighteenth-century belief in an improvable and progressively improving world." Dramatic economic changes fueled this optimistic outlook in the North. In the first half of the nineteenth century, the United States, through war and treaty with the French, the Spanish, the British, and the Mexicans, not to mention the Native Americans, had quadrupled the size of its national domain. The population doubled approximately every twenty-five years, aided by immigration on an unprecedented scale and supported by abundant natural resources as well as remarkable economic growth. After 1815 a revolution in transportation and communications encouraged regional specialization of production for an expanding national market. It also stimulated the growth of a factory system based on the division and specialization of labor and mass production by power-driven machines. By midcentury the soaring efficiency of American industry had given the United States the highest standard of living in the world.[7]

Such astounding material success generated a corresponding sense of confidence in the cultural attributes of the "miracle" section and a calling to carry those values—the recipe for success—to less fortunate realms. Many Northerners in the age of Manifest Destiny believed that the nation was ordained to play a leading role in "the progressive, dynamic process" that was history.[8] One Northern newspaper expounding on the "westward march of empire," editorialized that down the ages, progress in civilization had gone toward the setting sun and had culminated in the "discovery" of America:

> When Fulton launched his paddlewheels on the Hudson, and started off for Albany against wind and tide, America was just beginning to go. When the daguerreotype was perfected in New York, America was just beginning to see. . . . When Morse transmitted words hundreds of miles along a wire in a moment's time, America was just beginning to talk. It is no idle boast that we are 'Young America.' . . . Six thousand years have been spent in education, and now we are just entering upon our career.[9]

America was just coming into its own as a standard-bearer of light and civilization to the rest of the world. By the mid-nineteenth century, however, the vision of a triumphant national spirit sweeping all obstacles to Yankee-style material and moral progress from its westward path seemed threatened by the "great national curse of slavery" that had "practically ruined one-half of the nation." Kansas quickly became the focal point of a larger struggle that pitted Southern slave-holding interests against the free labor doctrines of men like Massachusetts entrepreneur, educator, and legislator Eli Thayer. At an anti-Nebraska meeting in Worcester, this future Republican congressman disclosed before an enthusiastic audience, his long-conceived plan to carry the "contest between Freedom and Slavery" out of legislative halls and into the prairies of the West. His proposed weapon was an emigrant aid company that would take to Kansas the "free labor trophies" of churches and schools, printing presses, steam engines, and mills, and "in a peaceful contest convince every poor man from the South of the superiority of free labor." [10]

The charter of Thayer's projected company, passed by the Massachusetts legislature and signed by the governor on April 26, 1854, created a corporation authorized to issue capital stock to an amount not exceeding $5 million. Thayer, through personal solicitation, drew the corporators of his proposed company from an influential coterie of Whiggish, unionist, anti-abolitionist industrialists, Free-Soil politicians, philanthropists, and moral reformers. They included, among others, Congressmen Stephen C. Phillips and Charles Allen; distinguished journalists C. Hazewell and Richard Hildreth; future governor of Massachusetts Alexander Bullock; future U.S. vice president Henry Wilson; philanthropist Samuel Grisewold Howe, who founded the Institution for the Blind in Boston; and temperance advocate Otis Clapp, "born of the best blood of New England." Three of these men—Hildreth, Bullock, and Clapp—joined Thayer and Edward E. Hale, a Unitarian minister of Worcester and one of the earliest recruits to the cause, in serving on a committee that reported a plan of organization for the company in May 1854. The original charter was laid aside because it elicited objections on the ground that it committed the stockholders to personal liability well beyond the amount of their actual investment. Instead, the corporators adopted a series of articles providing for the temporary organization of the Massachusetts Emigrant Aid Company as a private association under trustees, and opened books of subscription in Boston, Worcester, and New York.[11]

Immediately after, Thayer gave himself up to a whirlwind of meetings with "merchants in their counting rooms, businessmen upon the streets," and clergymen in the study of Theodore Parker, urging them to attend his promotional addresses at Chapman Hall in Boston. Thayer later wrote that he made the census of the United States his textbook and the basis of his appeals: "My themes were the commercial, industrial, and economic disadvantages of slavery. These arguments were effective with the Northern people. Such interests . . . more than any pity for the African, impelled the West to fight for the outlet of the Mississippi river." Toward the end of one of his Chapman Hall meetings, a man in the rear of the room rose and offered a subscription of ten thousand dollars toward the capital stock of the company. He was John M. S. Williams, of the business firm of Glidden and Williams, a Virginian by birth. Charles Francis Adams, son of John Quincy Adams, followed suit with a contribution of twenty-five thousand dollars. The company had already found yet another bulwark of financial support in its future treasurer, Amos A. Lawrence, the forty-year-old heir to the business establishment that founded the towns of Lawrence and Lowell, Massachusetts. One of the Chapman Hall meetings became the occasion for the beginning of a long and fruitful association between Thayer and Charles Robinson, a physician from Fitchburg, Massachusetts, who in August 1854 became the company's general agent in Kansas at an annual salary of one thousand dollars and subsequently the free-state governor of the territory. Favorably impressed with the countryside of Kansas during an earlier visit through the Mississippi valley en route to California, Robinson accepted a commission from the company to explore the territory with the objective of selecting suitable sites for colonization.[12]

In July 1854 the old articles of association, revised under the title Articles of Agreement and Association, became the basis for the official organization of an unincorporated joint-stock company with a capitalization of two hundred thousand dollars under the charge of a triumvirate of trustees consisting of J. M. S. Williams, Eli Thayer, and Amos Lawrence. Dr. Thomas Webb of Providence, a science and history enthusiast, and author of the influential pamphlet *Information for Kansas Emigrants,* became the secretary of the company; Lawrence was elected treasurer. In February 1855 a new charter authorized by the Massachusetts legislature incorporated the enterprise as the New England Emigrant Aid Company, with a capitalization of $1 million, and introduced organizational changes. John Carter Brown, head of the merchant house of Brown and Ives of Providence, Rhode Island, and benefactor of Brown University, lent the organization the prestige of his name by consenting to assume its presidency.[13]

Before long, the NEEAC launched a campaign to disseminate information about Kansas among prospective emigrants through promotional tours, pamphlets, and the columns of sympathetic publications. Echoing the free labor exaltation of the dignity of labor, the *Herald of Freedom*, the Kansas newspaper established in October 1854 as the official organ of the NEEAC in order to combat "the advancing hordes of Southern chivalry and their human chattels with the aid of the press," proclaimed labor to be "a necessity and a duty, . . . among the great blessings of man," and urged the East to send forth "500,000 farmers, mechanics, and artisans." Kansas offered a perfect opportunity for wage earners to realize the free labor dream of property ownership through individual effort. "The whole prosperity of the country hangs on the cordial cooperation of labor and capital," the *Herald* opined. Of what use was a mill without persons to attend to it, or a manufactory without mechanics? On the other hand, what could a mechanic accomplish without tools? The NEEAC organ quoted Gov. Andrew H. Reeder as saying, "The stone mason, bricklayer, carpenter, plasterer, laborer, and lime burner can lay the foundation of a fortune here the first year. We shall pay out in the territory nearly a million dollars in building and a man can be earning the highest wages, and getting a good farm at $1.25 an acre." Every man from New England who preempted 160 acres of land would "close up so much of soil against slave labor" and win the twin objectives of economic independence for himself and freedom for the territory, and hence "commerce for the east." The rise in real estate value of localities where cities sprang up "almost by the touch of enchantment" around the NEEAC's mills, schools, and churches was expected to yield a profit on the company's investments.[14]

The NEEAC would protect prospective homesteaders from the "stupendous system of knavery" operated by "runners" and other travel agents. It would provide emigrants with low fares, inexpensive food, and shelter while they were building permanent homes, as well as advice on acquiring valuable claims. The immediate introduction of a variety of mechanical arts among the settlers, as well as a company-sponsored press, school, and church, would prevent the forfeiture of their children's "morals and intelligence" by the "life of semi-barbarism" characteristic of the West. The civilizing mission of Thayer's venture was particularly significant in light of his expectation that the emigrants would consist largely of lower-class European immigrants and the poorer population of the eastern cities. The organized emigration of free labor would serve the cause of the nation at large by creating "a cordon of the sons of liberty to the Gulf of Mexico" who would furnish a market for the manufactures of the "commercial states." Thayer underscored the importance of founding new and free states bound forever to Massachusetts by "the strongest ties of gratitude and filial love: . . . especially will it prove an advantage to Massachusetts if she creates the new state by her foresight—supply the first necessities to its inhabitants, and open in the outset, communications between their homes and her ports and factories." [15]

On behalf of the trustees of the company, Lawrence instructed Robinson to recommend prospective appointees to serve as local agents in territorial towns—men who had an honorable standing in the community, but not "prominent politicians, especially not abolitionists." Strongly unionist, the men who steered the ship of organized emigration in New England had little sympathy with abolitionism, especially of the disunionist brand. Implicit in the philosophy of their enterprise was the aspiration to mold the South and the West in the image of the progressive Northeast. As Samuel C. Pomeroy, an agent of the company in Kansas wrote, "the hope and expectation is that this system will extend the institutions and society of the East to the more fertile prairies of the West." According to the *Herald,* the company knew "neither North, South, East, or West to the exclusion of the remainder." The *Herald* echoed one of the assumptions underlying the experiment in free labor when it asserted, "Remove the [poor, non-slave-holding] population of the South to Kansas and let them see labor made honorable, as it is among the pioneers from the North and the East, and there is no doubt many persons thus sent out would give their votes for making Kansas free."[16]

Thayer's attitude toward the "latter day fanatics," as he called the Garrisonian abolitionists, reflected the relatively conservative character of his program and the suspicion, indeed outright hostility, with which the Northern business class regarded William Lloyd Garrison and all that he stood for.[17] Commenting on alleged abolitionist attempts to incite servile insurrection, Thayer wrote thirty-five years after the curtain had closed on Appomattox, "they appear . . . to have desired to demonstrate with their characteristic logic their love for the African by making him a murderer. . . . If their gusty fury had only possessed cyclonic power, they would have wrecked the government, abolished the pulpit and the church, and shattered into fragments the civilization of this continent." Amos Lawrence, "the soul of the enterprise," was one of those Boston "cotton Whigs" whose experiment with organized emigration was seen by historian Thomas H. O'Connor as a "well-planned and seriously organized attempt by political conservatives to stop the spread of slavery without causing the disruption of the Union." As O'Connor pointed out, the cotton Whigs of Massachusetts had a great stake in the preservation of the Union. Their mills fed on Southern cotton, while the fortunes of Northern bankers and shippers were inextricably bound with the prosperity of the cotton kingdom. Ties of personal friendship and even kinship frequently cemented the economic relations between the cotton interests of the two sections. Thus, conservative Bostonians were apt to indict Garrisonian demands of immediate, unconditional, and uncompensated emancipation for jeopardizing the Union, and with it the economic stability of the nation.[18]

Nor did most of them find much common ground on the question of race with the abolitionists who professed, even if they did not always practice, the ideal of racial egalitarianism. When the Reverend Hale communicated the plans of organized emigration to T. H. Cunningham, a respectable citizen of Boston, the latter responded:

> I shall be very glad to see such a society as the one of which you speak set on foot in a proper manner, for it would do much good

independently of any political and moral question. . . . But I have no sympathy with abolitionism. As a great evil I detest slavery, but what will you do with the blacks when it is abolished? They cannot hold their own, and if given a fair land, would ruin it and relapse into African barbarism. I have the same kind of antipathy, although not so great in degree, to a black man or woman, that I have to a monkey.[19]

George W. Brown, the publisher of the Kansas *Herald of Freedom,* wrote Hale that it was not his intention to "engage in a slavery discussion." His primary objective was to furnish eastern friends facts and figures about Kansas. "If the country is desirable," he went on, "I trust there will be a heavy emigration, and through its instrumentality we will secure freedom to Kansas." The *Herald* maintained that immediate and unconditional abolition would destroy the master, and turn the slave "loose upon the world, ignorant, and wholly unqualified for the responsible duties of life." [20]

Garrison apparently did not like the leaders of organized emigration any more than they liked him. The *Boston Liberator* took the *Herald* to task for its disclaimer of abolitionist principles and for its espousal of emancipation through the apprenticeship system after the fashion of Pennsylvania and the Northern states. Garrison deprecated the NEEAC's scheme as visionary. The eastern emigrants themselves did not escape the ire of the fiery abolitionist's pen. He declared that freedom in Kansas was a lost cause because, among other reasons, most settlers were not emigrating "to be martyrs in the cause of the enslaved negro, nor to sacrifice their chance for a homestead on the altar of principle, but to find a comfortable home for themselves and their children." While in the East, these men and women "gave little countenance to the antislavery cause at home . . . and they were poisoned more or less with the virus of colorophobia. If they had no pluck here, what could rationally be expected of them in the immediate presence of the demoniacal spirit of slavery?" [21]

Whatever Garrison's misgivings about the NEEAC, organized emigration won, for the most part, the endorsement of organized religion in the North. While free labor advocates decried chattel bondage as

an impediment to material progress, many Northern evangelicals opposed slavery for undermining the nation's claim to be the vanguard
of worldwide spiritual advancement. Not all of them, of course, agreed
on the wisdom of immediate, unconditional, and universal abolition, or
on the means of accomplishing that goal. The New York–based American Home Missionary Society, founded by the merger of Presbyterian,
Congregational, Dutch Reformed, and Associate Reformed churches
in 1826 to pioneer the evangelization of America on a national scale,
favored a gradualist approach to emancipation. Indeed, as a national
organization, the AHMS avoided making any definite pronouncement
on the fractious issue of slavery until the growing strength of antislavery sentiment in the society's financial strongholds in the North and
West, coupled with the withdrawal of support by the Southern churches,
forced its hand on the question in the mid-1850s. In response to a series
of questions relating to the organization's stand on slavery put forth in
1844 by Lewis Tappan, celebrated merchant, philanthropist, and antislavery leader of New York, AHMS secretary Milton Badger replied that
the society drew only a small part of its support from the slave states,
where it maintained no soliciting agents. It issued its missionaries living
in the South no special instructions to preach against slave-holding and
as an eleemosynary institution reserved no power to lay down terms of
church or ministerial fellowship.[22]

Such equivocation on a profound moral issue deeply disturbed a
band of radical evangelical abolitionists, profoundly influenced by the
Finney revivals. In 1846 this predominantly Congregational group created a new society, the American Missionary Association, to protest
against the AHMS's prevarication on black bondage. William Jackson,
a distinguished businessman, antislavery politician, philanthropist, and
reformer from Newton, Massachusetts, became the first president of
the organization. George Whipple served as its corresponding secretary
as well as the chief editor of its official organ, the *American Missionary*. A "Lane Rebel," Whipple had completed his theological training
under Charles Grandison Finney and John Morgan at Oberlin College.[23]
Simeon Smith Jocelyn, the former pastor of a Negro Congregational
church in New Haven, Connecticut, became the AMA's secretary of

home missions in 1853. Lewis Tappan assumed charge of the association's treasury.[24]

These men steered the AMA along what historian Clifton Johnson has described as a "Christian abolitionist" course on the slavery issue. Unlike the antichurch abolitionists of the Garrisonian brand, who advocated the severance of all connections with the allegedly corrupt organized religions, the Christian abolitionists worked to reform churches immediately and completely from within by excommunicating slaveholders. Indomitably committed to racial egalitarianism, they castigated the AHMS's acquiescence in Negro pews and segregated communion services in Northern churches. At its tenth annual meeting in Fulton, New York, in September 1856, the AMA declared, "Nothing is more evident than that God has connected the destiny of this nation with its treatment of the colored man . . . [and] we may expect the Divine blessing in our efforts to maintain free institutions only as we require them for all." The Christian abolitionists were equally critical of the American Colonization Society, which they suspected was the brainchild of Southern masters wishing to rid the country of free blacks. "I cannot," the association organ asserted, "as a servant of Jesus Christ, afford any aid to a countryman, be he white or black, to find a home in another country where his opportunities will be diminished for becoming a Christian." [25]

In their attitude toward African Americans, the Christian abolitionists of the AMA represented the most progressive fringe of the variegated antislavery spectrum in the North. Yet as firm believers in the efficacy of political and constitutional mechanisms for the redress of national wrongs, they did not subscribe to the Garrisonian critique of American society as a fundamentally flawed institution in which slavery constituted only the worst sin. Instead, these reformists maintained that slavery was an anomaly in a basically good though divided society, which abolitionism would unite and strengthen by removing a deviant feature. The leaders of the AMA, many of them men of substance, shared in important respects the outlook of an evolving Republican worldview that celebrated the materialism, social fluidity, and enterprise of a prosperous Northern social order based on "the dignity and opportunities of free labor." The evangelical abolitionists shared with other supporters of the free labor doctrine a commitment to bring the "wild West" under the progressive influence of Yankee civilization.[26]

In contrast to the AMA's commitment to immediatism, the antislavery Christians of the AHMS supported gradualism. Despite its "very correct abstract views of the evil of slavery," the society continued to aid slave-holding congregations on the ground that it would be easier to reform masters who remained within the church than those who were beyond church influence. The sectional polarization of opinion on slavery in the tumultuous decade before the Civil War, however, compelled the AHMS to take a tougher line against the South's peculiar institution than it had previously done. In 1850 it upheld its missionaries' right to deliver antislavery sermons in accordance with the dictates of their conscience. In 1853 it denied missionary commissions to slaveholders, although it continued to concede their Christian status. The same year, the Albany Congregational Convention's passage of an antislavery resolution became the occasion for a protracted debate among antislavery evangelicals over the AHMS's position on slavery. The society argued in its own defense that the only evidence for the charge that it aided the system of slavery by "supplying it with the sanctions of religion" was that it paid part of the expenses of preaching the Gospel in the slave states in some "forty or fifty cases." The *American Missionary* countered that Christian abolitionists objected not to preaching the Gospel in the slave states but to preaching a "partial Gospel," as well as failing to discipline church members guilty of perpetuating slavery in any manner whatsoever: "There are . . . many that take no interest in the welfare of the slave who will be ready enough to declare their satisfaction with [the AHMS's] present position. Let no Christian abolitionist be among their number." [27]

Although the AMA denounced the AHMS for its ambiguity on the subject of black bondage, it shared the society's vision of an evangelical version of Manifest Destiny. Both groups agreed that the spiritual regeneration of the American nation was a prerequisite for the deliverance of the world to Christ. At the eighth annual meeting of the AMA, the association's secretary of home missions, Simeon S. Jocelyn, highlighted the intricate relationship between his nation's destiny, the character of the association's home missions, and their relevance to the Christianization of the world.[28] Likewise, the American Home Mission Society recognized "something remarkable" in the history of the American people, which singled them out as "privileged with a high Christian destiny." The very position of the American continent on the globe, "extending from sea to sea, grasping the commerce of two oceans, taking hold with powerful hand of all the three elder continents" bore testimony to its unique mission. So did the remarkable career of the prosperous race that inhabited it, observed the Rev. Azariah Eldridge of New Bedford, Massachusetts, in an address before the AHMS in 1853. "By the direction of Providence," he observed, "[this remarkable race] poured down from their home in the North, with broad breasts bare, white limbs agile and forceful, yellow locks streaming to the wind, and the mistress of the world [ancient Rome] was swept from her eminence before them." England owed her prominence in the family of nations to the members of this chosen race, he went on. When at last the same people crossed the Atlantic to occupy the Western Hemisphere, they launched America on its meteoric rise to world power status. "This race . . . is in the ascendant among mankind," he continued. "The Lord chooses to preserve it and cause it to flourish. Black men bow down, red men fade away before it. . . . Shall not Saxon America, whose enterprising citizens are abroad over land and sea . . . filling the whole world already with her influence, shall she not be evangelized? . . . If thoroughly evangelized, we might . . . standing here do nothing but shine, like a city set on a hill and the whole world would slowly become full of light."[29]

From the evangelical perspective, the South's peculiar institution posed a twofold problem. In the first place, slavery was totally contrary to Christian morality, an obstacle to the salvation of the poor slaves' immortal souls, a corrupter of their masters' morals, and as such, a sin that required national expiation. Second, the acquiescence of a Christian nation in such gross violation of the "higher law" weakened the credibility of the evangelical cause abroad and did incalculable harm to the image of the Christian religion in non-Christian eyes.[30]

Thus, when the "heartless Slave Power conspirators" attempted to cast their sinful net over the western "Eden of the world" by overturning the Missouri Compromise, the evangelicals championed a movement of "Christian Emigration" to assist the various eastern emigrant aid companies in their endeavor to settle the endangered West with free labor. The pages of the *American Missionary* and the *Home Missionary*, the official organs of the AMA and the AHMS, respectively, resounded with vivid descriptions of the "fair heritage" awaiting worthy settlers in Kansas territory: bountiful prairies, trout-filled rivers, and green beltings of timber. It would be a "burning shame" to allow "this fair heritage" to "degenerate into another Virginia." By 1859, when Bleeding Kansas had ceased to be the talk of the nation, the AMA had commissioned eight missionaries and the AHMS fourteen, to wage a two-pronged battle against the "twin evils of slavery and Romanism" in the territory.[31]

Rev. Charles B. Boynton, editor of the *Christian Press* and secretary of the American Reform Book and Tract Society, used the columns of the *American Missionary* to make an emphatic plea for the predominance of the religious element in the forthcoming struggle for freedom in Kansas. It was imperative that organized emigration be no less than Christian emigration—true Christians moving as missionary colonies and planting churches at important points with "strong, capable men at their heads. . . . They would at once be radiating points of influence and centers around which society would form itself."[32] For the Christian abolitionists believed that the will of God would determine the ultimate outcome of the crusade for a free Kansas.

The AHMS argued that planting Christian colonies in Kansas would yield rich dividends not only from a moral standpoint, but also in pecuniary terms. The society suggested that each westbound minister gather about him a small company of "staunch men and good families," who would secure and settle a large tract of land and organize a church and school to nourish their evolving community. The advantages offered by the institutions of civilized society and those arising from the sobriety and intelligence of the original settlers would attract a superior class of emigrants: "all of the right sort receive a warm welcome, and they are ready, of course, to pay a somewhat higher price for their lands, for the sake of such good neighborhood. If speculators and other undesirable persons apply for land also, there is 'none to sell,' and so the original advantages of the community remain unimpaired, until it has acquired a fixed character and strength to maintain it against all comers." Indeed, as far as the settlers from New England were concerned, a major advantage of migrating in parties under the auspices of the emigrant aid companies derived from the opportunity to select their neighbors. One such emigrant wrote the editor of the *Herald of Freedom* that but for his association with the NEEAC he might have found himself in "a settlement of Dutch or Irish not at all agreeable." [33]

Meanwhile, the exhortations of the missionary bodies were beginning to bear fruit. In response to an advertisement in the *American Missionary* inviting correspondence from ministers interested in accompanying colonies to Kansas or Nebraska, the Oberlin-educated clergymen Samuel L. Adair and Amos A. Finch wrote the AMA expressing their desire to serve the cause of freedom in the territory. Adair was first commissioned by the AMA as pastor of the Congregational Church at Lafayette, Ohio, in November 1851, and was a life member of the association. Finch had been affiliated with the Wesleyan Methodist Conference of Michigan for about five years when he transferred to Cedar Falls, Iowa, in 1853; there he "labored with his hands and preached on the Sabbath." In October 1854 the AMA appointed both ministers to further its goals in Kansas, pledging $500 a year in aid to Adair and $350 to Finch. A month later it commissioned the Rev. John H. Byrd, formerly its missionary at Sicily, Ohio, to supplement the efforts of Finch and Adair in the territory at an annual salary of $500.[34]

From Lafayette, Ohio, Adair reported that the organization in August 1854 of the Kansas Emigration Aid Association of Northern Ohio at Oberlin—very likely inspired by the example of the Massachusetts company—had excited much local interest. Even so, "substantial farmers— the bones and sinews of a colony for religious enterprise, . . . men of religious principle and property" were hesitant to emigrate to a territory whose prospects lay shrouded in uncertainty. The minister was prevented from traveling to Kansas with the Oberlin company as he had originally planned by the delay in getting the enterprise under way. Instead, the Adair family joined the second colony of emigrants sent out by the NEEAC in September 1854 at Chicago.[35]

Adair's wife, Florella, and their seven-year-old-daughter went ahead

to St. Louis by railroad with a group conducted by Aid Company agent
Charles H. Branscomb at the customary reduced rate secured for the
transportation of emigrants by the company.[36] When the NEEAC party
continued its journey to Kansas City by steamboat on the Sabbath, Florella refused to acquiesce in this violation of the Lord's Day, staying
on in St. Louis until the following Tuesday. The Reverend Adair and
his twelve-year-old son arrived in St. Louis two weeks later, on October 20.[37] The *American Missionary* registered a strong protest against the
Aid Company's disregard for the sanctity of the Sabbath: "it grieved us,
it grieved ministers here, . . . it weakened the moral influence of the
whole scheme and discredited New England," whereupon the president
of the company assured the AMA that the violation of the Sabbath was
against the known wishes of his organization.[38]

At Kansas City the Aid Company contingent acquired a valuable
addition to its ranks in the person of the Rev. Samuel Y. Lum. A former
student of Oberlin College and the Union Theological Seminary, Lum
was pastor of the Congregational Church in Middleton, New York, when
he received a commission from the AHMS to preach in Kansas.[39] The
home missionary subsequently merged his fortunes with those of the
NEEAC settlers and aided them in founding the free-state stronghold
of Lawrence. Kansas City on the western border of Missouri was the
point where the forwarding agents of the Aid Company received, stored,
and reshipped freight and baggage belonging to the settlers, and served
as "bankers in cashing and forwarding drafts drawn on the company
by its general agents." [40] The company-owned Gillis Hotel offered weary
pioneers of free-state sentiments a welcome respite from their travels.

Kansas City was also the headquarters of the company's financial
agent in Kansas, Samuel C. Pomeroy. A member of an established family
of Southampton, Massachusetts, Pomeroy had, by the time his association with the company began in August 1854, dabbled in antislavery
politics. He had played a role in the formation of the Liberty Party
and served as a Free-Soiler in the Massachusetts legislature.[41] It was
at Kansas City that prospective settlers, armed with Pomeroy's advice
on suitable settlement sites, left their families in the safety of Missourian towns and embarked on trips of exploration in the wilderness
beyond. For Kansas City was, as the *Herald* noted, "the landing place

of the emigrants to Kansas—the point where they left steamboats and all public conveyances behind, and taking covered wagons, went on to build homes in the unbroken prairies beyond." [42] For prospective homesteaders who arrived in this Missouri River port, the western adventure had truly begun.

2

"Wolves of the Border" and Other Men of the "Wrong Stripe": The South in Kansas—1

While the bulwarks of Yankee-style morality and freedom were taking shape in the vicinity of Lawrence and Topeka, proslavery colonies rooted in unabashed commercialism and political ambition sprang up to the north and the east.[1] The slaveholders' Kansas strategy hinged on what they saw as beating the "abolitionists" at their own game by combining "fanaticism and moneymaking" in a variety of ventures ranging from illegitimate invasions of territorial polls to Yankee-like movements of colonization through joint-stock emigrant aid companies.[2] Before long, however, the profit incentive vanquished, or at any rate severely dimmed, ideological zeal in several proslavery strongholds. If, as one writer has suggested, "the southern program depended upon making Kansas a country of large estates" conducive to coerced gang labor, the frenetic proslavery business activity in the territory gave no indication of it.[3] Along the Missouri border through the length of the new land, friends of the South founded towns that competed vigorously with each other as well as with free-state enterprises for settlers, railroads, and trade, at the expense of political principle in some cases. In the attempt to out-Yankeeize the Yankee, some of the most vigilant defenders of slavery abandoned their fanaticism and embraced instead not only moneymaking but, occasionally, alliances with its most skilled practitioners, the hated Yankees themselves. This installment of the Southern saga in Kansas discusses the makings of the violent prelude to that ultimate rapprochement. In the process it seeks to shed some light on the dynamics of proslavery activism leading to the establishment of a Missouri-elected territorial government in Kansas. At the same time it attempts to demonstrate the potential of cleavages within a business-minded pro-Southern leadership for fostering intersectional relationships grounded in economic interest. In other words, the following story highlights aspects of the proslavery phenomenon that contributed to the ferocity of sectional conflict in Kansas Territory, as well as those that made eventual reconciliation possible.

The settlements of Atchison and Leavenworth on the western bank of the Missouri River became prime players in the intra-proslavery race for economic success and political influence. The roots of that rivalry reached into the same deeply divided political soil of Missouri that helped spawn the repeal of the 1820 Compromise itself. David Atchison, in pursuit of a Senate seat from either Missouri or Kansas, burst upon the frontier in a flurry of proslavery activism in the summer of 1854. A hard contest awaited him on the undulating playing field across the Missouri River. As though he did not have enough opposition to contend with from the East, a group of entrepreneurs from his very own Weston, more Bentonite than Atchisonian, beat him to some of the finest land in the new territory to found its first town—Leavenworth. In June 1854 thirty-two Weston citizens, including three ministers, four lawyers, five doctors, two printers, four merchants, one surveyor, two army officers, one army clerk, and the rest farmers, laid out a settlement three and a half miles below the government military post of Fort Leavenworth on the right bank of the Missouri, where elm-covered bluffs sloped westward into gently rolling prairie, interrupted by an occasional hill. This fertile, well-drained country had long attracted the attention of Missouri border counties like Platte. News of the Delaware Indians' cession of this country to the federal government by treaty in May 1854 triggered a "land rush" from the Missouri border, even before the ceded lands had been surveyed, much less auctioned off to the highest bidder as the treaty required.[4]

The Yankee minister Charles B. Boynton, on a trek through the Nebraska country, reported that more than twelve hundred "squatter sovereigns" had "set up their thrones" on the Delaware lands. The seat of this squatter kingdom was the town of Leavenworth, which, one month before the sale of town lots in October, boasted "one steam-engine, naked as when it was born, but at work sawing out its clothes . . . four tents, all on one street, a barrel of water or whiskey under a tree, and a pot, on a pole over the fire. Under a tree, a type-sticker had his case before him, and was at work on the first number of the new paper [the *Kansas Herald*], and within a frame, without a board on side or roof, was the editor's desk and sanctum."[5]

Support of this pioneer town building project transcended sympathies on the thorny slavery issue. Not all original town-company proprietors favored Dixie's peculiar institution; among the dissenters was Frederick Starr, an AHMS clergyman originally from Rochester, New York. Starr returned to the East under proslavery pressure in the early stages of the Kansas conflict, but his fellow New York–born Leavenworth proprietor and secretary of the board of directors, H. Miles Moore, not only stayed but went on to make a mark in Kansas free-state politics. Moore had studied law at Rochester, New York, and practiced his craft in Louisiana before moving to Weston, Missouri, where he served on the editorial board of the *Weston Reporter*. Along the way he acquired a few slaves. Moore had not been in the territory long, however, before he abandoned his original pro-Southern position for free-state activism.[6]

Leavenworth's proslavery connections did not deter territorial governor and future free-state leader Andrew Reeder from reserving shares in the town-company, which, according to H. Miles Moore, he never paid for, any more than he fulfilled his promise to make Leavenworth territorial capital: "The boys often laughed about the trick—that Reeder had Yankeed the trustees out of those town shares."[7] Notwithstanding its proslavery reputation, the town of Leavenworth appeared anxious not to sacrifice economic interest to political principle. The *Leavenworth Register* warned "fanatics either from the North or South, East or West" to keep away and called upon "businessmen with capital, farmers with cattle . . . , enterprising young men, mechanics, especially brick makers, plasterers and stone masons" to make homes in the community.[8]

From the Atchisonian perspective, Leavenworth's attempt to project a neutralist image was disconcerting, not only for its potential impact on Atchison's political fortunes but also as a threat to the senator's economic interests in the territory. The town's appropriation of some of the "best lands" across the river, coupled with the commercial advantages that might ensue from a nonpolitical position made Leavenworth a formidable rival to the town the Atchisonians founded in July, named, appropriately enough, after the Southern knight-errant himself. Atchison town fathers Benjamin and John Stringfellow and Peter T. Abell soon busied themselves providing for their new enterprise all the accoutrements that distinguished a "real" town from a "paper" town: a store, a ferry, a hotel, a newspaper, and a railroad charter. The Missourian George Million, recipient of a thousand-dollar share in the town-company in exchange for his claim on the townsite, had long operated a flatboat ferry on the Missouri. Indeed, it was his ferry that transported the Challis brothers, future Kansas businessmen, accompanied by Abell, to Atchison to survey the prospects of building a store there. George T. and Luther Challis, natives of Imlaystown, New Jersey, more recently clerks in a dry goods store at Booneville, Missouri, promptly accepted Abell's offer of a town lot and fulfilled their side of the bargain by building a cottonwood store in the upcoming town. Other saviors from the evanescent fate of "paper towns" soon emerged: a hotel, several stores, shops, and saloons and a virulently proslavery newspaper, the *Squatter Sovereign*.[9]

The Atchisonians' Whiggish taste for business was not entirely out of character, despite the distaste they evoked among pro-Benton commercial interests in St. Louis. In Missouri's contentious pre-Nebraska political world, Atchison had apparently shared a somewhat ambivalent relationship with the soft-wing of the Missouri Democracy, which in collusion with States' Rights Whigs attempted to use "Bourbon Dave" in their bid to foil the reelection of "Old Bullion Benton" to the U.S. Senate in 1844.[10] Whether Atchison remained immune to the Soft's wooing, he appears to have shared a close relationship with at least one prominent Whig-turned-Know-Nothing physician who held extensive property in western Missouri.

Anxious to prevent the infliction of the "gold standard on this country . . . thereby put[ting] the dollar above the man" through "the hallucinations of Tom Benton," John Gano Bryan played a leading role in the Whig-Softs-engineered supersession of Old Bullion by a proslavery Whig candidate, Henry S. Geyer, in January 1851. An entrepreneur with wide-ranging interests in railroads, town development, mining, and banking, the doctor counseled Southerners "to place factories in the South" as the best way to deal with the tariff question: "then we will all become Protectionists, and the wealth created in the South will remain there instead of flowing northward." This Henry Clay Whig–colonizationist appears not only to have had a hand in Atchison's political ascendancy in the 1840s but also to have supported his cause in Kansas with men, money, and arms. For emancipation without deportation would bring upon the United States the fate of "every country in the world that was ever cursed by negro slaves," the doctor claimed. "The negro always eats up the man through the crime of amalgamation, and the country loses its civilization, its manhood and its sciences, so soon as the kink in the hair, the low receding forehead, the flattened nose and the swarthy skin disfigures the more perfect of the human race." [11]

It was perhaps the Soft's rumored affinity for Atchison that, in the wake of the Nebraska bill, prompted talk of a Whig-Atchison alliance in the Senate race of 1855. The charter of the Bank of Missouri was due to expire in 1857, and the Whigs wished to have it renewed. Whig circles began to reverberate with reports of a "sell out, lock stock and barrel" on the part of St. Louis Whigs. "Bank and niggerism" would, one Whig feared, "put Atchison in." Yet Benton's commercial home turf of St. Louis was distinctly uncomfortable with Atchison's extreme pro-Southern position. [12]

Indeed the political grapevine had it that Old Bullion was prepared to forsake his commitment to bullionism in an attempt to thwart an "antis [anti-Benton] Whig" alliance. One Whig wrote another: "You know the bargain has been for the antis to give us banks, repeal the usury laws — satisfy St.Louis in short, and the Whigs to give them Atchison for Senator." The same Whig went on to disclose the fact that Old Bullion had offered "to do as much" and wanted nothing in return. [13] For whatever reason, the "antis Whig" alliance fell through. In a last-ditch effort to maintain a united front, the States' Rights Whigs deserted Davy for one of their own — Atchison's close friend and former law associate Alexander W. Doniphan. The Missouri legislature, unable to decide among Atchison, Benton, or Doniphan at its January 1855 joint session, adjourned without electing a senator. [14]

These political developments accentuated commercial rivalries between the Bentonites and the Atchisonians looming simultaneously on the Kansas side of the Missouri River through the summer and fall of 1854. It was hardly surprising, therefore, that soon after the passage of the Nebraska Bill, western Missouri should reverberate with sounds of the Leavenworth-Atchison competition. In marshaling local opposition to Leavenworth, the Atchisonians combined appeals to republicanism, anti-abolitionism, and nativism.[15] The disappearance of four slaves from Weston in July, one of them belonging to Peter T. Abell, became the occasion for calling a Stringfellow-inspired meeting of "good citizens" to expose "negro stealers" in their midst under the cognomen "a Know-Nothing." Subsequent meetings, circulars, and notices in the press emanating from the same source denounced the Leavenworth town project as a monopoly of moneyed interests heavily tinged with the dark heresy of abolitionism. One Jas. H. McHolland, apparently a partisan of the Atchison camp, warned Missouri's "plain folk" that "Mr. Gist [Leavenworth town-company president] has this humbug thing well got up,"

> He has lawyers and doctors,
> With preachers on hand
> To swindle the yeomanry
> Out of their land.[16]

The subsequent exchange between Leavenworth town-company members and their detractors assumed distinctly nativist overtones. Leavenworth promoter Oliver Diefendorf warned the "chivalrous sons of Kentucky" that their would-be protector McHolland was really an alien imposter named Mulholand, who commanded an army of "brother Irishmen . . . alien and unnaturalized" that voted illegally at his bidding to "bring about results contrary to the wishes of U.S. citizens by birth and adoption." McHolland denied these charges and made a few of his own, alleging that his "libeller" was a "German-born, German-bred, non-naturalized alien" who had abandoned his original name—Diefendorfer—"rather too German . . . for a recreant of the fatherland."[17] These nativist-odorous charges carried over into clashes between two Weston groups whose membership overlapped significantly with that of the rival town-companies of Leavenworth and Atchison across the river: the Platte County Self-Defensive Association and the Weston Citizen's Meeting.

Founded in July 1854, the Atchison-inspired and led Platte County Self-Defensive Association was a secret society committed to clearing Missouri's neighborhood of abolitionists and colonizing the territory with proslavery persons. It resolved to uphold slavery in language that would have done any "positive good" proslavery polemicist proud. The "herrenvolk democrats" of Platte County sounded a theme that the pro-slavery side in Kansas constantly played on: black bondage was neither a moral nor a political evil because "it makes color, not money the mark which distinguishes classes. To white, the color of the freeman, it at-taches all the privileges of a higher class . . . from which the poor white laborer is excluded in those states where his color gives no privilege, but money marks his class." The association also urged local merchants to trade exclusively with "the cities of slaveholding states." [18]

The Self-Defensives' influence in western Missouri did not go un-challenged. Representatives of Weston's mercantile community led, sig-nificantly enough, by Leavenworth town-company president George W. Gist, protested the Atchisonians' violation of their "domestic quiet" and "good name" in distinctly Bentonite language at a Citizen's Meeting in Weston on September 1, 1854. The Citizens proclaimed their love of the Union, called upon merchants to trade with whoever brought the most advantages to "buyer and consumer," and asserted their faith in the "dignity of labor" as it did not "necessarily detract from the moral [or] intellectual character of man." [19]

Partisans of the Self-Defensives dismissed the opposition as consist-ing "mostly of foreigners" with "Dutchy" names and a few "bred and born abolitionists." These men might appeal to "all the Irish and Dutch grocery keepers in Weston, but never can they get a true Missourian . . . to countenance them." Especially odious was "the leader of this gang . . . the political priest" and Leavenworth proprietor Frederick Starr, who strove to "excite" political gatherings "composed principally of the lower class of Irish and Dutch . . . against such a champion of South-ern rights as General [Benjamin] Stringfellow." Another special target of the Self-Defensives' wrath was Leavenworth town-company secretary

H. Miles Moore — "an inflated youth with barely enough mother wit to take him through the world." [20]

Earlier on, Moore had almost come to blows with Benjamin String-fellow over the latter's alleged fulminations against free labor at a meeting of the Self-Defensives. The Citizen's response to the Self-Defensive's remarks on that occasion prompted a protracted struggle between the Bentonite and the Atchisonian for mastery over the hearts and minds of Missouri's working people through the medium of the press. Readers of the *Weston Reporter* learned that Stringfellow, in his remarks on the North, had denigrated all men "who labor[ed] for their daily bread" as slaves since the days of Abraham, and all such women "whores . . . from necessity." A free Kansas would force the general to emigrate wherever his "color was respected," where his sons would grow up to be "honorable gentlemen" and his daughters "virtuous women." Stringfellow, enraged by these charges, accosted his alleged libeler at a store, but settled for a resolution of the controversy through word rather than duel.[21]

The Atchisonian urged Missouri's "working men" to pay no heed to the "lies" of an abolitionist "mouthpiece," a "living definition of a 'white slave.' " He, Stringfellow, had simply purported to refute the notion that slavery was a political or moral evil by suggesting that it "elevated the white man, however poor, by right of his color to the privileges of a freeman." Such sentiments were unacceptable to the abolitionist as well as to "the same animal under another name, freesoiler. . . . They love the negro so well, they would have him free; love the white so little, they would have [him] slave. They think the whites make better slaves than the blacks." Stringfellow, on the other hand, was not willing to have a white man or woman call him master. The "poorest ditcher in the bogs of Ireland" who dug in the mire for his daily wages toward the noble end of feeding a starving family regarded with contempt "the powdered footman of the Lord Lieuten't with his master's livery on his back!" So too the poor washerwoman who "over her washtub earn[ed] her shilling a day" scorned the bedizened chambermaid in the "cast-off finery of her mistress" who dared not sit in her mistress's presence. Such was the menial condition to which white people were reduced where there were no "negroes to perform . . . servile duties." To the antislavery charge that the Slave Power threatened to enslave all men, irrespective of color, polemicists for chattel bondage responded that the color white was not only an insurance against slave status, but a guarantor of membership in the South's sociopolitical aristocracy, whereas in the free states the almighty dollar reduced poor whites to slaves of the rich.[22]

The alleged abolitionist mouthpiece, H. Miles Moore, struck back against Stringfellow's "wholesale charge against the Benton party" with equal venom. The Bentonite claimed that while he despised abolitionists as the "most contemptible of the human family," he shared "an equal contempt for a low-flung, red-mouthed fire-eater" who sought the "utter destruction . . . of our Glorious Confederacy." Calling attention to Stringfellow's charge that free-soilers "think the whites make better slaves than blacks," Moore urged "laboring men and mechanics, . . . and ye who employ men to labor for you" to reflect upon Stringfellow's charge: "if all are freesoilers that employ white men to work for them . . . why then, all who employ white labor must be slaveholders, and all those of you who labor must be slaves." Such an insinuation was "a scandal and a reproach upon the laboring classes."[23]

Yet the Atchisonian metaphor of the poor but independent Irish ditcher contemptuous of the slavish liveried footman was a compelling one to many prospective "squatter sovereigns" in western Missouri. Filtered through the rabble-rousing speeches of Atchison and Stringfellow, news of the eastern entrepreneurs' highly capitalized project to export "hired paupers" to do their abolitionist bidding in the vicinity of Missouri assaulted the independent sensibilities of many self-sufficient western Missourians, accustomed, according to David Thelen, to a sense of personal control "within a world held together by personal networks and patronage." Some of these men owned a few slaves; a few hoped to, some day; many others had little use for Negroes, slave or free. Indeed, in 1848 John Gano Bryan, the slave-holding Whig physician and entrepreneur who helped finance Atchison's operations in Kansas, had urged guests at a levee hosted by him to support Henry Clay for president. Such leading Missouri Democrats as Gov. Thomas Reynolds and Claiborne Jackson, future author of the rabidly proslavery Jackson resolutions, heard the doctor say that he would urge them to vote for James G. Birney if only "Mr. Birney and his followers would advocate sending the negroes to Africa."[24]

Several of Bryan's fellow Missourians no doubt agreed. They may even have said so, like the doctor, in private. "Nigger-loving . . . underground railroad–digging" fanatics from the East perverting such principles, were, however, a different matter. Their propensity to "steal and run off slaves" represented an external assault on Missouri's domestic institutions — an insult no self-respecting yeoman loyal to his home and hearth could tolerate. As Amos Reese, who voted illegally in the Kansas territorial legislature elections on March 30, 1855, explained to a congressional committee investigating the territorial electoral frauds of 1854 and 1855, the so-called border ruffians greeted the news that a Northern emigrant aid society planned to "carry and control the elections upon the subject of slavery and . . . to control the institution of slavery in Missouri" with indignation: "It was looked upon as an intermeddling with our own business by foreigners."[25] Especially if those foreigners were "the miserable scum of cities, packed up and transported like slaves at the will of a master," for "the double purpose of abolitionism and land speculation." Especially if the invaders were, as one Southern sympathizer fumed with antireformist zeal, an "ungodly crew of abolitionists, seditionists, infidels, socialists, Bloomers, vegetarians, women's rights women, philosophers, Jacobin reformers, Fourierites . . . men in petticoats and women with beards included."[26]

Proslavery rhetoric contrasted an alleged paradox of white slavery in the much-vaunted free North with the color-based social democracy of the slave South. The "purchased voters" of the East on the one hand and their proud squatter-king adversaries of the South on the other supplied the symbols and proofs of that contrast. The "loafer, the thief . . . drones of society" could never be squatters, proclaimed the Atchison *Squatter Sovereign;* "the brave, energetic, industrious" alone could aspire to that privilege: "Such were the men who first landed on the rock of Plymouth, who erected their cabins on the banks of the James, who penetrated the swamps of Carolina. The sires of Adam and Hancock, of Washington and Jefferson — these were squatters."[27] The proslavery squatter sovereigns of Kansas were thus no less alacritous than their free labor foes in laying claim to their share of the nation's pioneer and revolutionary heritage, including its Pilgrim component.

The arbiters of proslavery opinion, in an attempt to broaden their appeal, portrayed free-soil machinations as representing at once a somewhat abstract challenge to states' rights "under the constitution," as well as a more personal insult to every yeoman-squatter's sense of honor and capacity for self-government. The Atchison *Squatter Sovereign* cast the *New York Tribune*'s reference to "the swindling farce of popular sovereignty devised by [Lewis] Cass in 1848" in an interesting light: "Popular sovereignty is, in the opinion of [Horace] Greeley, [Andrew] Reeder and the abolitionists, 'a swindling farce'!! What say you squatters from Indiana, Illinois, Ohio and Michigan? Is it a 'farce' to say you are capable of self-government? Are you, men from non-slave-holding states, ready to admit that you are less competent to make laws for your own government . . . than the citizens of New York or Pennsylvania, or Greeley and Thayer?" [28]

The freemen of Missouri, urged David Atchison, must resist the designs of Thayer, that master of "white slaves," to make laws for Kansas through "hired minions" with "Colt's repeating pistols" at their hilt, "hell in their hearts and blasphemy on their tongues." To Missourians, the Kansas question was not one of "theory or conscience" as it was to their adversaries, Benjamin Stringfellow added. Rather, it was "a matter of home, of bread." It was also a matter of the Union. Missourians, by thwarting "higher law" fanaticism were "not only defending their own homes but the Union itself," for if the abolitionists succeeded in their objective of freeing Kansas as a stepping stone to the destruction of slavery in Missouri, Arkansas, and Texas, they would bring about "the speedy dissolution of the Union," Atchison's henchman warned.[29]

The Atchisonians' proslavery rhetoric produced impressive results at the polls in Kansas. Soon after his arrival, Governor Reeder divided the territory into sixteen districts and called an election for territorial delegates to Congress in November 1854. On that occasion, as well as at the election of the territorial legislature ordered by Reeder after a population census had been taken in March 1855, hundreds of Missourians rallied to the standard of their home, their bread, and the Union, egged on, their foes claimed, by promises of free whiskey and barbecues. They traveled to Kansas on horseback, and on foot, by wagon, and by carriage, to secure the triumph of the proslavery party through brazen fraud. While Southerners applauded Missouri's bold defense of their cause, Free-Soilers of all stripes expressed outrage at the border ruffians' crime against Kansas.[30]

According to tables printed at the time, of the fifty-three members and officers of the "Missouri-elected" legislature, the largest group — nineteen — claimed to be natives of Kentucky or Tennessee; seventeen hailed from the Upper Southeast, including Virginia and Maryland, five were from Missouri, four each from the midwestern and Mid-Atlantic states, one from Kansas Territory, and only three from the Lower South. The occupational distribution of these men suggested that for a majority of them land did not constitute the primary source of livelihood: although twenty-three claimed to be farmers, equally as many described themselves as professionals in the areas of law, medicine, and engineering. Six were merchants; one was a printer-artisan. The mean age of these men was 34.37.[31]

The "bogus" legislators of Kansas may not have been drawn, for the most part, from the South's planter elite, although several no doubt aspired to that status. They were certainly highly solicitous of slaveholding interests in the territory. One AMA missionary's fear that these men would "doubtless enact the most fanatical proslavery laws" was well founded. When the territorial legislature met at its first session at Shawnee Mission, it expelled the few free-state members who represented the districts where Governor Reeder had ordered reelections, reinstating the original proslavery victors. Over Reeder's veto, it adopted a series of statutes in defense of slavery, decreeing death for anyone convicted of inciting slave rebellion or aiding fugitive slaves, and imposing prison sentences on those who questioned the legality of slavery in the territory. Free-state men were barred from holding office or exercising the right to free speech.[32]

The "free for all balloting" that brought a Missouri-elected legislature to power in Shawnee Mission also supplied proslavery towns with a useful tool in their internecine struggle for preeminence on the Missouri's west bank. The election of a county seat for Leavenworth was a case in point. Two towns besides the city of Leavenworth coveted this distinction. The thriving settlement of Kickapoo, eight miles above Fort Leavenworth, replete with "all the paraphernalia of civilization and ambition" including mills, stores, saloons, and a newspaper, the *Kansas*

Pioneer, was "a pet of General Atchison." Delaware, located six miles below Leavenworth on the Missouri River, was an equally promising rival. But judging by the size of resident-voter population, Leavenworth deserved to be county seat. Delaware and Kickapoo, however, had evidently imbibed valuable lessons in proslavery election management from the March 1855 election to the territorial legislature. On election day, October 8, 1855, "the ferry boat ran free between Weston and [Atchison's favorite] Kickapoo," with the result that Kickapoo outvoted Leavenworth by two hundred. Not to be outdone, Delaware enticed voters from Clay and Platte Counties with announcements of free transportation to the town and a lavish barbecue on election day topped off by a big ball at night. When the party ended, Delawareans triumphantly presented the outcome of their polls: nine hundred votes for Delaware (population sixty)—a lead of one hundred over Kickapoo. Much to Leavenworth's chagrin, the territorial court ruled in favor of Delaware—an exercise in consistency as far as "waiving irregularities" in territorial elections was concerned.[33]

3

From the Pulpit and the Plow to the Sharps Rifle: Pioneer Life in the "Eden of the World"

If political preference was a function of sectional origin, pro-Southern forces would have prevailed at the polls in March 1855 even without help from Missouri. A territorial census completed the same month revealed that Southerners were a clear majority in Kansas. An analysis of the demographic profile of the territory based on the census records of 2,979 free males whose sectional or national origins could be determined suggests that almost 58 percent of them came from the slave states, while 22 percent had formerly resided in the Northwest, comprising Illinois, Indiana, Iowa, Michigan, Ohio, and Wisconsin. Emigrants from the Mid-Atlantic states, including New York, New Jersey, and Pennsylvania, constituted 8.4 percent; those from New England 6.3 percent of the population surveyed. Approximately 5 percent were foreign born (see tables 1–8).[1]

Missourians, accounting for nearly 85 percent of all Southern emigrants, settled in the largest numbers in the breaks of the heavily timbered bluffs along the western bank of the Missouri River and the fertile country beyond. Embracing the counties of Brown and Doniphan on the Nebraska border, this Missouri-dominated belt tapered southeastward to include the river district of Atchison, before fanning southward into the Leavenworth area, bounded on the south by the Kansas River. Covering Electoral Districts Fourteen, Fifteen, and Sixteen, this region was home to nearly 45 percent of the territory's emigrants from Missouri. Another Missourian stronghold lay in the second tier of counties south of the Kansas River along the territory's eastern border, in the vast Electoral Districts Five and Six. Well drained by the Neosho and other waterways, this area was the theater of several notorious incidents that shaped the gory image and reality of the Kansas conflict, including the Pottawatomie and Marais des Cygnes massacres. The typical male settler from Missouri was likely to be a farmer in his twenties, no doubt aspiring to ascend the ladder of agricultural prosperity through the acquisition of fertile land and, in some cases, slaves as well. Seventy-five percent of all emigrants from across the border claimed to be farmers. Mechanics and artisans, at 6 percent, came in a distant second, while merchants and small commercialists including hotelkeepers and grocers, concentrated heavily in the more "commercial" environs of Leavenworth and Atchison, accounted for only 3.6 percent. Professionals—broadly defined in this survey as lawyers, doctors, teachers, preachers, and engineers—were relatively scarce among the Missourians, although disproportionately represented in their leadership. The approximately 7 percent who listed no occupation in the March 1855 census may have been ready recruits to the roving territorial militias.

One chronicler of Bourbon County history made a distinction between men of the "very worst class . . . poor white trash, few of whom made any pretense to citizenship" and "bonafide" settlers, the "true squatter sovereigns," who, although proslavery in politics, "had no more design . . . of a criminal crusade in order to accomplish their political ends than did Stephen A. Douglas himself." Firm unionists for the most part, they "lived and died under the flag of Clay and Benton, either the one or the other of whom had been their household God since the days of their youth."[2] This assessment was corroborated by Nancy Wade, a Missourian born of Kentucky pioneer parents. She recalled that her fellow Missourians in Douglas County were usually "home-seekers." A majority were young men under twenty-five years of age, non-slave-holding and unionist, as well as negrophobic, as another observer noted.[3] Several came to recoup lost fortunes. A few were lawyers with "great ideas of their ability to make successful farmers . . . who in their imaginations had counted their cattle upon a thousand hills."[4]

It is reasonable to expect that Nancy Wade, like the controversial Atchison, was not alone among the Missourians in her possession of a

Kentucky lineage, for as one writer has observed, "Missouri was the natural outlet for the moving population of Kentucky, and to come to Kansas would be to come but one step further."[5] Indeed, Kentucky, along with Tennessee, contributed the second largest Southern group in the territory—about 8.4 percent of the total slave state population. The greatest cluster of these emigrants was concentrated in District Five, south of the Kansas River. The occupational distribution of this population was similar to that from Missouri, with 75 percent engaged in farming and 7 percent in craftsmanship and the mechanical trades. However, it included a larger proportion of professionals (6.3 percent) and fewer commercialists (1.4 percent) than the Missourians did.

The Upper Southeast, consisting of Virginia, Maryland, Delaware, and Washington, D.C., and the Lower South—defined as the rest of the slave states, excluding Missouri, Kentucky, and Tennessee—contributed an equal proportion of the total slave state population—about 4 percent and 3 percent, respectively. The Virginians and Marylanders were more widely dispersed than settlers from the Deep South, with the largest number of them settled in the cosmopolitan Third District, where northeasterners made up approximately 44 percent of the population. Moreover, upper southeasterners included a lower proportion of farmers (approximately 55 percent) and a higher proportion of professionals and commercialists (approximately 8.5 percent and 11 percent, respectively) than other slave state groups did. Virginians continued to trickle into Kansas after the spring of 1855, their sentiments on slavery distinctly uncertain. With Virginia contributing more emigrants to free Ohio than to slave Kentucky, which the Old Dominion supposedly settled, the *Boston Daily Advertiser* remarked, "there is more reason to expect a [more] considerable emigration of free labor from Virginia than of slave labor from it." Newcomers from Virginia to Kansas in 1856 included a free-state colony under a United Brethren minister on the one hand, and a company of mechanics and farmers who fought on the side of the "border ruffians" before their return to the East, on the other.[6] Nearly 40 percent of all Lower South emigrants in 1855 staked claims among fellow slave-staters in Districts Five and Six, and like them were predominantly farmers (74.5 percent). Professionals and artisans occurred in equal proportions in this group—about 6 percent each.

At the opposite end of the scale of numerical preponderance from Southerners were the foreign born. Settlers born in the British Isles including Ireland, as well as those born in Germany, Denmark, Hungary, Switzerland, France, or Canada, exhibited a geographical and occupational distribution rather different from that of native-born settlers.[7] Only 36 percent of them claimed to be farmers; 23.7 percent pursued some sort of mechanical or artisan trade. Almost 29 percent either described themselves as laborers or listed no occupation. Small wonder, then, that over half of all foreigners surveyed settled in the commercially oriented Sixteenth District, the seat of Leavenworth, which no doubt offered artisans and laborers greater employment opportunities than more sparsely settled areas. Since farming was not an inexpensive proposition in the West, it is reasonable to speculate that the low proportion of farmers among foreign immigrants suggested that they were, as a group, perhaps materially worse off than native-born immigrants.

The northwestern presence in Kansas in the spring of 1855 was fairly evenly distributed between Yankee and slave state strongholds. The First Electoral District, where the combined forces of settlers from New England and the Mid-Atlantic states made up 48 percent of the residents, claimed a larger number of all northwesterners surveyed than any other single district. In this Yankee-dominated belt, hugging the south bank of the Kansas River, 118 northwesterners, accounting for just under 18 percent of all settlers from their section, constituted 30 percent of the population, slightly outnumbering those from New England. On the other hand, the predominantly Southern-settled Districts Five and Six adjacent to Missouri together drew nearly 25 percent of the total northwestern contingent in Kansas. In occupational distribution, northwesterners occupied something of a middle ground between their slave state compatriots on the one hand and northeasterners on the other. As with all groups, most tilled the soil for a living. However, at over 64 percent, farmers made up a lower proportion of the northwestern males than that of Southerners (75 percent except for the Upper Southeast), but occurred more frequently than among the Yankees (approximately 52 percent). On the other hand, the percentage of the second largest northwestern occupational group—artisans and mechanics—at 12.6 percent, was higher than that for Southerners (5 percent) but lower than that for northeasterners (23 percent). The distribution of the third largest vocational category, the professionals, at 7 percent, bore a closer resemblance to that of the Southerners than the Yankees. Merchants and laborers occurred with approximately equal, and not very great, frequency: 2.9 percent and 4.5 percent, respectively. About 6.7 percent of northwesterners did not list any occupation.

If there was a northeastern heartland in Kansas, it was centered in the western portion of the territory's First District extending along the southern bank of the Kansas River as far west as "the first watershed ravine . . . above the town of Lawrence." The fertile, open prairie of Douglas County drained by the Kansas and Wakarusa Rivers, straddling the western half of District One and nearly all of District Two, was home to the largest group of Yankees west of the Missouri. Over 61 percent of all New Englanders and nearly 30 percent of all those from the Mid-Atlantic states together constituted approximately 48 percent of all males surveyed in District One. The contiguous Second District, embracing part of Douglas County, and the Third District, vigorously antislavery around Topeka, both south of the Kansas River, claimed nearly 20 percent of all northeasterners. On the whole, emigrants from the Mid-Atlantic were more widely dispersed through the territory than their fellow settlers from New England. Thus, New York, New Jersey, and Pennsylvania contributed nearly 9 percent of the total population of the reputedly proslavery District Sixteen, home to the thriving commerce of Leavenworth.

The occupational profile of the northeastern emigrants resembled that of the upper southeasterners more closely than any other sectional group. Farmers predominated universally, but as with settlers from Virginia, Maryland, Washington, D.C., and Delaware, less completely than among other groups: 48 percent of all Mid-Atlantic settlers and 55 percent of all New Englanders worked the land. The proportion of professionals was roughly equal in all three groups, varying from 9.5 percent to 11 percent, but artisans and mechanics occurred much more frequently among the northeasterners. Whereas only 3 percent of upper southeasterners were skilled craftsmen, more than one of every four New Englanders and one of every five from the Mid-Atlantic was one. Thus non-farmer Yankees included more artisans than professionals, while the reverse was true of upper southeasterners. The surprisingly low percentage of merchants and small commercialists (approximately 5 percent of all those surveyed from New England and 3 percent of those from the Mid-Atlantic) defied the stereotype of the Yankee shopkeeper.

This overall northeastern occupational profile based on the 1855 Kansas territorial census did not exactly parallel that of the NEEAC emigrants. A survey of 195 heads of household belonging to three spring 1855 parties revealed a startling preponderance of artisans and mechanics over farmers. While artisans made up almost 55 percent of this group, farmers came in a distant second at 28.7 percent. A little over 8 percent of the arrivals claimed to pursue careers related to the courtroom, the classroom, and the pulpit. At 2.56 percent, the proportion of merchants and small commercialists mirrored the relatively insignificant presence of the mercantile community in the general northeastern population. This occupational profile suggests the picture of a people moving west in order to re-create a republican utopia rapidly changing in their native states into a world of clock, steam, and wage labor. A profound irony was at work here. The very economic forces that prompted an optimistic faith in the possibility and desirability of spreading Northern-style progress to distant lands also threatened to strip craftspeople of their traditional skills and undermine their economic independence, long thought to be essential for republican virtue. The NEEAC attempted to reconcile the goals of its industrial leadership and artisan emigrants by taking recourse in the classic free labor rationalization for wage labor: such labor was a temporary expedient for free and self-disciplined agents, a means to the ultimate and attainable goal of property ownership, especially where free land abounded. The *Herald of Freedom* had, in January 1855, anticipated a large spring emigration of "tradesmen and mechanics who have been supporting themselves by hands or wits [and who] now seem determined to avoid so uncertain a support and obtain an interest in the soil." The NEEAC organ feared that "capital will not be as abundant as men."[8]

An overwhelming majority of the pioneer women appear to have accompanied their kinsmen to Kansas as wives, daughters, and sisters.[9] A tiny fraction, however, immigrated independently. Thirty-year-old Malinda, a white widow from Arkansas, moved with her family of six children to make a living as a seamstress in the new territory. Two free black women—fifty-year-old Mary Pascal of Missouri and twenty-one-year-old Sarah Johnson of Pennsylvania, apparently set themselves up as cooks in the Ninth Electoral District. The census records at least one instance of a rather unusual "occupation" among women: the wife of a fifty-year-old hotelkeeper from Missouri was listed as being engaged in "witchery." The occasional occurrence of women described as "widows" and "old maids" testifies to the existence of a modest contingent of single women among the territorial population. James H. Fleming of District Six, a twenty-one-year-old farmer from Indiana, "wants a wife," the census taker recorded. Whether Fleming found the mate he sought is not known. At any rate, the territorial sex-ratio was not on his side. A survey of 3,465 native-born white men and women above the age of twenty-one in March 1855 reveals there were 214.71 men for every 100 women. Settlers of Missourian nativity enjoyed the most balanced sex-ratio (182.79:100), followed by those hailing from the Northwest (206.74:100). Northeasterners on the other hand, included a lower proportion of women than any other group with the exception of the upper-southeasterners. Thus, while New England sent out fewer than 28 women and the Mid-Atlantic fewer than 33 for every 100 men, Virginia, Maryland, Delaware, and the District of Columbia collectively contributed approximately 25 women per 100 men (see table 9).

Life in the "Eden of the world" proved to be something less than a bed of roses, as the pioneers discovered fairly early in the course of their western adventure. For one thing, Thayer's hope that organized emigration would afford the morally delinquent urban poor of the East an opportunity to improve their fortunes and character remained largely unrealized. Rev. Samuel Adair noted that many of the settlers arriving in Kansas City under the auspices of the various aid companies were disappointed to discover that emigration was a more expensive proposition than they had expected: "It cost . . . $5 a week board at the only hotel worth anything in the place, $1 a day for horsekeeping . . . flour [cost] $9.50 per bar, corn meal $1 per 50 lb., potatoes from $1.35 to $1.50 and very scarce . . . beef about $6 per cut." Moreover, disease and death stalked the emigrants every inch of the way. Adair hired "some rooms" in Kansas City, Missouri, to accommodate his family for a month while

Table 1 Occupational Distribution of Free Males by Section/State in Electoral Districts 1 through 17, March 1855

State: Missouri

Electoral District	Occupation*							
	Farmer	Artisan	Merchant	Professional	Laborer	Other	None	Total
1	49	2	2	1	0	0	7	61
2	84	6	0	3	0	0	9	102
3	9	0	1	1	0	0	0	11
4	15	0	2	0	0	0	0	17
5	237	2	3	2	0	2	7	253
6	97	7	4	1	3	7.	0	119
7	12	2	2	2	0	0	1	19
8	10	5	3	2	0	1	6	27
9	3	0	1	0	3	1	0	8
10	24	2	1	0	0	0	1	28
11	20	2	3	1	1	1	0	28
12	22	3	6	5	6	0	3	45
13	29	2	2	0	0	0	15	48
14	223	22	6	4	14	2	2	273
15	148	19	8	4	1	0	29	209
16	93	15	9	10	23	5	14	169
17	18	2	0	6	0	1	11	38
Total	1093	91	53	42	51	20	105	1455
Mean	64.3	5.35	3.12	2.47	3	1.18	6.18	
Standard Deviation	72	6.55	2.59	2.59	6.08	1.92	7.53	

* Artisan: includes mechanics.
Merchant: includes Indian traders, grocers, hotelkeepers, and small commercialists.
Professional: includes doctors, lawyers, engineers, teachers, and clergymen.
Laborer: defined broadly to include unskilled and non-artisanal labor, as well as services not covered in the professional category, e.g., plasterer, bricklayer, teamster, cook, and ferryman.
Other: miscellaneous categories of work ranging from fiddle-playing to government service.
None: free males identifiable by section who listed no occupation.

Source: Kansas Territorial Census of March 1855, reprinted in *1855 Territory of Kansas Census*, 2 volumes, transcribed and compiled by Kansas Statistical Publications, Overland Park, Kansas.

Table 2 Occupational Distribution of Free Males by Section/State in Electoral Districts 1 through 17, March 1855

Section: Upper South-West*

Electoral District	Occupation**							
	Farmer	Artisan	Merchant	Professional	Laborer	Other	None	Total
1	10	0	1	0	0	0	1	12
2	12	0	0	1	0	0	1	14
3	9	2	0	1	0	0	0	12
4	1	0	0	0	0	0	0	1
5	32	1	0	1	0	0	1	35
6	13	2	0	1	0	1	0	17
7	1	0	0	0	0	0	0	1
8	2	1	0	0	0	0	1	4
9	0	0	0	1	2	1	0	4
10	2	0	0	0	0	0	0	2
11	0	0	0	0	0	0	0	0
12	1	1	0	1	0	0	0	3
13	4	0	0	0	0	0	0	4
14	7	0	0	0	0	2	0	9
15	5	1	0	0	0	0	0	6
16	9	2	1	3	4	0	0	19
17	0	0	0	0	0	1	0	1
Total	108	10	2	9	6	5	4	144
Mean	6.35	0.59	0.12	0.53	0.35	0.29	0.24	
Standard Deviation	7.72	0.77	0.32	0.78	1.03	0.57	0.42	

* Includes Kentucky and Tennessee.
** Artisan: includes mechanics.
Merchant: includes Indian traders, grocers, hotelkeepers, and small commercialists.
Professional: includes doctors, lawyers, engineers, teachers, and clergymen.
Laborer: defined broadly to include unskilled and non-artisanal labor, as well as services not covered in the professional category, e.g., plasterer, bricklayer, teamster, cook, and ferryman.
Other: miscellaneous categories of work ranging from fiddle-playing to government service.
None: free males identifiable by section who listed no occupation.

Source: Kansas Territorial Census of March 1855, reprinted in *1855 Territory of Kansas Census*, 2 volumes, transcribed and compiled by Kansas Statistical Publications, Overland Park, Kansas.

Table 3 Occupational Distribution of Free Males by Section/State in Electoral Districts 1 through 17, March 1855

Section: Upper South-East*

Electoral District	Occupation**							
	Farmer	Artisan	Merchant	Professional	Laborer	Other	None	Total
1	8	1	1	0	0	0	0	10
2	2	1	0	3	0	1	0	7
3	12	0	2	0	0	0	0	14
4	1	0	0	0	0	0	2	3
5	6	1	1	0	0	0	0	8
6	4	0	0	0	0	2	0	6
7	0	0	0	0	0	0	0	0
8	1	0	0	0	0	0	0	1
9	0	0	0	1	0	1	0	2
10	0	0	0	0	0	0	0	0
11	1	0	0	0	0	0	0	1
12	1	0	2	0	2	0	1	6
13	0	0	0	0	0	0	0	0
14	0	0	0	0	0	0	0	0
15	1	0	0	0	0	0	0	1
16	2	0	2	2	2	1	1	10
17	0	0	0	0	0	2	0	2
Total	39	3	8	6	4	7	4	71
Mean	2.29	0.18	0.47	0.35	0.24	0.41	0.24	
Standard Deviation	3.29	0.38	0.78	0.84	0.64	0.69	0.55	

* Includes border slave states of Delaware, Maryland, Virginia, and Washington, D.C.

** Artisan: includes mechanics.

Merchant: includes Indian traders, grocers, hotelkeepers, and small commercialists.

Professional: includes doctors, lawyers, engineers, teachers, and clergymen.

Laborer: defined broadly to include unskilled and non-artisanal labor, as well as services not covered in the professional category, e.g., plasterer, bricklayer, teamster, cook, and ferryman.

Other: miscellaneous categories of work ranging from fiddle-playing to government service.

None: free males identifiable by section who listed no occupation.

Source: Kansas Territorial Census of March 1855, reprinted in *1855 Territory of Kansas Census,* 2 volumes, transcribed and compiled by Kansas Statistical Publications, Overland Park, Kansas.

Table 4 Occupational Distribution of Free Males by Section/State in Electoral Districts 1 through 17, March 1855

Section: Lower South *

Electoral District	Occupation**							
	Farmer	Artisan	Merchant	Professional	Laborer	Other	None	Total
1	0	0	0	1	0	0	0	1
2	6	0	0	0	0	2	0	8
3	1	0	0	0	0	0	0	1
4	3	1	0	0	0	0	0	4
5	3	0	0	0	0	1	0	4
6	15	1	0	0	0	0	0	16
7	0	0	0	0	0	0	0	0
8	2	0	0	0	0	0	0	2
9	0	0	0	0	0	0	0	0
10	1	0	0	0	0	0	0	1
11	0	0	0	0	0	0	0	0
12	0	0	0	1	1	0	0	2
13	1	0	0	0	0	0	0	1
14	2	0	0	0	0	0	0	2
15	1	1	0	0	0	0	0	2
16	0	0	0	1	2	1	0	4
17	3	0	0	0	0	0	0	3
Total	38	3	0	3	3	4	0	51
Mean	2.24	0.18	0	0.18	0.18	0.24	0	
Standard Deviation	3.56	0.38	0	0.38	0.51	0.55	0	

* Includes all slave states excluding those covered in Tables 1, 2, and 3.
** Artisan: includes mechanics.
  Merchant: includes Indian traders, grocers, hotelkeepers, and small commercialists.
  Professional: includes doctors, lawyers, engineers, teachers, and clergymen.
  Laborer: defined broadly to include unskilled and non-artisanal labor, as well as services not covered in the professional category, e.g., plasterer, bricklayer, teamster, cook, and ferryman.
  Other: miscellaneous categories of work ranging from fiddle-playing to government service.
  None: free males identifiable by section who listed no occupation.

Source: Kansas Territorial Census of March 1855, reprinted in *1855 Territory of Kansas Census,* 2 volumes, transcribed and compiled by Kansas Statistical Publications, Overland Park, Kansas.

Table 5 Occupational Distribution of Free Males by Section/State in Electoral Districts 1 through 17, March 1855

Section: Northwest*

Electoral District	Occupation**							
	Farmer	Artisan	Merchant	Professional	Laborer	Other	None	Total
1	74	15	0	14	0	1	14	118
2	37	3	0	0	0	0	1	41
3	12	6	1	1	0	0	2	22
4	16	2	1	2	0	0	4	25
5	86	1	4	3	0	1	1	96
6	56	6	2	1	0	1	1	67
7	9	5	0	2	1	1	0	18
8	4	0	1	0	0	0	2	7
9	2	10	0	2	1	0	0	15
10	12	0	0	3	0	0	0	15
11	0	0	0	0	0	0	0	0
12	29	7	0	3	6	0	2	47
13	15	0	2	1	0	0	3	21
14	32	5	0	1	0	1	0	39
15	0	6	0	2	12	0	4	24
16	42	18	8	10	10	6	7	101
17	3	0	0	2	0	1	3	9
Total	429	84	19	47	30	12	44	665
Mean	25.2	4.94	1.12	2.76	1.76	0.71	2.59	
Standard Deviation	25.5	5.17	2.03	3.57	3.67	1.45	3.50	

* Includes Illinois, Indiana, Iowa, Michigan, Ohio, and Wisconsin.

** Artisan: includes mechanics.

Merchant: includes Indian traders, grocers, hotelkeepers, and small commercialists.

Professional: includes doctors, lawyers, engineers, teachers, and clergymen.

Laborer: defined broadly to include unskilled and non-artisanal labor, as well as services not covered in the professional category, e.g., plasterer, bricklayer, teamster, cook, and ferryman.

Other: miscellaneous categories of work ranging from fiddle-playing to government service.

None: free males identifiable by section who listed no occupation.

Source: Kansas Territorial Census of March 1855, reprinted in *1855 Territory of Kansas Census*, 2 volumes, transcribed and compiled by Kansas Statistical Publications, Overland Park, Kansas.

Table 6 Occupational Distribution of Free Males by Section/State in Electoral Districts 1 through 17, March 1855

Section: Mid-Atlantic*

Electoral District	Occupation**							
	Farmer	Artisan	Merchant	Professional	Laborer	Other	None	Total
1	33	19	3	6	2	2	10	75
2	7	1	0	3	0	1	0	12
3	20	12	0	2	0	0	0	34
4	3	0	0	0	0	0	0	3
5	15	0	1	2	0	2	0	20
6	5	0	0	1	0	0	0	6
7	8	7	0	0	0	1	0	16
8	4	0	0	0	0	0	0	4
9	4	3	1	1	4	0	0	13
10	1	0	0	0	0	0	0	1
11	0	0	0	0	0	0	0	0
12	4	2	0	0	1	1	1	9
13	0	0	0	1	0	0	0	1
14	1	1	0	1	0	0	0	3
15	4	3	2	3	0	0	0	12
16	9	9	1	5	8	2	3	37
17	2	0	0	0	0	1	2	5
Total	120	57	8	25	15	10	16	251
Mean	7.06	3.35	0.47	1.47	0.88	0.59	0.94	
Standard Deviation	8.28	5.25	0.85	1.79	2.05	0.77	2.41	

* Includes New Jersey, New York, and Pennsylvania.

** Artisan: includes mechanics.

Merchant: includes Indian traders, grocers, hotelkeepers, and small commercialists.

Professional: includes doctors, lawyers, engineers, teachers, and clergymen.

Laborer: defined broadly to include unskilled and non-artisanal labor, as well as services not covered in the professional category, e.g., plasterer, bricklayer, teamster, cook, and ferryman.

Other: miscellaneous categories of work ranging from fiddle-playing to government service.

None: free males identifiable by section who listed no occupation.

Source: Kansas Territorial Census of March 1855, reprinted in *1855 Territory of Kansas Census*, 2 volumes, transcribed and compiled by Kansas Statistical Publications, Overland Park, Kansas.

Table 7 Occupational Distribution of Free Males by Section/State in Electoral Districts 1 through 17, March 1855

Section: New England*

Electoral District	Occupation**							
	Farmer	Artisan	Merchant	Professional	Laborer	Other	None	Total
1	52	38	6	11	3	4	2	116
2	17	0	0	2	0	0	0	19
3	13	8	0	0	0	0	0	21
4	0	0	0	0	0	0	0	0
5	6	1	0	0	0	0	0	7
6	2	0	1	0	0	0	0	3
7	0	0	0	0	0	0	0	0
8	1	0	0	0	0	0	0	1
9	0	1	0	0	0	0	0	1
10	10	0	0	1	0	0	0	11
11	0	0	0	0	0	0	0	0
12	0	0	0	0	0	0	0	0
13	0	0	0	0	0	0	0	0
14	1	0	0	0	0	0	0	1
15	0	1	0	0	0	0	0	1
16	2	0	3	1	1	0	0	7
17	0	0	0	1	0	0	0	1
Total	104	49	10	16	4	4	2	189
Mean	6.12	2.88	0.59	0.94	0.24	0.24	0.12	
Standard Deviation	12.5	8.98	1.54	2.58	0.73	0.94	0.47	

* Includes Connecticut, Maine, Massachusetts, New Hampshire, Rhode Island, Vermont.
** Artisan: includes mechanics.
  Merchant: includes Indian traders, grocers, hotelkeepers, and small commercialists.
  Professional: includes doctors, lawyers, engineers, teachers, and clergymen.
  Laborer: defined broadly to include unskilled and non-artisanal labor, as well as services not covered in the professional category, e.g., plasterer, bricklayer, teamster, cook, and ferryman.
  Other: miscellaneous categories of work ranging from fiddle-playing to government service.
  None: free males identifiable by section who listed no occupation.

Source: Kansas Territorial Census of March 1855, reprinted in *1855 Territory of Kansas Census*, 2 volumes, transcribed and compiled by Kansas Statistical Publications, Overland Park, Kansas.

Table 8 Occupational Distribution of Free Males by Section/State in Electoral Districts 1 through 17, March 1855

Electoral District	Foreign-born* Occupation**							
	Farmer	Artisan	Merchant	Professional	Laborer	Other	None	Total
1	1	0	0	0	0	0	0	1
2	0	0	0	0	0	0	0	0
3	7	3	0	0	0	0	0	10
4	2	1	0	0	0	0	0	3
5	1	0	0	0	0	0	0	1
6	1	1	0	8	0	0	0	10
7	0	0	0	0	0	0	0	0
8	0	0	0	0	0	0	0	0
9	0	0	0	0	0	0	0	0
10	1	0	0	0	0	0	3	4
11	0	0	0	0	0	0	0	0
12	3	1	0	0	0	0	1	5
13	6	0	0	0	0	0	6	12
14	0	0	0	0	0	0	0	0
15	15	11	0	0	0	0	1	27
16	17	19	7	0	32	2	1	78
17	1	0	0	0	0	0	0	1
Total	55	36	7	8	32	2	12	152
Mean	3.24	2.12	0.41	0.47	1.88	0.12	0.71	
Standard Deviation	5.08	4.96	1.65	1.88	7.53	0.47	1.52	

* Includes men native to Canada, Denmark, England, France, Germany, Ireland, Mexico, Switzerland, and Wales.

** Artisan: includes mechanics.

Merchant: includes Indian traders, grocers, hotelkeepers, and small commercialists.

Professional: includes doctors, lawyers, engineers, teachers, and clergymen.

Laborer: defined broadly to include unskilled and non-artisanal labor, as well as services not covered in the professional category, e.g., plasterer, bricklayer, teamster, cook, and ferryman.

Other: miscellaneous categories of work ranging from fiddle-playing to government service.

None: free males identifiable by section who listed no occupation.

Source: Kansas Territorial Census of March 1855, reprinted in *1855 Territory of Kansas Census*, 2 volumes, transcribed and compiled by Kansas Statistical Publications, Overland Park, Kansas.

**Table 9 Sex-Ratio of Native-born, White Population over 21 Years
by Section, March 1855***

Section/State	Men	Women	Men per 100 Women
Missouri	1115	610	182.79
Kentucky/Tennessee	136	49	277.56
Upper Southeast	71	18	394.44
Lower South	54	19	284.21
Northwest	583	282	206.74
Mid-Atlantic	219	71	308.45
New-England	186	52	357.69

*   This survey excludes figures for District 14, where the ages of women were not listed, so there was no way of knowing how many were over 21 years old. The numerical break-down of native-born white men over 21 years by section/state in District 14 was as follows: Missouri: 272; Kentucky/Tennessee: 12; Lower South: 3; Northwest: 38; Mid-Atlantic: 3; New England: 2. These figures were deducted from the total number of native-born voters from all electoral districts for each section/state represented in table 9. Thus, the survey excludes figures for both men and women in District 14. For sectional distribution of Kansas voters in March 1855, see Hickman, "Reeder Administration," 2, 450.

   The territorial sex-ratio may, in fact, have been more balanced than my survey suggests, since several men undoubtedly married or were accompanied by young women under 21 years. However, since there was no way of distinguishing these women from young children, I omitted them from my survey.

Source: Kansas Territorial Census of March 1855, reprinted in *1855 Territory of Kansas Census*, 2 volumes, transcribed and compiled by Kansas Statistical Publications, Overland Park, Kansas.

he ventured into the wilderness on his own. Unfortunately, two attacks of diarrhea stalled his plans for a while. When Florella fell sick, the notoriety of frontier quacks prevented the Adairs from calling in a physician. Fortunately, "the Lord" sent them one in the person of Dr. Hummon, a slaveholder of Maryland, who had taken stock in the Pennsylvania and the New York Emigrant Aid companies. He called to see a lady of his acquaintance, who was staying with the Adairs until her husband, an agent of the Pennsylvania company, returned from an exploratory trip into the territory. Dr. Hummon, who successfully treated the Adairs' ailments, professed to be a Free-Soiler. His numerous slaves had turned down his offer of a passage to Liberia, so he planned to take them "to some colored colony in some free state, and make provision for them for a time, and then let them look out for themselves."[10]

Thanks to the ministrations of the slave-holding physician, Adair recovered sufficiently to embark on a tour of the prairies south of the

Kansas River in the company of A. G. Jones, colporteur of the American Tract Society. Fortified with clothing, buffaloes, and blankets, the pioneer missionaries traveled on horseback about twenty miles each day. They slept at night wrapped in buffalo robes and blankets to protect them from the "constant, piercing, prairie wind[s]," which "expel almost all the calorie that a man has in him." On one occasion, Adair and Jones, led astray from their path by a storm, found refuge in the home of the mixed-blooded John Tecumseh "Ottawa Jones," where Jones the colporteur suffered a return of diarrhea.[11] Ottawa Jones, a member of the Baptist Indian Mission, was married to Jane Kelley, a white missionary from Maine. The Joneses were under a commission from the government to help establish the Ottawas on their new reservation in Franklin County, given them in exchange for their Ohio lands.[12] Ottawa Jones maintained a large farm well stocked with "cattle, horses, hogs, and comfortable buildings," which afforded weary emigrants a welcome opportunity to replenish their strength before they went on their way. On the Sabbath, Adair accompanied his host to the mission church where the clergyman engaged in a fruitful dialogue with a group of friendly Indians through the medium of an interpreter. Antislavery for the most part, this band of Indians "came forward of [its] own accord and shook hands warmly." [13]

Like Adair, John E. Stewart, a Methodist minister from New Hampshire and a member of the fifth party of the NEEAC, left his family in Missouri, loaded an ox team with tools and provisions, and started for Kansas in the company of a few other prospective homesteaders.[14] Another New Englander who had expected to "plunge into vast forests or roll monotonously over boundless prairies without a single mark or sign to recall to the mind images of the beautiful scenes and the home feeling" he had known in New England, was pleasantly surprised by the variegated landscape that met his eye. The country had a "civilized" appearance that challenged comparison with the "most delightful localities of the East." The chronicler of these impressions assured his compatriots at home through the influential medium of the *Herald of Freedom* that "a white cottage now and then, and occasionally a church steeple would at once convert this lovely country into another New England, without the long struggle with rocky, obdurate soil, and forbidding forests and wintry storms, which so severely tested the spirit of our Puritan ancestors." [15] The material discomforts of cold winds and poor accommodation, however, appear to have rendered the Stewart company somewhat more oblivious to the natural beauty of their adopted home on their first trek across the country. Indeed many of the young men returned east, Stewart later recorded.

Three days of "hard travel" across an Indian reservation brought Stewart and his companions within sight of Lawrence. One northeastern pioneer described his first impression of Lawrence thus:

> passing with our mule team slowly along over the open prairies yet unincumbered with fences, a row of small cabins appeared over the brow of a little eminence, and we saw for the first time, a city without an omnibus, theater, or grog shop. We told the driver to take us to the best hotel. Imagine a roof about forty feet long, placed on the ground with no walls to support it; composed of thatch, with the gable ends of sod; a door in one end, with a small window each side of it; a table running down the middle of the room, with a row of berths on the side . . . ; the ground carpeted with saw-dust for a floor. Such is our *Hotel*.[16]

Although the hotel attracted "much laughter and hard swearing," its clients were thankful for the shelter it offered. Unfortunately the conveniences of the hotel were not available to the Stewart company on their first visit to Lawrence. Those hardy pioneers huddled together with two hundred others in a "building made of poles and hay," called "the Church." [17]

Lawrence, destined to go down in the annals of territorial Kansas as the leading bastion of free-state activism, was established by the members of the first two NEEAC parties in September 1854. In organizing their town association, the New Englanders joined forces with a band of western pioneers who had preceded them to the vicinity and were encamped a few miles west on the California Road. Among these emigrants, whose "heart and homes at Mt. Gilead, Ohio, had always been open to the slave seeking safety," was the attorney S. N. Wood who proved to be an invaluable recruit to the antislavery cause in Kansas. The little home that Wood built on Main Street for his wife, Margaret

Lyon, and their young sons, Dave and Will, became forever "the refuge of the sick and the dying; no applicant for shelter and care was ever turned away from their door, though Mrs. Wood often looked as though she must sink under the many burdens," recalled a fellow frontierswoman Sara T. D. Robinson. "The Eastern people did well to learn of the Western people this open handed hospitality," Sara concluded. Daughter of prominent Massachusetts Whig leader Myron Lawrence and wife of NEEAC agent Charles Robinson, she gained distinction in her own right by authoring *Kansas: Its Interior and Exterior Life* — an acclaimed record of the early pioneer experience. In the early days of settlement, the women of Lawrence did "all they could to make life home-like" in the "thatch hotels christened with high sounding names," which served as the venue of "Peace parties" and other gatherings around which the social life of the community revolved. Sabbath services led by the Reverend Lum in the dining room of one of them became the occasion of "decorous assemblages" rivaling gatherings in eastern homes. Dr. Robinson usually rang the great dinner bell to announce the hour.[18]

Such was life in the nascent town of Lawrence when Stewart settled in its environs. Adair ultimately took a claim in Osawatomie, on the Osage River at the junction of the Marais des Cygnes and Pottawatomie Creek. This free-state settlement was originally founded by a party of New Yorkers belonging to the New York Kansas League in late 1854. Samuel C. Pomeroy, as trustee for the New England Emigrant Aid Company, held a one-third interest in the town-company formed in January 1855.[19] On March 22, 1855, the Adairs moved into a log cabin, eighteen by twenty feet and equipped with a chimney built with sticks and mud, on their claim. Amos Finch was not as lucky. When the Finch family arrived in Lawrence in early November 1854, there was no house to go into, save "a large tent thatched with prairie hay, which was very uncomfortable during the cold nights." Finch wrote Jocelyn, "we had to sleep on the ground . . . and get along without any fire, until I could go about fifty miles to the Missouri River, and get us a stove after which we were more comfortable, though very much crowded." Six months later, Finch moved to Osawatomie about half a mile from Adair's claim. The lower cost of living at Osawatomie and a controversy over town lots in Lawrence prompted the transfer.[20]

By September 1855 the AMA had appointed five missionaries to Kansas, all but one of whom were concentrated in free-state areas south of the Kansas River. Harvey Jones staked a claim three-fourths of a mile west of the town of Wabaunsee. Situated seventy miles west of Lawrence and surrounded by plenty of good farming land and timber, this town promised to be a more inviting field for evangelical preaching than the older, more thickly settled areas further east, where ministers were "numerous and at a discount." Launched by members of the fourth party of NEEAC emigrants in November 1854, Wabaunsee achieved fame as the headquarters of the Beecher's Bible Rifle Company, a unit of the free-state militia. John Lowry settled in Council City (later Burlingame), the only free-state colony founded entirely independently of the NEEAC through the efforts of a group of Pennsylvanians traveling under the auspices of the American Settlement Company, an affiliate of the New York Kansas League.[21] The sole AMA minister to make his home among friends of slavery was John H. Byrd, who settled in Leavenworth City.[22] Since most of these settlements were small, the missionaries traveled to various points around their base of operations.

Occasionally, a community applied to the AMA for aid in sustaining a "true Gospel" in their midst. Ebenezer Disbrow of Bloomington invited Henry H. Norton, the association's missionary in Lodi Station, Illinois, to preach in his neighborhood ten miles from Lawrence. The New York–born, Oberlin-educated Norton arrived in the territory in July 1856. He organized one church in Bloomington and one in Kanawaca before his death the next year. The AMA commissioned Jonathan Copeland, formerly of Peterboro, New York, to fill Norton's position in the region of Lawrence and Topeka. In the meantime, Henry Morell, a Frenchman educated in Switzerland, arrived in the territory under the misapprehension that a company of three hundred French persons had settled in Council City. Although disappointed in his intended mission, he decided to remain in Kansas under a commission from the AMA to replace Lowry at Council City. He ran into serious problems of communication with his congregation, eventually prompting them to seek his replacement by an English-speaking minister.[23]

By April 1858 three of the missionaries had moved to fresh fields. Amos Finch moved to Indianapolis, and Henry Morell to Superior.

Byrd relocated to Atchison, "formerly the strongest proslavery region in the territory," where, he reported in his 1857 annual report, "until this spring scarcely a sermon had been preached. . . . But within a few months, eastern men have made extensive purchases of town property . . . so that the complexion of the community is decidedly changed."[24] The location of the Christian abolitionist missionaries suggests that they sought primarily to strengthen rather than create antislavery sentiment. Perhaps anticipating the limited scope the movement offered for the use of moral suasion upon diehard proslavery men, the AMA envisioned for its missionaries the function of providing moral support to the more active combatants for freedom. From the start, therefore, the AMA determined to send missionaries to minister to the souls of free-state colonists on their way to the territory under the auspices of the eastern emigrant aid companies, "to go with them and strengthen and cheer them, . . . while giving to them and their children the free and pure Gospel of Christ . . . share with them in their sacrifices and ultimately rejoice with them in their triumph."[25] The emigration companies welcomed the missionary clergymen, believing that their presence enhanced the reputation of local settlements and lent an aura of morality and respectability to the free-state movement as a whole.

The Christian abolitionists in Kansas fought the Slave Power most visibly by establishing churches that did not fellowship slaveholders, although the lack of funds for building purposes severely hindered this endeavor. During 1857 AMA missionaries aided in the formation of six churches, most of them Congregational. Other instruments for the conversion of souls included Sabbath schools and Bible classes. These were often poorly attended, however, because of frequent outbreaks of sickness in the community, the lack of suitable schoolhouses, and transportation problems especially in inclement weather. Harvey Jones wrote the AMA headquarters in New York that he would "very much like to add . . . books of an antislavery character" to the Wabaunsee Sabbath school collection, but did not know how to procure them.[26] In the aftermath of each spurt of frontier violence and sectional strife, the missionaries helped "relieve temporal distress" by disbursing clothing and other provisions donated by eastern benefactors.

Missionaries sometimes contributed their mite to the promotion of

Christian emigration by traveling east (for settlers from the East were most likely to be of "the right stripe") and disseminating information about conditions in the territory. In early 1857 Norton spent eight months touring the free states "as far east as Connecticut" delivering public lectures on the geographical, political, and religious condition of Kansas, and felt that he had been instrumental in stimulating emigration of the "right sort" to the territory.[27]

The burden of the antislavery missionary devolved upon clergymen who were willing to attack black bondage from the pulpit. The October 1855 issue of the *American Missionary* contained a brief of an antislavery lecture that may have been intended to provide guidelines to home missionaries. The author devoted the first part of the lecture to delineating the peculiarities of American slavery as distinct from Hebrew servitude, Russian serfdom, and Turkish slavery; the next part to an exposition of the damage wrought by American slavery to the slave, to the non-slaveholder of the South, to the slaveholder's family, and to the moral and religious institutions of the whole Union. He went on to place the onus for slavery's persistence and growth on the free states, enumerating acts by the federal government that ensured the perpetuation of the institution — the purchases of Louisiana and Florida, the annexation of Texas, the Fugitive Slave law, and the abrogation of the Missouri Compromise. The North buttressed slavery still further by "submitting to pro-slavery dictation in the management of missionary enterprises and Sabbath schools" and by allowing literature published by the American Tract Society to be expurgated of any allusion to the sin of slavery. The author went on to argue that churches that received slaveholders into fellowship without requiring repentance or reformation were themselves guilty of the abomination of slave-holding. In conclusion, he outlined steps the North could take to eliminate the blight of slavery from national life, arguing that abolition would advance the cause of liberty and Christianity the world over.[28]

Given the odds arrayed against the frank expression of Christian abolitionist doctrines — "the high handed iniquity of government and of the Missouri slave-holding legislature of Kansas and their laws of blood and persecution" — it is unlikely that the Kansas missionaries devoted entire sermons to such explicit, systematic denunciations of the peculiar institution.[29] In 1859 Byrd reminded Jocelyn, "considering the peculiar state of things here, you counselled me not to make the subject of slavery too prominent in my Sabbath labors, while my ordinary efforts were to be faithful and persistent against it." But evidence of the missionaries' persecution by proslavery activists suggests that they were by no means silent about their Christian abolitionist convictions in word any more than in deed. Byrd's views on the "nefarious institution of slavery" expounded in a Sabbath sermon within the inhospitable environs of Leavenworth, provoked a proslavery proposal to give him a coat of tar and feathers if he dared to preach in town again. The missionary's radical proclivities did nothing to endear him to the defenders of slavery, who, he reported, ranked abolitionists below murderers, and professed in "Missouri fashion," to "class such men as [William H.] Seward and [Salmon P.] Chase with horse thieves."[30]

Byrd reported that at one meeting of the proslavery party in Leavenworth City, he was "traduced and vilified," and that a letter addressed by him to the President of the United States, which had been republished in a proslavery newspaper, was called for and read. According to the Christian abolitionist, "Mr. Calhoun, Surveyor General of the Territories said he knew me well in Illinois, that I was utterly devoid of character. That among those who knew me, I was accounted more loathsome than the rotten carcass of a dead horse. That I stank so of abolitionism that the people of that state could not be persuaded to touch me with a line of tongs 20 feet long. . . . This harangue of a drunken office-holder would be recorded as truth by the delegates from various parts of the territory, and will go the rounds of the proslavery papers, I suppose." Byrd was apparently not present at the meeting during Calhoun's speech but called on his detractor the next morning to introduce himself as the man whom Calhoun had slandered. Calhoun replied "in confusion" that Byrd was not the man he had known in Illinois.[31]

That did not, of course, persuade proslavery sympathizers to leave the missionary alone. In August 1856 he was taken prisoner by the enemy about the same time that a Missouri newspaper published the following extract: "We learn that a notorious abolitionist named Bird [sic] has been taken into custody. Preparations are making to take care of other birds of the same plumage." Although Byrd, by virtue of his location,

was the most vulnerable to proslavery chastisement, the other missionaries did not escape persecution. Finch, in the course of his wanderings
around the Neosho, came upon a proslavery trading post, the owner of
which informed him that he had two prices, "one for white men, and
one for abolitionists."[32]

For a majority of the preachers of Christian abolitionism, to live in
predominantly free-state communities may not have been as challeng-
ing as to settle amidst confirmed friends of slavery. Yet many free-state
men in Kansas were enemies of abolitionism. It must have taken courage
to adhere unswervingly to a position of racial egalitarianism in communities where the Black Law feeling was often the raison d'être of
free-statism. Moral revulsion against slavery among free-state emigrants
did not necessarily translate into sympathy for the African American.
Indeed, Byrd claimed that James H. Lane, "the most prominent and
efficient free-state man in the territory," was accustomed to declaring
in his speeches, "I look upon this nigger question just as I look upon
the horse or the jackass question. It is merely a question of dollars
and cents."[33]

Adair reported that he had been excluded from the house of a professed Free-Soiler from Ohio where he had earlier preached twice, because, he was, according to the man, an "abolitioner." The Ohioan told
Adair, "you pray as if you would have the slaves all set free at once,
and were in favor of their having their rights among us—a doctrine
which I do not hold, and which I am unwilling shall be preached in
my house." Much disheartened by the display of negrophobia, Adair
observed, "their free soil is free soil for white, but not for the black.
They hate slavery, but they hate the negro worse. Their language is, 'if
we must have niggers here, let them be slaves, not free.' . . . I meet
very many in these territories who hold these views. The ignorance of
some of these men is most profound. I could relate some most amusing
conversations and discussions held with them, did time permit."[34]

Christian abolitionism derived its greatest significance from its exertions, in the face of insuperable odds, on behalf of a cause that implied
true progress in the context of the time, namely the spirit of universal
brotherhood of man. Christian abolitionist rationale refused to blame
the victims of oppression for vices engendered by an unjust institution.

The *American Missionary* argued that if slaves were dishonest as alleged, "why should not they be, under such examples as are set before them from infancy? Robbed of their rights and of the fruits of their labor, it is natural enough that they should imitate their masters and become robbers themselves, if indeed taking some of these fruits can justly be considered robbery." [35]

The missionary clergymen frequently drew on their experiences with people of color in order to buttress their pleas for racial egalitarianism. Finch was favorably impressed with a slave woman who lived on her master's claim a few miles off the Santa Fe road. Having stopped at her log cabin for the night in the course of his tour of the Neosho region, the minister partook of a meal "prepared [by the woman] in a short time and in first-rate order." The mother of four "bright looking" girls, the woman expressed a great desire to educate her children and "to be free," although she had a good master. Finch wrote his headquarters, "I have often thought that this system [slavery] was ungodly, but never realized it as clearly as at this time. [The slave woman and her husband] were parents who . . . were capable of accumulating a respectable property, and of educating their children . . . who are deprived of the honest earnings of their entire lives. . . . Can a person be a Christian and refrain from praying for these poor suffering beings?" To John Lowry, the answer was a clear No. This clergyman risked more than personal unpopularity by arguing against Negro exclusion in a debate sponsored by the Pioneer Institute Lyceum in Council City. Byrd refused to turn out colored children from the Sabbath school at Atchison where he preached, and often read letters and wrote replies for colored families, earning the name "nigger preacher." His consequent exclusion from the Union Meeting House hindered his ministry.[36]

There is plenty of evidence to suggest the Christian abolitionists in Kansas played a part in the operation of the territory's underground railroad (UGRR), which in the three years after 1855 apparently carried three hundred Missouri bondspeople to freedom through Lawrence and across Iowa into Canada.[37] The firebrand abolitionist John Brown of Osawatomie, a half brother of Florella Adair, led numerous raids across the border in pursuit of this mission. Much influenced by the Adairs' flattering portrait of Kansas in their letters to his family, John Brown and his sons left Ohio to try their fortunes and combat "Satan and his legions" in the territory in October 1855.[38] On a bitterly cold Christmas night in 1858, John Brown arrived at the Adairs' doorstep in the company of eleven fugitive slaves whom he had rescued from a Missouri plantation. Having sought in vain to find a refuge for the bondspeople during their journey to Osawatomie, Brown requested Adair to shelter them. The clergyman consulted his wife on the wisdom of complying with that dangerous plea. She responded, "I cannot let those poor slaves perish. Bring them in." According to one chronicler who drew extensively on Adair's testimony when writing about some of Brown's engagements many years later, the next morning, "the negro men were secreted in cornshacks and the negro women were safely packed away in the house. The following night they were taken to a cabin about four miles west of Lane, where they were concealed for more than a month, while officers were riding the country in every direction in search of John Brown and the kidnapped slaves." [39]

Adair was evidently not alone among the Christian abolitionists in his readiness to offer a sanctuary to slaves in flight from bondage. Byrd's role as a conductor on the UGRR earned him a great deal of proslavery antipathy. One of the preacher's more notable exploits involved the rescue of a slave woman and her child awaiting passage to the South from an Atchison hotel room in 1859. Isaac Maris, a fellow conductor, later recalled: "Mr. Bird [sic] . . . took [the bondswoman] and her child or was the means of her walking out of the hotel," and riding off on a horse "in broad daylight." The missionary delivered her to her next "station," where she lay "secreted on some boards laid over the joists of a one-room cabin" for a few days before she continued on her successful escape to Canada. Meanwhile, Byrd's house in Atchison was searched on suspicion of the clergyman's role in the rescue. The master of the fugitives claimed that he had decisive evidence that "that preacher Byrd stole her." Byrd wrote the AMA in response, "I doubt the matter of his evidence, but if his theory was true it does not appear that he has any remedy at law. The Fugitive Slave Law refers to slaves escaping from one state or territory to another and there is no local law on the subject, either Congregational or territorial. So it appears that underground railroad traffic in territorial slaves is a legitimate business." [40]

The wife of Reverend Finch harbored a fugitive slave girl for a day and a half in his absence, prompting the proslavery *Leavenworth Herald* to comment scathingly on the "hired emissaries of such despicable traitors as Eli Thayer, Amos Lawrence, . . . among whom the wives of Reverend gentlemen . . . are tolerated after taking to their bed and their own arms a stinking negro wench, only selecting a wench instead of a buck because it was she that made first application—judging whom from the past, we may early look for a flourishing crop of young mulattoes as members of ministerial families."[41]

The AMA missionaries' outspoken radicalism on the race question may have alienated more discrete and pragmatic elements within the northeastern free-state contingent. The NEEAC organ, the *Herald of Freedom,* maintained that emancipation through apprenticeship would serve "the best interests of all concerned." It is thus no wonder that the company preferred to associate with less "ultra" missionary bodies than the AMA. A typical alliance involved the Rev. Samuel Y. Lum of the American Home Mission Society. When the impecunious Lum family arrived in Kansas in September 1854, General Pomeroy took the missionary by hand "as a true brother, and from his own pocket," helped him to meet his initial expenses. Lum joined the Lawrence Association and held the first service in the settlement on October 1, 1854. On the fifteenth of the same month, when the Plymouth Congregational Church of Lawrence was founded, he conducted its first service in the Pioneer Boarding House, a hay tent owned by the New England Emigrant Aid Company. Lum reported that the members of his church were, for the most part, prominent members of New England churches, "men who have been influenced to come here, not mainly from a desire of wealth, but to plant the standard of the Cross in this fair land." A congregation of about a hundred met in the general sleeping apartment of the Company, "a room about 50 by 20 feet, made of poles, and thatched with prairie grass" on the Sabbath. The colony "in mass meeting" invited Lum "to supply their pulpit for a year."[42]

Lum's ties with the emigrant aid company are hardly surprising in view of the fact that the company's stance on antislavery was in greater harmony with that of the AIIMS than with the position of the AMA. The Christian abolitionist Amos Finch complained that Lum treated him "coolly," perhaps because "we don't exactly agree with regard to certain matters pertaining to the great questions of reform. . . . He expresses his views in opposition to the position taken by the AMA. . . . I do not regard Mr. Lum as sound antislavery in his operations here." What was more, "Mr. Lum will not come out in daylight and say he is for the black law, but gives his decided influence in favor of those who take that position . . . because it is expedient to do so," Finch charged.[43]

In April 1855 the AHMS commissioned C. E. Blood of Springfield, Illinois, to supplement Lum's efforts in Kansas. On the advice of George Park, the Free-Soil editor of the *Parkville Luminary*, Blood located in the vicinity of a city site selected by a party of New England emigrants between the Blue and the Kansas Rivers known as Juniatta. The AHMS clergyman requested NEEAC agent Samuel Pomeroy to send up the Big Blue one of the best companies that should emigrate to the territory. Early in the spring of 1855 a band of many "excellent men" arrived and subsequently formed, in collaboration with a group from Cincinnati, the town of Manhattan, located six miles from Juniatta, at the mouth of the Big Blue. Blood was favorably impressed with the moral standards of the emigrants. Those at Juniatta were "fair specimens of the best New England character," while the settlers of Manhattan were "*mostly* religious people" who maintained a Sabbath school and prayer meeting. By December 1856 Blood was able to report the existence of a substantial free-state majority in western Kansas—at Manhattan, Zeandale, and Ashland, which now fell within the limits of his expanded missionary field.[44]

The 1855 spring emigration from New England brought a further accretion of strength to the AHMS contingent in the territory. Rev. Richard Knight, for one, left Springfield, Massachusetts, with the Hampden County Colony for Kansas in April 1855. In the course of a short and ill-fated stay in the territory, during which the friendly attentions of General Pomeroy alleviated his troubles somewhat, the minister was forced to shift his operations to Topeka when sickness depopulated his original preaching spot on the Neosho in the summer. On twice becoming the victim of "domestic bereavement," he returned to the East with the remainder of his afflicted family in March 1856.[45]

The society commissioned Lewis Bodwell of New York to replace

Knight at Topeka in July 1856. Bodwell's Kansas experience began omi-
nously with his arrest by the proslavery "law and order party" upon his
arrival in the territory after a journey across Iowa on foot. After his re-
lease by the "bogus" authorities, the minister settled in Topeka where he
preached his first sermon as the regularly appointed minister of the predominantly New England "Free" Congregational church on October 26,
1856. Bodwell had more cheerful news to report than his predecessor.
The character of the community where he made his home bore a "true
New England stamp." A vigilant Temperance Society flourished and
an "Institute" replete with a valuable library and weekly debates had
usurped the barroom as the chief attraction of the settlement.[46]

The following account of Bodwell's typical day, in the missionary's
own words, illustrates the diverse concerns that daily demanded the
clergymen's attention:

> Saddled my horse and rode four miles before breakfast, to procure
> a workman whose presence was necessary by the usual hour for
> work. [Bodwell was overseeing the completion of a church for his
> congregation.] Next, five miles more to visit a ministerial neighbor
> who was very ill. Thence, three miles to order at one place some
> lime, at another to find a man to load it, and at a third to order some
> stone from the quarry; then back to the church, two miles; thence
> to another quarry to help roll on a load of stone. From there, . . . [I
> called] upon a church member who was lying very ill; back to the
> quarry, and helped load more stone, and finally, a four mile ride
> home. On another day I was stopped in the midst of a similar round
> of duties to attend a funeral three or four miles away, across the
> river—a journey necessarily made on foot. . . . Scarcity of laborers
> and of means to pay them lays upon him who would see any such
> work go on, the necessity of donning his working suit, and putting
> his own hands to the work.[47]

Ill health compelled Lum to resign his pastoral charge of the congregational church at Lawrence in 1857. In the meantime, the clergyman
undertook extensive tours of exploration into the remote wilderness of
the interior in search of promising new missionary fields and was soon
urging the AHMS to expand its ministerial force to keep pace with the

tide of population rolling into the territory: "In little over three years," he wrote, "the wild unbroken prairie is teeming with life crowded with busy intelligent farmers, and the towns springing up as if by magic are crowded by thousands of earnest businessmen and mechanics," who required the restraining influences of the Gospel more than ordinary immigrants. Several new towns were being laid out and experience demonstrated that "those towns give most evidence of permanent prosperity, where the earnest faithful preacher was on the ground *at the very beginning.*" Accordingly, in 1857 the AHMS dispatched to the territory four ministers who had formed a "Kansas Band" at the Andover Theological Seminary the previous year. Sylvester D. Storrs, Grosvenor C. Morse, Roswell D. Parker, and Richard Cordley had, since the summer of 1856, held weekly prayer meetings and examined reports from the "battlefield" of Kansas.[48]

In the autumn of 1857 Storrs settled in Quindaro, the "port of entry" for Kansas and called "Yankee Town" because it was founded by New England people. The missionary reported that a majority of the citizens of Quindaro were in favor of the Black Law, which forbade Negro children to attend school with the whites. The few "colored" children in Quindaro were "well-behaved and very anxious to learn." Since their numbers were too small to warrant the establishment of a separate school, Mrs. Storrs spent time every week giving them "gratuitous instruction." Morse organized a Congregational Church in Emporia, a township located near the junction of the Cottonwood and Neosho Rivers, "one of the finest agricultural districts in the territory" and peopled by industrious young men, as intelligent as any the missionary had seen back East. Those emigrants who hailed from west of the Ohio River, however, had religious characters that were "anything but good."[49]

Parker accepted the challenge of Leavenworth, "the most important and perhaps the most difficult missionary field in the territory."[50] By November 1858 this settlement had grown into a bustling town with over 9,000 inhabitants, including 79 lawyers and 38 doctors, 2 theaters, 5 weekly papers, and 4 dailies; it was the destination of over 300 steamboat trips in six months, carrying freight worth $67,000. It was however, also the home of 200 liquor shops, 7 billiard saloons, and 3,000 Germans who ran an "infidel association" and violated the Lord's Day by raising the American flag at their five public gardens, dancing to bands of music, engaging in fencing and gymnastic exercises, and drinking lager beer. Thus, "between the Germans and the steamboats," the faithful at Leavenworth could "hardly be said to have a Sabbath." In the midst of this "seething sea of sin," nine evangelical churches maintained a tenuous hold on survival. The dauntless Parker rose to the challenge of Leavenworth. A total stranger to the town, the missionary hired a hall upon arrival, advertised himself in the papers and began preaching. By November 1858 he had organized a Congregational Church of twenty-eight members in concert with a few Congregational and New School Presbyterian brethren.[51] In the meantime, Cordley replaced Lum at Lawrence. By May 1859 a host of new commissions — F. M. Serenbetz at the German settlement of Humboldt, Paul Shephard at Big Springs and Tecumseh, O. L. Woodford at Grasshopper Falls, D. F. Judson and Warren Mayo at Minneola, and G. S. Northrup at Geneva — had driven the number of clergymen sustained by the AHMS in Kansas to fourteen.[52]

In the initial period of settlement, the AHMS missionaries appeared to be more anxious to combat the "baneful effects of Unitarianism" and other "wild heresies," which threatened to "crowd orthodoxy out of Kansas." Direct strictures against slavery were a lot rarer and began to appear in their letters only as the outrages perpetrated by the Slave Power assumed serious proportions. Apparently the clergymen believed that freedom was clearly linked with a pure gospel, so that efforts to preserve and propagate religious orthodoxy would automatically bring about the progress of antislavery doctrines.[53]

The road to "true religion" in Kansas was a rocky one indeed. The evangelical cause as a whole faced formidable foes in the general collapse of the restraints of civilized society, in the near universal "worship of Mammon," and the disruptive influence of political chaos within the territory. Within a few months of his arrival in the territory, a disillusioned Lum was forced to change his opinion on the general character of the emigration to the West. Even those raised in the moral-religious traditions of the East, "when outside the restraints of eastern society" acted out of "the native depravity of the human heart." Profanity was commonplace, and the sound of the rifle and the axe desecrated many a Sabbath.[54] Along the Missouri River especially, good morals were "as little known among the boatmen as crystal drops in its turbid waters." During the season of navigation, boats arrived and left, landed and received freight on the Sabbath as on other days of the week. Storrs lamented that he did not know of a Sabbath-keeping boat on the river and prayed for the provision of alternative means of transportation: "There has been much traveling done on the Sabbath on this river, both by ministers and laymen. . . . The ministers perhaps thinking that they could *preach* away their guilt in so doing." [55]

Some clergymen strayed even further from the path of righteousness. One of the "old settlers of Osawatomie, a deacon in the Baptist church, one who had heretofore been most decided in temperance, antislavery, and all reforms," built a large hotel and applied for a license to sell liquor.[56] Grog shops proliferated in the vicinity of such a model settlement as Lawrence at an alarming rate, while at Quindaro, in as many as three instances men from New England engaged in "that heinous business" of rum selling.[57] The crux of the problem, as Storrs saw it, lay in the fact that "the peculiarities of the West exist here in an intense form. . . . If a man is given to profanity, he becomes extremely profane, if to Sabbath-breaking, few restraints are brought to bear upon him, if to intemperance, he is seldom urged to reform. I cannot say that men are really much *worse* in Kansas than in New England, but wickedness is less concealed, everyone doing openly what he desires." [58] This confession was rare among New England ministers, who generally held up their section as a model of propriety and piety.

On his arrival in Topeka, Bodwell found the prospects of building a church somewhat poor. Of the three trustees of the church building fund, one was slowly recovering from a severe illness, another had repaired East to spend the winter, and the third was a prisoner on trial at Lecompton with other free-state men. The swelling tide of emigration called for more commodious houses of worship, forcing ministers to preach at different places at different times, exacerbating the problem of securing a permanent audience. The faithful of Manhattan were forced to congregate in a log cabin without floors or windows, "to which the light of heaven had no access, except by avenues which would admit equally the winds and storms of winter." At Lawrence the hall that had served as the venue of public worship was, in due course, converted into barracks for soldiers.[59]

The *Home Missionary* reproached businessmen and men of property in the West for allowing the churches, which enhanced the quality of their family life and the value of their property, to "look wistfully" to "the hills of New England" for support. The general run of emigrants were poor young men who had exhausted all their resources in making the trip to Kansas. They could do little in the way of financing churches and schools or even assuming the entire burden of ministerial support. But in a money-scarce economy, contributions of labor and produce sometimes replaced cash payments. At Manhattan, young men subscribed fifty dollars each to the church building fund, to be paid in "hauling and other work." Some gave lumber or logs, and others the use of teams, stone and lime.[60]

Territorial Kansas became a battleground for another kind of tussle that arrayed the materialism of a pervasive speculative spirit against the progress of "a pure gospel." Missionaries frequently referred to claim disputes among settlers: "Many claims are cut up badly. Some lose their timber, some their prairie, some lose both; . . . I often think of the Psalmist's expressions: 'The Lord is my portion' 'Thou maintainest my lot.' Truly blessed must that soul be that finds itself in possession of such a claim." Practical needs, however, dictated the acquisition of earthly claims as well. The Byrds applied to the AMA for a loan of four hundred dollars to pay for their valuable claim of 160 acres near Leavenworth City. They lived in a log cabin, and had ten acres of land "well enclosed," on which grew "an excellent crop of corn."[61]

Most clergymen were obliged to supplement their ministerial salaries with subsistence farming. The Yankees were heir to a Puritan religious tradition fraught with the paradoxical requirement that man attend to his worldly calling faithfully, without allowing material success to interfere with the higher love of God.[62] The missionaries found themselves engaged in a delicate balancing act to prevent their moral obligation to do well on earth from degenerating into an ungodly lust after material wealth. Not all were successful in this endeavor. One clergyman lamented: "Ministers metamorphosed into keen speculators are strewn all over the territory." This observer had counted as many as fourteen such "*ex*-ministers" of various denominations in Lawrence. Even some of those who were still in service had "got one foot in." He continued:

the transformation from a preacher to a speculator is gradual and unconscious. The preacher first seeks to "get a home of his own," which of course is proper. But he finds the word "home" in Kansas a very expansive term. It may mean a log cabin, seven by nine, or a claim, a few town shares, a sawmill, etc. I am convinced that the efficiency of the ministerial force of all denominations taken together is reduced at least one-half by this diversion of its energies.[63]

The Christian abolitionist contingent in Kansas suffered a casualty in the losing battle with materialism when Reverend Finch succumbed to the temptations of speculation and resigned from the AMA in 1860.[64]

Few missionaries went as far as Finch. A majority of the clergymen, however, had to devote some attention to secular pursuits because they were perennially plagued by financial distress. As far as the home missionaries were concerned, the lack of a regular mail service, combined with the AHMS rule that drafts in payment of missionaries could be forwarded only upon the receipt of satisfactory reports of labor at specified intervals, almost invariably occasioned delays in the dispatch of paychecks. As Blood explained to Badger, the AHMS policy of payment spelled acute financial embarrassment for one situated as he was, 190 miles from a post office regularly receiving mail:

I write my report, for instance, at the close of the Quarter. It is perhaps three weeks before I have an opportunity to send it to the Post Office. It is three weeks longer reaching New York. Then owing to the irregularity of the mails I may receive my draft in three weeks or I may not in eight as in the present case it is eight and a half weeks since we have had a mail. Then when I receive the draft, we have no bank or moneyed merchant to cash it, and perhaps I must send by private conveyance to Kansas City, Missouri, or Parkville to get it cashed, and in three weeks longer I may get my money. All this time I have been living on credit and making promises which I have not been able to fulfill.[65]

In many instances, the Christian abolitionists received only a part of the amounts pledged by the people toward their support, while the diminished receipts of the AMA's treasury during periods of economic downturn, as in 1857–58, made it difficult to pay the portion assumed by the association. Harvey Jones' parishioners undertook to raise $130 for his support. Since money was scarce, they paid him in produce and labor, much to the minister's inconvenience, since the produce was paid at the settlers' own price and often in commodities the clergyman did not need. The destruction of free-state property during the "border warfare" compounded the general poverty of a majority of the settlers, often making it impossible for them to redeem their pledges of ministerial support.[66]

Occasionally, settlers appealed to their minister for material aid when drought ruined their crops, when sickness prevented them from working, or when the scarcity of money made work unavailable for wage earners. Thus Serenbetz incurred a debt of $194 for the relief of his poor German parishioners at Humboldt who turned to him as their "only guide and protector." At other times, a minster's congregation came to his aid in his moment of distress. When Brownlee and his wife lay ill in bed, his brethren from Superior came over en masse and cut and stacked a sufficient quantity of hay for the Brownlees' cattle. They came "richly laden with good things to eat," so that their minister had to prop up his table for once and everyone had a "merry, bustling time for two days."[67]

Besides economic insecurity, numerous other tribulations beset missionary work on the frontier. The clergymen devoted a disproportionate amount of space in their periodic reports to recounting the physical discomforts of life in the wilderness. Lum's house, which according to the missionary was "said to be as comfortable as any," had no floor or walls, "nothing but a bare 'siding' and that so open as to give us views of the country in almost any direction." John Lowry was even less fortunate than Lum. He spent several weeks with his son in an ox wagon covered with cloth. They cooked out in the open, and rainstorms frequently obliged them to go to bed without supper. If howling wolves did not keep them awake, hungry ones prowled around their wagon in search of crumbs, so that the minister had to take care not to leave his books outdoors. "I am now seated on the bare ground with a trunk for a writing table and the wind blowing so hard that I can scarcely hold my paper and prevent it blowing away," Lowry wrote Jocelyn.[68]

The Finch family did not fare too well in the beginning. In July 1855 the minister wrote:

We put up a small log house without one foot of lumber, split out stiff for floors, doors, and window casing, and were under the necessity of going into our house before we had the large cracks filled up. Yesterday, there came up a tremendous rain-storm with heavy winds, so that . . . [there was] not a dry thing [left] in the house. . . . I have been obliged to prepare a field in which to keep my pony and cow. Labor is so high that my means will not admit of hiring much. Provisions of all kinds are also very high here; flour is $16 per barrel, sugar from 10 to 12 cents per pound. . . . So you see that it takes something to live in Kansas.[69]

Not infrequently, disease and death through exposure and a poor diet—if not violence—cast a heavy pall of gloom over a missionary's home. Harvey Jones lost his only child and Henry Morell his wife to the ravages of disease.

A territory in the throes of political anarchy offered poor grounds for the hope that the Bible and the ballot box would be effective weapons in achieving the victory of freedom and religion. Although the AMA advised its missionaries in Kansas "not to become mixed up with military companies," Norton reported that the exigencies of war had forced the "best Christians," even ministers of the Gospel, including himself to take up arms. And who could blame clergymen confronted with "an invading and infuriating army of 3,000 men under desperate leaders" for resorting to the "only natural means of defense: prayer and good rifles"?[70]

Rev. John Stewart, formerly of New Hampshire, would undoubtedly have agreed with Norton. The Methodist minister had managed to survive the winter of 1854–55 without getting into debt by working for wages making rails. An abundance of wild ducks on the Wakarusa Creek near his claim assured his family a regular supply of meat. The following spring, the purchase of a cow, a "tolerable crop" of corn and vegetables from five acres of prairie, and a "temporary stable" filled with cornstalk to feed the cow had placed the Stewart family on the path to economic self-sufficiency when the advent of proslavery outrages in the district compelled the minister to forsake the Bible and the plow for a supply of Sharps rifles. Similar harassment in the Ogden area near Fort Riley persuaded another NEEAC emigrant, Lemuel Knapp of New York, that "a deep scheme" of proslavery inspiration "was laid to prevent [free-state settlers] from planting." In pursuit of this "plan," Knapp believed, his "woodpile which was a very large one" and very nearly his house as well, were set aflame, and his fences burnt, while he himself was made to "dance attendance on the bogus courts as witnesses or jurymen" often on cases about which he knew nothing. "The consequence of this," he complained to the National Kansas Committee established in 1856 for the relief of free-state settlers, "was that a large part of the seed I intended to sow, was planted too late to be productive and what little grew was destroyed by a large herd of cattle that came down from the Republican fork, when we were all sick, and unable to drive them off." [71]

Stewart remarked in his statement to the Kansas Committee, "we came here to work, not to fight . . . to plant fields and build up towns, to erect schools and churches. . . . The proslavery party . . . mistook our quiet disposition for cowardice. How vividly they were mistaken, the history of our battles will prove. We do not like to fight, but we can and will fight desperately when there is no other alternative." They were as good as their word, as the engagements of the Wakarusa Liberty Guard, a free-state military company formed in Stewart's community, demonstrated. The company dispatched J. B. Abbott, a maker of gold pens, who had emigrated to the territory under Aid Company auspices to "make a home . . . in a free state," to the East to procure arms. Likewise, the fifty-year-old Pennsylvanian Samuel Anderson had plowed nine acres of his claim bordering the south fork of the Osawatomie Creek when news of the impending siege of Lawrence in May 1856 stalled his farming career for a while. As a member of John Brown Jr.'s company, and subsequently the captain of the free-state Pottawatomie Guards, Anderson devoted his attention to drilling his men each week, preparing them to "hold themselves in readiness," in the event of an emergency.[72]

Obviously the world of the small commercial farmer envisaged by the northeastern free labor ideologues as an oasis of New England culture in the moral wilderness of the West, if it existed at all, was in serious turmoil.

4

"A Model New England State"

When Henry Ward Beecher, the pastor of Brooklyn's Plymouth Congregational Church and widely acknowledged as the "spokesman of middle-class America,"[1] described the antislavery crusade in Kansas as a battle between civilization on the one hand and barbarism on the other,[2] he was both molding and reflecting the sentiments of a significant segment of the Northern public. The agents of the free-state campaign invested the armed men who confronted each other on the prairies of Kansas with stark, contrasting images that struck a deep chord in the culture of Victorian America with its concern for all-around human progress. On one side of the battle line stood "men of liberty, Christianity, industry, arts, and of universal prosperity"; on the other, "the waste and refuse materials of a worn out slave state population," whose civilization rested upon "a rifle, a horse, a hound, a slave, tobacco and whiskey . . . and an annual uproarious camp meeting." A hint of class consciousness lent anti-Southernism a pungent edge. The wretched human tools of slavery deviated not simply from the standards of Northern society, but from those of Northern middle-class society. The British journalist Thomas H. Gladstone described the plunderers of Lawrence in May 1856 thus: "Men, for the most part of large frame, with red flannel shirts and immense boots worn outside their trousers, their faces unwashed and unshaven, . . . wearing the most savage looks and giving utterance to the most horrible imprecations and blasphemies." To Gladstone, the men's attire appeared to symbolize the incongruity of proslavery barbarism coupled with Yankee gentility: "Some displayed a grotesque intermixture in their dress, having crossed their native red rough shirt with the satin vest or narrow dress-coat pillaged from the wardrobe of some Yankee, or having girded themselves with cords and tassels which the day before had ornamented the curtains of the Free-State Hotel."[3]

The urgency of a free-state victory in Kansas derived, in part, from the need to prevent the virgin West from relapsing into ugly primitivism of the kind described by Gladstone. NEEAC agent Samuel C. Pomeroy observed in his welcoming address to Gov. Andrew Reeder in October 1854 that the treasures of Lawrence—that oasis of New England culture in Kansas—consisted not of "wealth . . . computed by dollars and dimes," but of "the facilities for high intellectual and moral culture," planted by the fathers of New England in "the infancy of the [American] Republic," to stand as the "great bulwarks of Freedom and Happiness." New Englanders came, as their forbears "who sought liberty in the Mayflower" had done, bringing with them "the Bible in one hand, and the spelling-book in the other, with the high purpose of laying the one upon the altar of a Free Church, and the other upon the desk of a Free School."[4]

Pomeroy's words summed up significant elements of the Kansas crusade's appeal among middle-class white Northerners. Refracted through the lens of leading antislavery players in the embattled territory, the contest for a free Kansas emerged as more than simply an attempt to defeat slavery at the polls. It seemed to have been inspired by a larger social vision that sought to weave the threads of Protestant civilization and republican liberty bequeathed by New England's Pilgrim fathers into a uniquely northeastern tapestry of "Americanism" over the morally and economically vulnerable West. This broader goal required remaking the motley crew of "deviant" elements, whom the diverse factions of northeasterners encountered in the West, into model specimens of New England society by setting a good example.

Expounding on the motives that inspired that "new discovery in Political Economy"—the New England Emigrant Aid Company—the *Herald of Freedom* informed its eastern readers that a large proportion of the emigrants to the territories consisted of the lower orders of European society who were "entirely destitute of the institutions of Christianity or education." Eli Thayer also hoped, by his venture, to induce the migration of the "poorer population" of the eastern cities, "necessarily vicious" by virtue of their poverty. These elements were very likely to breed settlements rife with infidelity and vice. Under these circumstances, the "enterprising sons of New England . . . although casting a longing eye from our sterile soil and cold climate to the fruitful fields of the far West choose rather to remain and struggle with scarcity." The NEEAC would resolve this dilemma through the vehicle of organized emigration — an important concept in free labor circles. Northerners would win the West because they would emigrate in colonies with their civilization intact rather than as isolated individuals dispersed hither and yon. By their stellar example, they would, moreover, reform and refine aberrant elements in the territory.[5] The emphasis on transplanting the "trophies of free labor" in the frontier reflected a desire to inculcate the middle-class morality and enterprise of New England in the West. The institutions of "civilized eastern society" were not only important vehicles for cultivating the qualities of "honesty, frugality, diligence, punctuality, and sobriety," which the Protestant ethic and Republican outlook exalted as essential to success in one's calling,[6] but also promoted the "general freedom of the human mind," which contained the key to human progress.[7]

In a lecture delivered at Lawrence on the occasion of the seventy-ninth anniversary of the U.S. Declaration of Independence, NEEAC resident agent and future free-state governor Charles Robinson drew the audience's attention to the diverse historical legacies of the North and the South. While Virginia, the oldest state in the Union, took root in the "most plentiful, sweet, fruitful, and wholesome soil of all the world," Massachusetts was settled on a sterile soil and in a forbidding climate by men made of "sterner material than was the soil or the climate." Virginia drew "her nourishment at the breast of parental kindness," developed a religion "congenial" to the mother country, sent her youth across the Atlantic to drink at the "fountains of science in England," and built an ostentatious lifestyle around luxuries imported from Europe. The rugged New Englanders, on the other hand, assailed by the rigors of nature and the oppression of the British crown, were thrown upon their own resources.[8]

Passing over the difficult issue of how Virginia, "dandled in the lap of complaisance," came to claim so prominent a share in the nation's revolutionary heritage, Robinson went on to record the important fact that "the same year that the Puritans effected their landing at Plymouth, a cargo of slaves was imported into Virginia." The subsequent course of Southern history afforded the rest of the country "valuable instruction." The future Republican congressman drew on the census of 1850, as well as on the testimony "not of abolitionists, not of hot-headed fanatics, but of slaveholders, southern politicians, and southern divines," like Cassius M. Clay and Thomas F. Marshall of Kentucky, and the Rev. William Henry Ruffner of Virginia, to demonstrate that slavery had led the South down a path of "indolence, ignorance, vice, and whiskey." Would the people of Kansas allow their adopted home— "the Eden of the world"—to take the southern route over the northern one of "enterprise, intelligence, skill, morality, sobriety, and universal thrift"? The juxtaposition of these sectional attributes left no doubt concerning the link between morality and economic progress in free-state rhetoric.[9]

The NEEAC substantiated such rhetoric by complementing its hotel and mill-building activities with enterprises to enhance the intellectual and moral life of Kansas Territory. In Lawrence, a frame house known as the Emigrant Aid Building served as schoolhouse, church, town hall, and the premises of the company's Lawrence office, until 1857. Robinson paid the instructor her salary out of his own pocket in 1855.[10] By November 1854 Robinson had laid out the grounds for a college, but Amos Lawrence advised him to first build a school to prepare boys for college. "You must sweep the state with a Yorktown broom, made in Trenton," the NEEAC treasurer urged. In laying the foundation of a sound system of education in Kansas on the model of New England, Lawrence was, however, anxious to avoid what he considered at least one pitfall of the New England system, namely the "over-education" of women. He wrote Robinson that a projected preparatory school "should be for boys and not for girls. . . . My own impression is that we have fallen into a great error here in Massachusetts, of late years, by raising the standard of female education so high that the physical development has been checked, the constitutions weakened." The women of New England made "good scholars and good school mistresses," but were too "unhealthy and weak" to bear strong children. "While we are refining the intellect, we are injuring the stock," Lawrence feared. He had no faith "in the utility of giving diplomas to women, except for good house-wifery, for courage and for raising good families of children."[11]

Lawrence's misgivings about the over-education of women reflected a crucial aspect of the middle-class mentality born of industrial capitalism. The advent of wage labor in the antebellum North solidified the doctrine of separate spheres for "public" man on the one hand and "private" woman on the other. The family, stripped of its earlier economic function as a unit of production, assumed new importance as an organic refuge from the turbulent, amoral, self-interest driven world of commerce beyond.[12] The "cornerstone" of this pious haven of affection was, the *Herald of Freedom* noted,

> the virtue of women. . . . Must we not trace all other blessings of civilized life to the doors of our private dwellings? Are not our hearth-stones guarded by holy forms of conjugal, filial, and parental love, the cornerstones of Church and State — more sacred than either, more necessary than both? Let our temples crumble, let our public halls of justice be levelled with the dust; but spare our homes! Let no socialist invade them with his wild plans of community.[13]

Slavery's desecration of the sanctity of the family posed as serious a violation of a cardinal value of progressive Northern society as did the socialists' communitarianism. The *Herald of Freedom* underscored the pro-Southern ruffians' contempt for the family, white as well as black, in its observations on the different character of the two belligerent camps after the Wakarusa War: one was a "besotted rabble . . . sleeping off the fumes of intoxication. . . . The other was cool and collected . . . determined [to drive back] the devils incarnate *who boasted they would . . . ravish our wives and daughters.*" When the citizens of Lawrence took up arms, they did so in "defense of . . . their hearthstones, and their family altars," and their female kin.[14] For one mother, as the pivot of those relations in which "we find through life the chief solace and joy of existence," was "worth a thousand friends; one sister truer than twenty intimate companions. . . . Coldness may spring up; distance may separate; different spheres may divide"; but time only strengthened the ties of family, the NEEAC organ declared.[15]

Northern distaste for slavery was inextricably woven with faith in the rewarding complementarity of separate spheres in a mesh of cultural values that schools, like churches, were expected to transmit. Small wonder, then, that the NEEAC took its commitment to education rather seriously. Although Amos Lawrence's plan for a preparatory school for boys did not materialize, owing to trouble over land titles, the Boston businessman placed his hopes of replicating New England's intellectual facilities on the frontier in a college, to be known as the Free-State College. It would stand as a "monument to perpetuate the memory of those martyrs" of freedom who fell in the battle against slavery and would "radiate forever the light of liberty, of learning, of religion." [16] In pursuit of this goal, Lawrence established a trust fund of ten thousand dollars under the guardianship of Robinson and Pomeroy.[17] At the same time, in his correspondence with prominent territorial leaders, including Gov. John W. Geary, he suggested that part of the income from the fund be diverted to provide for the best possible system of common schools and Sunday schools in every settlement "in advance of the population." Attention to public education was the key to building a model state that would inspire "the old states to keep up a high standard of learning, virtue and patriotism." The *Herald* urged that schools throughout the territory uniformly adopt a set of books including the Town's series of readers and spellers, which were "the best extant, . . . and generally in use in New England, New York, and Pennsylvania." [18]

Northeastern emigrants were in the vanguard of the territorial temperance movement. The Lawrence City Association constitution incorporated an article prohibiting the sale of alcoholic liquor within the town limits. This provision was repeatedly flouted, prompting the city to submit the liquor question to a popular vote. Even though the temperance measure passed by a vote of 74 to 1, "tippling shops" continued to flourish. The ladies of Lawrence now rose to the occasion. In the summer of 1856, according to one sympathetic chronicler, they "first tried to buy out the stock on hand, exacting a promise that it should not be replenished. Failing in this, they took up the *hatchet* in defense of their right to inhabit peaceful . . . homes and to destroy that which was destroying their husbands and sons." The Lawrence Temperance Association attempted to buttress the women's efforts by appointing a committee to suggest "innocent and healthful amusements" as alternatives to drinking. One meeting voted dancing an acceptable pastime but rejected card-playing as immoral. In the meantime, alcohol consumption continued to prevail over more innocuous pursuits, prompting the ladies to renew their prohibition crusade in January 1857. An assemblage of forty temperance advocates visited several offending groggeries, whence they "saw and conquered." The opposition was reportedly led by a Franklin-returned "noisy rabble" that paraded down the streets of Lawrence in a wagon waving a half-barrel of whiskey and a red flag, earning the hearty denunciation of all "decent people." [19] Nevertheless, the intemperate who lost that particular skirmish won the larger war over alcohol in the territory.

In its endeavor to fashion the West after the pattern of the progressive, Protestant Northeast, the NEEAC found valuable allies in the evangelical opponents of slavery. Several of the AMA leaders were prominent men in business and banking, railroad promotion, and antebellum reform.[20] Steeped in the values of the free labor doctrine, they combined their commitment to Christian abolitionism with attempts to inculcate into frontier society the very qualities that Republican ideology exalted through the vehicles of free churches and Sabbath schools. The evangelical emphasis on a new morality grounded in personal self-government harmonized well with the individualistic ethic of the emerging wage-labor-based capitalist order, with its abandonment of "the old relations of dependence, servility, and mutuality." [21]

The more conservative American Home Missionary Society shared the sociocultural goals of the AMA, although it eschewed its radicalism on the race question. A multidenominational clerical convention held at the Free State Hotel in Lawrence on February 12, 1856, passed a series of resolutions, urging upon the settlers the observance of the Sabbath, the discountenance of alcoholic liquors, the formation of local Bible societies as auxiliaries to the American Bible Society, and the organization of Sunday schools. Lum served on a committee chosen to draft a constitution for an auxiliary Bible society. At a subsequent meeting, which opened with a prayer by Richard Knight, clerics from different denominations resolved to bury their sectarian differences in favor of a ministerial alliance to promote "the circulation of the Scriptures, the observance of the Sabbath, the causes of Freedom, Temperance and other moral reforms." Knight was one of the original signers of the constitution of the Kansas Ministerial Alliance, as the proposed society was called. Lum was elected an officer of the organization, while Ephraim Nute, a missionary of the American Unitarian Association, served as its secretary.[22]

In the meantime, at a meeting of citizens interested in building a church in Lawrence, E. B. Whitman reported favorably on the origin and progress of a movement initiated by the American Unitarian Association in the East to "furnish aid for religion and education in Kansas." Several of the "first men in Massachusetts" had responded to the appeal with generous donations. The pledge of between three and four thousand dollars by religious societies in Boston, Dorchester, Providence, Portsmouth, Salem, Taunton, Chicopee, Cambridge, and Waltham testified to the "interest felt in the people of Kansas by their neighbors and friends who had stayed home." Additional funds were expected to be raised for a church tower rendered essential by the gift of a bell and the promise of a clock. Individual parishes and congregations throughout Massachusetts had provided additional fixtures for the church: an elegant pulpit Bible, hymn books for the pews, and an organ.[23] Subsequently, the assembly adopted Charles Robinson's resolution pledging the Rev. Ephraim Nute the "zealous cooperation" of the citizens of Lawrence in establishing the Ministerial Alliance.[24]

The NEEAC cultivated its association with appropriate missionary bodies, believing that the projection of the free state cause as a religious-cultural crusade would elevate its moral tenor in Northern eyes. In 1855 the NEEAC proceeded to rally the Northern churches in support of its enterprise. A committee of clergymen headed by the NEEAC's chief propagandist and historian, Unitarian minister Edward E. Hale, issued a circular urging Northern divines to cooperate with the company in promoting the four great causes of "Freedom, Religion, Education, and Temperance" in Kansas by enlisting as life members of the corporation. The circular claimed that the company had established all the towns of consequence in the territory, except Leavenworth on the Missouri border. Divine service was maintained only in settlements founded under company influence; traffic in intoxicating liquors was severely limited in such communities; schools due to open in July 1855 at Lawrence, Topeka, Osawatomie, and Hampden owed their existence to the exertions of the company.[25] Although the circular was part of a fund-raising drive designed to replenish the Aid Company's nearly bankrupt treasury, its propaganda value for the image of the free-state cause in Kansas cannot be overlooked.[26] Amos Lawrence suggested that the Sharps rifles sent for the Aid Company settlers' defense be sold to men who were on the "right side of the free-state question" and that the money be donated to the Pilgrim Church in Kansas. "This will be even better than 'beating their swords into ploughshares,' " he wrote.[27]

The evangelical abolitionist endeavor to mold the frontier in the image of the genteel Northeast differed in one important respect from that of the NEEAC. The AMA conceived of a biracial "bourgeois Christian" order, which would offer both blacks and whites the opportunity for social mobility and economic independence through hard work. Its missionaries in Kansas did not balk at attacking racial injustice from the pulpit or at arguing against Negro exclusion in debates sponsored by territorial lyceums. They welcomed black children into their Sunday schools and harbored fugitive slaves in their homes, often at great risk to themselves and their families. Denigrated as "nigger preachers," many Christian abolitionists were barred from the homes of avowed free-soilers.[28]

The Rev. John H. Byrd held out Hiram Young, a former slave from Independence, Missouri, who had hired out his time, purchased his freedom, and made a fortune in wagon and ox-yoke manufacture, as a model product of the free labor system. Young employed white men and hired slaves, many of whom he assisted in buying their freedom. Although he was illiterate and employed a clerk to do his writing, he made all contracts and paid all monies. "And," Byrd concluded, "I understand that he possesses the confidence of the community as an upright and enterprising businessman."[29]

Unfortunately, not all freed slaves made smooth transitions into paid employment, and the missionaries demonstrated a lack of understanding of the cultural implications of slave experiences for the emancipated black worker. Slavery, as historian Eric Foner has pointed out, was not designed to "produce workers socialized to the discipline of capitalist wage labor." The chief engine of industry in a capitalist system, namely the desire to progressively raise living standards, was not relevant to freedmen with little experience with the marketplace and accustomed to existing at subsistence level under bondage.[30] But like the Northern "soldiers of light and love" who went south during Reconstruction to inculcate the values of thrift, hard work, and punctuality among the former slaves, Christian abolitionists had no doubt that the right kind of education would equip blacks to take advantage of the opportunity for economic success offered by a free labor system.[31] Their prescription for the smooth integration of former slaves into white society consisted of the provision of education and spiritual sustenance, rather than "forty acres and a mule" to the emancipated people.

In its venture to extend market agriculture to the West, the NEEAC, however, was willing to bow to the dictates of political expediency by supporting in public the exclusion not merely of slavery but of former slaves as well. If replicating Northern society on the frontier demanded that the territory be kept white in order to keep it free, the free labor entrepreneurs were willing to acquiesce in the adoption of a territorial Black Law. Thus the *Herald* editorialized that "as in the free states, if the country is peopled by the pure Anglo-Saxons, the arts of peace will flourish, genius will triumph, mind will conquer matter. . . . Every man will be a *citizen.*"[32]

On the eve of the March 30 elections of delegates to the Kansas territorial legislature, N. W. Goodrich, formerly of McKean County, Pennsylvania, used the columns of the *Herald* to urge settlers from all sections of the country to pay heed to their common interests in Kansas and not "Africanize" the territory. In what was obviously an appeal to the interests of non-slave-holding white working men from all sections of the country, Goodrich enquired, "What motive can you have in voting for slavery in Kansas? . . . Very few of you can expect to buy slaves. Their high price, . . . the risk you run of their loss of health and death, and running away makes the investment a hazardous one." Slave labor was, moreover, unprofitable and there was certainly "nothing so attractive or agreeable" about Negroes that justified their presence if they did not make efficient workers, which of course they did not. Surely one would prefer to hire a white man instead of a Negro? The introduction of slaves would create a serious shortage of labor in the territory, because white men would refuse to place themselves on a par with the Negro, and Kansas would never have enough slaves to meet the high demand for labor. The territory could place herself in as favorable a position as though "there was not a negro in America." If she did so, she would no doubt incur the wrath of ultra proslavery men who would lose the opportunity to "throw a portion" of the free black population out of the South, and of the abolitionists who "long[ed] for an occasional chance to take a negro by hand, and give him a cordial greeting." But the denunciation of the two "extremes of ultraism," argued Goodrich, testified strongly to the correctness of the "medium position" he championed.[33]

A logical corollary of the New England crusaders' tendency toward cultural imperialism was their prejudice against groups that deviated from Northern middle-class standards of acceptable behavior. In contrast with the Democratic tolerance of cultural pluralism, Republican ideology implied uniform standards, perhaps as a logical concomitant of a program of economic nationalism.[34] The values of the progressive Northeast defined such "national" or "American" standards; the Southerner and the western frontiersman, "backward" according to the Northern scale of progress, were considered deviant elements. The agents of free labor generally correlated the degree of an emigrant group's moral and material progress to its sectional, ethnic, or class affiliations. F. M. Serenbetz, the AHMS's missionary at Humboldt, was struck by "the average ignorance among those settlers coming from Illinois and the Southern states." Their inability "to read even the Bible" promised to keep the community's future Sunday school busy.[35] The Christian abolitionist clergyman Samuel L. Adair deplored the wide prevalence of profanity, Sabbath-breaking, and drunkenness in Osawatomie. The intemperate men, though, were "mostly southern or western," the missionary added.[36] The evangelical preachers from the East claimed that such elements dealt a deathblow to the moral standards of the communities where they settled.

When Yankee refinement clashed with western vulgarity, the heterogeneous free-state movement reeled under the strains of conflict among its often incompatible constituents. There was, for example, little love lost between the NEEAC sponsored *Herald of Freedom* and the acknowledged western organ, the *Kansas Free State*, both published at Lawrence. While the *Herald* came under fire from the caustic pen of Josiah Miller, the South Carolina–born, Indiana-raised editor of the *Free State* for being "conservative" on the slavery issue, the *Herald* alleged that the rival antislavery paper was a covert proslavery enterprise operated by a "drunken editor." To substantiate its allegations, the *Herald* quoted the *Free State* as having described the "border ruffians" who illegally stormed the polls during the election of the territorial legislature on March 30, 1855, as "as fine looking a class of Missourians as we have ever seen . . . well-disciplined and under the command of good leaders." The *Herald* went on to berate the western-run paper for "taking pains" to represent the people of Lawrence as "a set of poltroons who had no courage whatever on election day." What clinched the question of the *Free State*'s true allegiance, claimed the *Herald,* was its admission that "we mingled among the Missourians, . . . trying to . . . learn their plan of operation . . . [our policy] is to cultivate the acquaintance of proslavery men — to approach and converse with them in a gentlemanly manner, and we have thus formed a good many personal friends among them." [37]

In reporting the results of the March 30 elections, the western editor used the term "Squatter ticket" in preference to "proslavery ticket" in an attempt "to give the impression abroad that it was the actual settlers here" who nominated that ticket, the *Herald* alleged. In response to Miller's assertion that the "Squatter" candidates Chapman and Banks "were both free-state men and had been put on the ticket to carry the free-state Missourians and others," the eastern paper expressed surprise that the editor of a free-state journal should be "so thoroughly advised in regard to the secret motives of the enemy." Perhaps, the *Herald* went on to inform its readers, the explanation lay in the fact that "the proslavery party put their ticket in nomination the night previous to the election while encamped on the west side of this town, and that one of the editors of our ultra antislavery journal was also in the enemy's camp . . . laughing and joking about southern chivalry." [38]

It is significant that the *Herald* should have juxtaposed its challenge of the *Free State*'s antislavery credentials with allegations that the editor of the western journal was a habitual drunkard.[39] Slavery, violence, and whiskey were irrevocably interlinked as the salient attributes of the "enemy" in northeastern free state rhetoric. On one occasion, the editors of the *Free State* expressed surprise at having been cheated by merchants at Westport, Missouri, who "supposed they were trading with Yankees." The western paper declared, "We do not see how this could be, for certainly there are no two objects more unlike than ourselves and a pure Yankee." The *Herald* responded, "Yankees! Descendants of the Pilgrim Fathers! Sons of the heroes of the revolution! How do you like the tone of the Jesuits who sail under the flag of freedom, while they are more 'unlike' you who bear the true flag aloft than the most opposite objects in nature?"[40]

Nancy Wade, a pioneer settler from Missouri, who had preceded the NEEAC party to the site of Lawrence, later recalled that the western settler had "fully as much contempt for the Yankee as the Yankee had for him." This unionist Free-Soiler's first impression of a Yankee was that "of a long slim biped somewhat lacking in the upper story." She went on to explain, "You will better understand the reason for this impression when I tell you that many of the specimens from New England brought trunks filled with trinkets to trade to the settlers for land as they would trade with natives. One young New Englander offered me two silk handkerchiefs for a cow and would throw in a pair of scissors if I'd sell him the cow that gave the buttermilk." Western and Southern pioneers chafed at the Yankees' frequent characterization of them as coarse, boorish, whiskey-doused specimens of depravity.[41]

The *Free State* complained that everything published about the NEEAC contained a few sentences as to the " 'great civilization and refinement' . . . that the company is going to introduce into the territory. Western and southern men have become tired hearing the intimations that none of these things can come from any quarter except the East." The paper sarcastically admonished the "refined gentlemen [of the East]" to "make up their minds at once to consider western men as human beings, and conclude to associate with them," for, given the preponderance of western settlers in Kansas, New England would have "but a small share in making a model state or in framing its free institutions."[42]

While slavery was the primary object of free labor assaults, the northeastern evangelicals and entrepreneurs reserved a large portion of their vituperation for the "twin evil" of "Romanism." A flood of apparently unacculturable Irish and German Roman Catholic immigrants to U.S. shores had introduced a new factor in the political crisis of the 1850s. Native Anglo-Saxon Protestants often associated the newcomers with rising crime rates, inflated welfare costs, drunken brawls, a papal crusade against public education, and moral indifference to the sin of slavery, all of which militated against the very grain of Protestant progress.[43]

The *Home Missionary* reproduced a graphic report of the tragic "exemplifications of Popery" in which Ireland abounded — "troops of beggars, children in rags, . . . obstructing your path when you walk for pleasure, and distracting your thoughts when you pause for contemplation . . . in a land so favored of heaven." In an account reminiscent of the Republican portrait of Southern society, the *New York Independent* enquired rhetorically why there was no inducement for the capitalist or the practical farmer to come and settle among the people of Ireland: "Why from this scanty village population did sixty yesterday depart for America? . . . Why have the people themselves no higher inducement to live than the grub-worm that they would fain eat? Tell us, O jolly red-faced priest, with that score of beggarly women bending reverentially about you, what is the reason for all of this?" The Seventh Annual Report of the AMA furnished an explanation. It drew parallels between a priesthood that led "the poor victims of superstition by artifice and deceit" and slavery that "ruled by brute force," and denounced both systems for spelling "death" for the "individual, [for] national virtue, and prosperity. . . . The one burns the Protestant Bible, and the other by law prevents its use, by entirely denying education and books to the slaves. . . . Popery furnishes a large proportion of the drunkards and of the miserable men who traffic in intoxicating liquors, demoralizing, impoverishing, and destroying the people."[44]

The *Herald* pronounced the project of organized emigration based on free labor attractive to the American party, which would see in the enterprise a means of establishing the Protestant religion and the common school "on the confines of the Republic." A New York insurance agent named D. R. Anthony wrote his sister Susan that in the 1858 Leavenworth municipal election, "all of the whiskey, Irish Catholic and Douglas Democrats pulled together." The "large population of ignorance in the town" had raised the cry of "free white state for free white men." The New Yorker professed support for incorporating the word "white" in the Republican platform in Kansas in order to "combat the ignorance and prejudice of the Irish." He went on disgustedly, "The great cry now is nigger, nigger, nigger. I tell many who raise the cry that niggers in New York are better educated, more intelligent and industrious than they themselves are." Anthony wished Frederick Douglass would "come here and lecture." [45]

The friends of slavery in Kansas were quick to use the apparent nativism latent in Northern antislavery in conjunction with appeals to white supremacy in an attempt to woo potential supporters among European Catholic immigrants. The proslavery Atchison *Squatter Sovereign* reminded white immigrants in the territory that free-soilers were "in favor of keeping the poor white Dutchman or Irishman from coming among us, while they help the meanest Negro to run away from his master and then make a hero of him!" Referring to Massachusetts's recourse to personal liberty bills to thwart the Fugitive Slave Law, the *Squatter Sovereign* declared that "abolitionists love negroes so well that they punish their officers for obeying the law to remove them from their state! They hate white men so bitterly, they punish their officers for obeying the law which gives them a right to stay in their state! Such is the 'law and order' practiced by the abolitionists of Massachusetts. What think Irishmen and Dutchmen of 'law and order men' here? They are all alike." Yet there is no evidence to suggest that the anti–Roman Catholic sentiments of the northeastern evangelicals and entrepreneurs in Kansas translated into support of immigration restriction. Rather, free labor advocates like Thayer and the missionaries seem to have had ample faith in the power of eastern institutions to redeem the lowliest victim of adverse circumstances of class, religion, section, and ethnicity.[46]

Thayer's hope of achieving a peaceful conversion of proslavery men to the free-labor persuasion remained unrealized. A spate of gory conflicts over slavery and land claims in the territory that gave Bleeding Kansas its name belied the hope that the Bible and the ballot box rather than the bowie knife and the Sharps rifle would shape the Kansas struggle. Not only did pro-Southern excesses in the territory jeopardize the venture to plant vital elements of Protestant material and moral culture in the West, they raised the alarming specter of unrepublican "white slavery" reminiscent of eighteenth-century British tyranny.

5

"White Men Can Never Be Slaves"

In July 1855 Charles Robinson gave NEEAC emigrant and pen-maker-turned-free-state-militiaman J. B. Abbott of Wakarusa a letter of introduction to Eli Thayer in Worcester, Massachusetts, requesting Thayer to help Abbott procure arms for a military company formed in his district to stave off proslavery depredations. "In my judgement," Robinson wrote, "the rifles in Lawrence have had a very good effect, and I think the same kind of instruments in other places would do more to save Kansas than anything else." The Aid Company officials complied at once, because as Amos Lawrence observed, "when farmers turn soldiers, they must have arms." The battle for the territory had assumed a different course from that intended by the eastern exponents of antislavery. The musket had superseded the accoutrements of free labor as the most effective weapon of warfare. Free-state men, however, projected their recourse to violence as a last resort, reluctantly taken as a measure of self-defense against proslavery aggression. Through the columns of the *American Missionary*, the *Home Missionary*, and the *Herald of Freedom*, the free-state party emerged as the victim of senseless violence committed by the unprincipled minions of a ruthless Slave Power, actively abetted by a partisan administration in Washington. More importantly, as free-state politics in Kansas crystallized into resistance to the territory's "Missouri-elected quasi-legislature," the struggle against black slavery took on the aspect of a crusade against *white* slavery as well.[1]

In his address at Lawrence on the seventy-ninth anniversary of the U.S. Declaration of Independence, Charles Robinson called upon his fellow citizens to ask themselves who, where, and what they were. *Who* were they? Were they not free-born? Were not their *mothers* as well as

their fathers of Anglo-Saxon blood? Was not the right to govern themselves guaranteed to them by the "united voice of the United States?"
Where were they? Were they not in "the most beautiful country that
human eye ever beheld" situated strategically between the Atlantic and
the Pacific? Finally *what* were they? They were the "subjects, slaves of
Missouri." The free-staters frequently compared their subjugation by
a Missouri-elected quasi-legislature with the oppression of eighteenth-
century American patriots chafing under the tyranny of a British Parliament in which they had no representation. Responding to reports
that territorial governor Wilson Shannon had sworn to enforce the proslavery enactments of the bogus legislature to the letter, the *Herald of
Freedom* reminded its patrons that "it was the *attempt* to enforce an unjust law, backed up by the whole power of the British government, which
brought on the American Revolution." [2]

Reports on politics in territorial Kansas rang with the northeasterners' claims to be the true heirs to the nation's republican heritage.
In mobilizing antislavery sentiment against the South, the free-state
press made effective use of the parallels between the revolutionary generation's fears of a sinister design of enslavement on the part of the
mother country and the Northern states' apprehensions of a Slave Power
conspiracy to stifle liberty in the land.[3] The time had come when the
North must fulfill the historic mission of the former British colonies
as bearers of the torch of freedom for both white and black. Martial
exploits harnessed to this patriotic cause, especially if they culminated
in martyrdom, represented the essence of public-spirited civic virtue.[4]
A messianic commitment to republican liberty fused with concern for
Protestant morality and economic progress to constitute an American
creed that undergirded the Northern struggle for supremacy in Bleeding Kansas.

The New England Emigrant Aid Company took an active interest
in molding the contours of the free-state movement in Kansas. It encouraged its agents to assume political leadership, aided the antislavery
cause in the territory with advice and money, allowed the company office
in Boston to serve as the headquarters of a free-state propaganda dele-
gation that went East in February 1856, helped sell scrip issued by
a territorial executive committee set up to finance free-state politics,

supplied arms, conveyed funds raised in eastern communities for the free-state cause, and strove harder than ever in early 1856, when the conflict was rapidly gaining momentum, to stimulate the emigration of free labor to Kansas.[5] Numerous Aid Company settlers abandoned the plow to play an active part in actual combat as members of free-state military companies. Above all, a large section of the northeastern public viewed the Kansas conflict through the lens of the company's publication, the *Herald of Freedom.*

The American Missionary Association, on the other hand, directed its ministers in Kansas to be circumspect in political action, "lest it be truthfully said that they prize politics more than Christianity."[6] Nevertheless, Bleeding Kansas forged a "solemn and momentous" connection between politics and religion, prompting many antislavery clergymen to carry their campaign against the Slave Power outside the pulpit.[7] For example, John Byrd served on the platform committee of the free-state party. Adair won election to the senate of the free-state legislature in September 1857 and reported the loss of two Sabbaths while he was attending a meeting of that body in March 1858.[8]

Free-state contenders in the territory were deeply conscious of the propaganda potential of the tumultuous drama unfolding before their eyes. As early as January 1855, the Reverends Finch and Lum served with Samuel C. Pomeroy and others on the executive committee of the Kansas Free-State Society organized at attorney S. N. Wood's house to combat proslavery propaganda.[9] Charles Robinson underscored the importance of having slavery's enemies play their cards right: "I am not in the habit of looking upon the struggle as a local one," he wrote a friend back East. "I regard it as one in which the whole nation is involved, and hence I feel not a little anxiety that public sentiment in the North shall be such that when we strike the first blow, should we be compelled to, that moment will be seized to give slavery its death blow in our country."[10]

A close look at the politics of Bleeding Kansas and its aftermath facilitates an understanding of the republican filter through which antislavery news was interpreted to the Northern public. At the same time, it reveals that occasional switches in sectional alliance belied the impression of the struggle as a clear-cut, bipolar contest between hermetically sealed factions. Furthermore, the observations of the actors and actresses themselves on the political furor in their adopted home furnish a sense of the frenzied excitement that gripped the territory as it bled. They afford interesting insights into the perceptions and reactions of the settlers to the various events in the orgy of violence that interrupted their daily business of staking claims, building log houses, harvesting their corn, pursuing their true vocation, indeed of living and breathing.

The election of March 1855 inaugurated an era of violent political confrontation over slavery that gave new meaning to familiar frontier conflicts over land claims in Kansas. The Democratic president Franklin Pierce, anxious not to alienate his powerful Southern allies, turned a deaf ear to Governor Reeder's pleas to denounce proslavery fraud at the polls. Instead, he blamed the NEEAC for fomenting sectional strife in Kansas and dismissed Reeder from his gubernatorial office, ostensibly on charges of land speculation. In his place, the president appointed Wilson Shannon of Ohio, who upheld the legitimacy of the Shawnee legislature, much to the chagrin of free-state men and women in the territory. Adair reported that the "bogus assessor" paid his settlement a visit, but that only two persons gave him a list of their property—"one a pro-slavery man and the other, a rum-seller." Adair apparently told the assessor that he had nothing for him but contempt, as he did for all other officers of "that mob elected legislature." The assessor met with the same reception at almost every house, the clergyman claimed.[11]

Meanwhile, Charles Robinson, perhaps motivated by the combined desires to further company interests, serve the cause of free-soil, and advance his own political fortune, spearheaded a movement to mobilize the growing antislavery sentiment in the territory generated by proslavery excesses during and after the March 30 election. In this mission, he was joined by the flamboyant, quintessential frontier politician, Indiana-born Democrat-turned-free-soiler James Henry Lane, as well as the more urbane deposed governor, Andrew Reeder.[12] Fortified by the arrival of the first batch of Sharps rifles at Robinson's request, free-state delegates met at Big Springs on September 5, 1855, organized a free-state party, and set a date in October for the election of a territorial delegate to Congress, for which office they nominated Andrew Reeder. The former governor set the tone for the official free-state approach to the impending struggle when, speaking in response to his nomination by acclamation, he counseled peaceful resistance to the "tyrannical and unjust laws of the spurious legislature," and violence only as a last resort, in the event that all appeal to the "proper tribunal" for the protection of the people's "dearest rights" should fail: "Our position is one of asking only that the law be carried out." As Reeder paused, his audience drew a deep breath, and the next instant, the air was torn with cries of "Yes, we will strike, . . . white men never can be slaves." [13]

The Big Springs convention also denied "the stale and ridiculous charge of abolitionism" and adopted a platform of principles containing a "Black Law" provision barring "all Negroes, bond or free" from settling in the territory in the best interests of free white men. John Byrd, who served on the platform Committee, dissented from this capitulation to racism, but was overruled by the conservative majority.[14] In accordance with a resolution adopted at the Big Springs gathering, a constitutional convention meeting at Topeka in October drafted a free-state constitution for Kansas. The Topeka constitution prohibited slavery after July 4, 1857, and referred a Black Law provision to voters along with the constitution. On December 15, 1855, an election in which only Free-Soilers participated adopted the constitution and voted in favor of a general banking law as well as Negro exclusion.[15]

The breakdown of the free-state vote on the Black Law reveals that only three precincts rejected the law: Lawrence in electoral District One recorded 223 votes against black exclusion out of a total of 356 votes cast; Juniatta in the Seventh District and Wabaunsee in the Eighth, turned down the law 19 to 10, and 11 to 7, respectively. Elsewhere, negrophobia triumphed. Topeka registered a close vote—69 to 64 in favor of exclusion. The virulence of antiblack feeling, judged by the percentage of votes cast in favor of the Black Law, was strongest in the proslavery stronghold of District Sixteen, where all 73 votes recorded supported exclusion.[16] The size of the total vote was largest in District One (497), followed by District Five (263), and District Three (237). In the First District, where, in March 1855, northeasterners had constituted approximately 48 percent and westerners 30 percent of all free males surveyed, 49 percent of the voters rejected the law. In District Five, on the other hand, where in March, Missourians constituted nearly 60

Table 10 Free-State Vote on Negro Exclusion, December 15, 1855

District	Votes against Exclusion	Total Votes
1	245 (49.3%)	497
2	19 (12.3%)	155
3	66 (27.8%)	237
4	3 (4.2%)	72
5	49 (18.6%)	263
7	34 (45.3%)	75
8	12 (16.2%)	74
9	8 (8%)	99
10	1 (1.8%)	57
11	4 (8.3%)	48
13	1 (1.4%)	73
14	7 (46.7%)	15
15	2 (6%)	33
16	0 (0%)	73
17	2 (28.6%)	7
Total	453 (25.5%)	1778

Source: Daniel W. Wilder, *Annals of Kansas* (1886; reprint, New York, 1975), 90.

percent, westerners just under 23 percent, and northeasterners slightly over 6 percent of the population studied, only 18 percent voted against exclusion. In District Three, where six months earlier northeasterners had made up 44 percent and westerners 17.6 percent of the settlers surveyed, the percentage that voted against the Black Law occupied middle ground between Districts One and Five—27.8 percent.[17]

A month after the ratification of the Topeka constitution, free-state men elected a coalition government of former Whigs, Democrats, Republicans, and Know-Nothings, united only by their desire to see Kansas become a free-state, or at any rate to give popular sovereignty a fair chance. Charles Robinson became governor. Lieutenant Governor W. Y. Roberts of Pennsylvania and Congressman Mark W. Delahay of Maryland were both Douglas Democrats. A former slaveholder, Delahay was accustomed to saying that he would "as lief buy a negro as a mule," but opposed slavery on the grounds that the soil and climate of Kansas were not suited to bonded labor. The attorney general–elect, H. Miles Moore, was a National Democrat from Missouri, while Auditor G. A. Cutler was a free-state man from Kentucky. John Speer, the successful candidate for state printer, on the other hand, was an Ohio Republican. E. M. Thurston and S. B. Floyd, elected reporter and clerk of the supreme court, respectively, were "Squatter Sovereignty" Whigs.[18]

A free-state legislature convened at Topeka in March, adopted statutes, named U.S. senators, and petitioned Congress for statehood under the Topeka constitution.[19] Thus, by the spring of 1856, rival governments functioned at Lecompton and Topeka — symbols of the triumph of sectional over partisan politics in a crucial battleground for slavery. The "legitimate" one, fraudulently elected by proslavery forces, named John W. Whitfield as territorial delegate to Congress, while the unofficial Topeka government chose former governor Andrew Reeder. Congress refused to seat either candidate and appointed a committee headed by House member William A. Howard of Michigan to investigate the chaos in Kansas.[20]

The political test of wills over slavery was accompanied by a blood-bath in the prairies of Kansas that reinforced antislavery perceptions of Slave Power barbarism, while affirming the free-state commitment to public service in the form of military readiness. In November 1855 a twenty-two-year-old Free-Soiler named Charles W. Dow was cut down by a proslavery assassin's bullet while on a visit to the blacksmith's near Hickory Point in Douglas County. The murder, although prompted by a claims' dispute, assumed ominous political overtones before long, erupting into the famous Wakarusa War. The *Herald of Freedom* informed its readers that the culprit, Coleman, was "secreted by his proslavery abettors" to Missouri, where he surrendered to Westport's acting postmaster Samuel J. Jones, whom the territorial legislature had appointed sheriff of Douglas County. Dow had been a member of the Wakarusa Liberty Guard, the free-state military company on behalf of which Robinson had solicited Thayer's aid through J. B. Abbott.

John Stewart, one-time Methodist preacher from New Hampshire, now an active member of the Wakarusa Liberty Guard, testified before the National Kansas Committee that his military company summoned what the *Herald* described as a "people's" assembly to investigate the cir-

cumstances surrounding the "martyrdom" of Dow. Having concluded
that the murder was part of a "preconcerted plan of extermination," the
martyred man's fellow soldiers repaired to his grave. "No stone marked
the spot," Stewart wrote, "but the raised earth pointed out his resting
place. Silently we approached the grave, and the inmate seemed to say,
'I died a martyr, be firm, and fall like men rather than yield your rights.'
Never did soldiers fire a salute over a braver man . . . the only crime
he was guilty of towards his murderers was his firm free-state principles." Soon thereafter, Sheriff Jones, attended by a "posse of fourteen
others," arrested Jacob Branson, who had participated in the free-state
meeting held to "enquire into the facts" of the murder. The warrant
for Branson's arrest on grounds of "security of the peace" was issued
by Hugh Cameron, "a professed free-state man" who was sworn in as
justice of the peace by three Douglas county commissioners appointed
by the mob-elected legislature. The free-state people were much cha-
grined to learn of Cameron's appointment as "scavenger for the people
of Missouri" and regarded him as "an Arnold" who had "sold himself
to the enemies of Freedom for a paltry office," and a "Judas" who had
"betrayed his own countrymen that he might glory in the appellation of
esquire." [21]

Cameron's case suggests that party lines in Bleeding Kansas were not
impenetrable. Economic exigencies and political expediency spawned
an occasional turncoat. The *Herald* reported that "the noisiest and the
most degraded lick spittle of the southern masters" in the "bogus"
legislature, had, a year ago, been "the most ultra free-soiler" of Ohio. In
Kansas, he was "quite as valiant in defense of slavery." A friend of the
renegade Free-Soiler disclosed that the latter disliked slavery as much
as ever, but that his family had been suffering for want of bread in the
territory, and to relieve them from distress he had accepted a nomination from proslavery men to a seat in the legislature.[22] The NEEAC
organ asserted that the most vitriolic denunciations of antislavery men
in the press usually issued forth from the pens of Northern apostates
whose only hope of "maintaining their position with proslavery men"
lay in becoming "more ultra than the most devoted fire-eater in the
South." Thus the author of an extract from the *Leavenworth Herald*,
which described Lawrence as "a vile sink hole of infamy and vagabond-

ism . . . inhabited almost exclusively" by negro-stealing fanatics, was, the *Herald* ventured to guess, a Northern "doughface." [23]

The Kickapoo *Kansas Pioneer*, exulting in the victory of the proslavery candidate in the election for territorial delegate in November 1854, observed, "[Northern] emigrants are but a short time among us when they begin to learn that the doctrines of southern men are correct. . . . Such men . . . will not be long in the South before they become slave-owners." The editor suggested that those Northerners who had not voted the proslavery ticket apply to a certain Mr. Rively, a merchant of Salt Creek Valley for a quantity of "an elixir manufactured expressly for the purpose of southernizing northern and eastern abolitionists." The *Herald* countered, "We wonder that our neighbors in Missouri . . . should object to eastern emigration, when the pioneer can so readily be molded to suit their caprice. Perhaps the elixir is expensive, in that possibly lies the secret of the opposition." If Northerners proved susceptible to Southern pressures, many former defenders of slavery—among them H. Miles Moore—grew disenchanted enough with the proceedings of proslavery men to switch their loyalties to the free-state party.[24]

Such volte-faces in allegiance must not of course obscure the sharp political polarization over slavery that prompted the Wakarusa War in Kansas to snowball into "a rehearsal for the Civil War." Following the issue of a warrant for Branson's arrest, Sheriff Jones accompanied by his posse arrived in Blanton's Bridge on Wakarusa Creek four miles south of Lawrence, where according to John Stewart, they "spent the afternoon smoking and drinking liquor, which they brought with them, and in the course of conversation which they had with different people, it leaked out that they were going to arrest Branson." When this news reached the ears of J. B. Abbott, he procured a horse and, accompanied by S. N. Wood, rode to Branson's house where the men learned that the sheriff had accomplished his mission twenty minutes earlier.[25]

A company of free-state men, including Stewart, then assembled near Abbot's house half a mile south of Blanton's Bridge and were in the process of formulating a plan of action to rescue Branson when the sound of approaching horsemen brought them to their feet. Cocking their guns against their shoulders, they filed across the road, bringing what turned out to be the sheriff's party of horsemen to a halt. When "bogus Jones" demanded an explanation, Abbott enquired after Branson. The man under arrest identified himself and complied with his rescuers' invitation to walk over to their party, countering the "bogus posse's" threat to "blow his brains out if he moved" with the reply, "I can die but once." According to Stewart, Jones "blustered a great deal . . . said he was no coward, and to prove it he challenged to a fight any one of our number, but we told him we did not fight for fighting's sake. S. N. Wood told him we were eastern paupers and asked him if we were not pretty good fellows. After some thirty minutes spent in this way, they departed, Jones declaring that in less than two weeks, he would bring 10,000 men up, and make us respect his authority." Branson's rescuers then fell in double file, and marched to Lawrence to the sound of drums.[26]

At four o' clock the same morning, Sara Robinson awoke to the "hurried tramp of a swift rider" followed by a loud knock upon the door of her house in Mt. Oread near Lawrence. Her husband enquired of the familiar voice under the window, "What is wanted?" S. C. Smith furnished the governor an account of Branson's rescue, concluding with the alarming news that runners had been dispatched to Missouri and a battle was going to be fought on the plains of Lawrence that morning. No sooner had Smith ridden away than the Robinsons heard "the sound of the drum and the quick words of the Captain" of the band of Branson's rescuers as they came over the hill south of the NEEAC agent's residence. A few moments later, Wood and his companions were ensconced in the Robinson home, relating the events of the previous night. Sara Robinson later recalled:

> I shall never forget the appearance of the men in simple citizen's dress, some armed and some unarmed, standing in unbroken line, just visible in the breaking light of a November morning. This little band of less than twenty men had, through the cold and open ground, walked ten miles since nine o' clock of the previous evening. Mr. Branson, a large man of fine proportions, stood a little forward of the line, with his head slightly bent, which an old straw hat barely protected from the cold, looking as though in his [hurried departure] from home, in the charge of ruffianly men, he took

whatever came first. The drum beat again, and the rescuers and rescued passed down to Lawrence.

Sara fell asleep soon thereafter, leaving her husband sitting in the parlor, deep in thought. On awakening the next morning to a rising sun and screaming coyotes in the valley, her first thought was that the Missourians had come.[27]

Sara Robinson's apprehension turned out to be far from groundless. John Byrd wrote the AMA that Governor Shannon, in response to an appeal by Sheriff Jones, had called upon all "good citizens" to assist the sheriff in the recapture of Branson. Although in fact the governor had summoned the Kansas militia, free-state observers claimed that "hundreds of Missourians" seduced by the offer of a dollar and a half a day, and a land warrant, had marched to Lawrence and encamped in the town's vicinity for a few days.[28] The intruders apparently found no pretext to initiate hostilities, because the citizens of Lawrence, in deference to the dictates of prudence, had decided not to harbor Branson's rescuers, only two of whom were Lawrence residents. Yet affairs were "assuming a serious aspect." A party of Missourians had broken open the U.S. arsenal at Liberty, Missouri, robbed it of guns and ammunition, and marched to the scene of conflict. These "lawless men" had apparently shot a man in cold blood near Lawrence and were said to have arrested Mr. Phillips, correspondent of the *New York Tribune* and a few other prominent residents of Lawrence. "The citizens of Lawrence and the neighboring towns are daily or frequently drilling their little bands," Byrd concluded.[29]

The free-state population of Lawrence was indeed preparing to meet the gauntlet thrown down by the governor by perfecting a military organization "not for the purpose of aggression . . . or to resist the *legally* constituted authorities," but simply to resist a mob invasion from Missouri, the *Herald* claimed. Robinson assumed command of the free-state militia, while a newly created Committee of Public Safety invited sympathetic fellow citizens to rally to the defense of the free-state cause. Despite rumors of the formidable strength of the enemy collecting at Franklin near the mouth of the Wakarusa, four miles east of Lawrence,

"our people," reported the *Herald,* "remained firm, cool, and collected."
Although most of them continued with their "several avocations" as
though nothing unusual was occurring, a closer inspection would have
revealed that they were "amply provided with weapons" and quite prepared to "rush to the scene of danger." Scouts came in every day with
fresh estimates of the enemy's strength and, on one occasion, to report
that Governor Shannon was assuming command of the "allied armies."
The *Herald* quoted a "gentleman direct from Missouri" as saying that
the whole state was "on fire" and there was no doubt it would "set the
Union in a flame." All business, except preparations for defense and collecting provisions for the free state army, was suspended. The NEEAC
organ's description of merchants, mechanics, and laborers, "seen with
arms upon their shoulders at all times . . . conscious of being in the
right," recalled the eighteenth-century revolutionary minutemen, prepared to defend liberty at a moment's notice.[30]

The *Herald* proudly proclaimed that while the wives and children of
proslavery men had been removed to Missouri, free-state women had
not shown "a particle of alarm. They KNOW their husbands and friends
are in the right, and if the issue shall come they will be found by our
sides defending their homes to the last extremity." As free-state companies from Bloomington, Wakarusa, Palmyra, and Topeka, very likely
armed with Sharps rifles, began to pour into Lawrence, public and private houses "overflowed" with soldiers. One evening, Sara Robinson
had been nearly asleep when "three young men with Sharps rifles and a
cheerful 'Good Evening' " entered her home. She set out a hearty meal
for them on the table—a custom she invariably followed as long as the
"war" lasted.[31] Margaret Lyon Wood, the wife of S. N. Wood, opened
her home to women who made cartridges for the men in "the hastily
thrown up trenches." Mrs. Wood and Mrs. G. W. Brown also accomplished the astonishing feat of smuggling in through the enemy lines a
keg of powder from across the Wakarusa.[32]

Religious meetings on the Sabbath were suspended in Lawrence, as
the hall was occupied by "an assemblage of citizens with rifles on their
shoulders." Reporting on the escalation of tension around Lawrence,
Adair alleged that Stringfellow and Atchison were with the governor and
were reported to have stated that they would leave only on condition that

the free-state military company be disbanded, the presses destroyed, the fifteen-thousand-dollar Union Hotel built by the New England Emigrant Aid Company demolished, and every man swear allegiance to the laws of the legislature. Adair wrote that the proslavery party threatened that if these conditions were not acceded to they would wage a war of extermination, not sparing a man, woman, or child. In the meantime, "all roads leading to Lawrence are guarded. Wagons going in have been plundered, and small companies taken prisoner. . . . Mails have been robbed, and all communication as far as possible has been cut off." In a subsequent letter, Adair conceded that much of what he had written about Governor Shannon in his previous communication was untrue. Shannon had never formally made any statement on the conditions of peace, which the leaders of the Missourians had demanded.[33] It is not hard to imagine how such inflammatory rumors about enemy-perpetrated inequities must have compounded the sense of impassioned outrage and tense foreboding that saturated the settlers' precarious existence in territorial Kansas.

Headlines in the proslavery press screamed out charges of treason and rebellion against the free-state party. The *Leavenworth Herald* accused the "abolitionists in arms against the laws of the territory" of receiving arms and ammunition from Massachusetts, of rescuing "criminals" from the hands of "the officers of the law," of burning the houses of proslavery men, and driving their families into the wilderness. "Truly," concluded the editorial, "a more infamous, lawless set of men never assembled together than these men are. . . . Still professing to be God-fearing, law-abiding, and order-loving men. Surely none but Yankee abolitionists could go to such heights and depths of duplicity, falsehood and hypocrisy. But these are the cardinal virtues of an Abolitionist, together with stealing."[34]

The *Herald* justified Branson's rescue on the grounds that to have sanctioned a citizen's arrest by a writ issued by "such a person" as Cameron would have been tantamount to "acknowledging the legality of that villainous legislature." Anxious to avert any armed confrontation that might damage their cause in the free states, the Lawrence Committee of Safety dispatched two representatives to Shawnee Mission in an attempt to seek Shannon's intervention in their behalf. A personal visit to the Missouri-dominated proslavery camp on Wakarusa Creek near Franklin persuaded the governor that the prospect of proslavery aggression and its potential for advancing the political fortunes of the Republican party in the approaching electoral campaign were serious enough to warrant the cessation of hostilities on both sides at once. Shannon ordered his militia generals to disband their forces, visited Lawrence, and concluded the compromise Treaty of Lawrence with the free-state party led by Lane and Robinson. The governor denied that he had called upon volunteers from Missouri to maintain the law, and the free-staters professed to have no knowledge of "any organization to resist the laws." [35]

Once the crisis passed, Robinson congratulated his fellow "soldiers" who had gathered in the town square to hear their commanding officers speak. The free-state leader exulted that in the face of a foreign foe, "the moral strength of our position was such that even the 'gates of hell' could not have prevailed against us, much less a foreign mob, and we gained a bloodless victory—literally may it be said of our citizens, 'they came, they saw, they conquered.'" The enemy was weak because despite their superior numbers, they were a "besotted rabble, who left their home in a neighboring state on a drunken revel, and who were glad for an excuse to return as soon as their casks of whiskey were emptied." Pitted against this mob were citizens "fighting in defence of their wives, their children, their hearth-stones, and their family-altars." [36]

Sharps rifles played no major role in settling the Wakarusa War, but if Pomeroy's testimony is accurate, whiskey played a part, however minor, in the conclusion of the peace treaty. Pomeroy wrote Thomas Webb, "I suppose you know that drunken fool Shannon after disbanding his troops from Missouri came to Lawrence, where we got him drunk and then he commissioned our officers and legalized all our proceedings in defending the town. I never saw a set of men who felt [so] completely *sold out* as do these Missourians." Pomeroy derived this last piece of information through his interaction with the "ruffians" themselves in Lexington where he had stopped en route to the East soon after the conclusion of peace. One of the first people the Aid Company agent met at the Lexington Hotel was the captain of a company of Missourians who had taken him prisoner during the Wakarusa War. Pomeroy "soon found that most of the officers of the War were in town" and would be glad to see him, and indeed they insisted that he have supper with them. The captain's men assured the agent that if he were better acquainted with the border ruffians, he should like them. They urged him to drink with them, but he declined. Although the atmosphere was very "rowdish" and all the men were "too drunk for decent society," Pomeroy felt "perfectly at home" and cleared up the Missourians' misconceptions about the Emigrant Aid Company. What was most useful about the encounter was that his new-found friends paid all his bills.[37]

Such display of interparty goodwill did little to overpower the legacy of Wakarusa, which spurred a fresh spurt of violence in the spring of 1856. The trouble began when Sheriff Jones was shot at and wounded in Lawrence after making futile attempts to arrest two of Branson's rescuers, S. N. Wood and S. F. Tappan. In response to charges from Judge Samuel D. Lecompte, the proslavery chief justice of the territory, the partisan grand jury of Douglas County indicted Reeder, Robinson, Lane, S. N. Wood, and others for treason, and recommended that the *Herald of Freedom* and *Kansas Free State* newspapers and the Free State Hotel at Lawrence "be abated as nuisances." The U.S. marshall for Kansas, I. B. Donaldson, issued a proclamation declaring that the citizens of Lawrence had resisted arrest and commanding "law-abiding citizens" to appear at Lawrence for "the execution of the law," much to the delight of men who detested the Yankee stronghold.[38]

Armed with five cannon, they besieged the town as the redoubtable Atchison raised the battle cry for Southern-style "law and order" in the following incendiary style attributed him by the *New York Tribune*:

Boys, this day I am a Kickapoo Ranger, by God! This day we have entered Lawrence with "Southern Rights" inscribed upon our banner, and not one damned Abolitionist dared to fire a gun. Now, boys, this is the happiest day of my life. We have entered that damned town, and taught the damned Abolitionists a Southern lesson that they will remember until the day they die. And now, boys, we will go in again, with our highly honorable Jones, and test the strength of that damned Free State Hotel, and teach the Emigrant Aid Company that Kansas shall be ours. Boys, ladies should, and

I hope, will, be respected by every gentleman. But when a woman takes upon herself the garb of a soldier by carrying a Sharps rifle, then she is no longer worthy of respect. Trample her under your feet as you would a snake! Come on, boys! Now do your duty to yourself and your Southern friends. Your duty I know you will do. If one man or woman dare stand before you, blow them to hell with a chunk of cold lead.

Historian Bernard Weisberger has thought it unlikely that "a man of Atchison's position would have permitted himself such a frenzied cocktail of profanity and bad grammar." Indeed, several years later the Missourian denied making the speech. Nevertheless, the searing impact of the infamous pro-Southern westerner's *reported* words—whether apocryphal or not—as a fresh testimonial of slavery's all-around intemperance is not hard to imagine, especially in the light of subsequent events.[39]

Atchison's boys did him proud, although they stopped short of blowing any abolitionist to pieces. Indeed the sack of Lawrence entailed only one casualty, and he was a proslavery man. Pomeroy later claimed that as chairman of the Committee of Public Safety he had insisted the free-staters take no action in their own defence until they could demonstrate to the public that the government was "powerless for protection." And so the city of Lawrence "stood still and saw . . . the few monuments of civilization which had been hastily erected . . . thrown to the winds or consumed in the flames!" Adair wrote about the episode two days after it had occurred: "I have now to say that Lawrence has been taken—the Hotel destroyed; Governor Robinson and G. W. Brown's houses burnt; the presses of the *Herald* and the *Free State* thrown into the river. All done by Missourians, Alabamians, Georgians enrolled as the militia of the territory, armed with U.S. arms, and acting under a U.S. deputy marshall." What was more, the worst was not over. Adair went on: "We have a company of Alabamians camped near us—some 60 or 70 in number. When sober, they say that they came here to settle and to make this a slave state. They are very sanguine they will succeed—tell great stories about what the South are going to do. But when they are drunk (and that is as often as they can get liquor to get drunk on), they are ready to fight and threaten and make a great noise."[40]

The Republican press and pulpit offered the "Sack of Lawrence" as fresh proof of slavery's natural bestiality, confirmed by simultaneous events in Congress. Senator Charles Sumner of Massachusetts launched a passionate two-day diatribe against the South's "crime against Kansas," singling out his absent colleague Andrew Butler of South Carolina for personal attack. Butler's unfortunate speech defect, which caused the senator to drool, received a rather unkind mention. Sumner charged that the South Carolinian had "chosen a mistress . . . who . . . though polluted in the sight of the world, is chaste in his sight—I mean the harlot, slavery."[41] To Butler's cousin, Congressman Preston Brooks, the senator from Massachusetts had done more than exceed the bounds of good taste. Two days after the speech, the younger South Carolinian responded to the Yankee's challenge of his family honor by caning Sumner into unconsciousness as he sat writing at his desk. Southerners showered Brooks with praise as well as decorative canes to replace the one he had broken on Sumner's head. To outraged Northerners on the other hand, the bleeding senator became a symbol of "bleeding liberty." The South's commendation of Brooks's dastardly deed proved that slavery was the real culprit, preached Rev. O. B. Frothingham at a Unitarian church in Jersey City: Slavery had taught Brooks "to meet reasoning with wrath, and to answer facts with the bludgeon." The South Carolinian's "cruel blows" were "directed . . . not at a single noble man who had spoken words of biting truth, but at the whole cause of freedom." Slavery made no distinction between persons; it would punish "an unruly Senator" in his chamber just as savagely as it would an obdurate slave upon a plantation: "Despising one race, it despises all races. . . . If it is right to beat and brutalize the black man, why is it not right to beat and brutalize the white man? If it is right to suppress free thought, free speech, and free will in the African, why not in the Saxon too?"[42]

Violence, however, was not exclusively a proslavery prerogative. At least not in the reckoning of Samuel Adair's brother-in-law John Brown. With a family history of mental instability, this committed, if misguided, abolitionist viewed himself as divinely ordained to "break the jaws of the wicked." And break their skulls he did. Incensed by the sack of Lawrence, he led a band of followers in the massacre of five proslavery men on Pottawatomie Creek on the night of May 24, 1856.[43] The free-state settlers of Osawatomie apparently did not rejoice at John Brown's deed unreservedly, as Jason and John, two of the old man's sons, later testified. The two younger Browns had been camping with a company of free-state men on Ottawa Creek, en route to Lawrence on a defensive expedition, when a man came riding up, "with his horse all foaming with sweat," and informed them that John Brown had killed five men on Pottawatomie Creek. This earned the brothers much antipathy from the rest of the company, which then dispersed. The brothers made their way to Osawatomie and found refuge with their uncle, the Reverend Adair. "At that time, we thought that Mr. Adair and family were the only friends we had in that part of the territory," recalled Jason Brown many years later.[44]

While Adair deplored the Pottawatomie murders as "base, barbaric, and horrible" in a letter to the AMA, he made no pretense at grieving over the loss of the victims, who he maintained had been "vile" in "character and conduct." One of them, William Sherman, was "pro-slavery, . . . very profane and drunken" and threatened free-state men with death if they did not leave the territory. Wilkinson, originally from Tennessee, started his career in the territory as a Free-Soiler, but ended up being elected to the bogus legislature on a proslavery ticket. As post-master, he caused the free-staters great annoyance by intercepting their newspapers—the *National Era*, the *New York Tribune*, and the like: "He hailed the Alabamians on their arrival, . . . and was supposed to be privy to their plots and threats." The Doyles "were said to be hale fellows with the Shermans in threatenings and efforts to drive off free-state men." They apparently warned the opposite party that "they would clear the entire region of the d—— abolitionists if they did not clear out in a few days. . . . They designed in this way to find claims for the Alabami-ans who were camped in the vicinity." The terror engendered by their threats prompted a Free-Soil family to flee their home and spend the night in the open prairie. The women and children of two others, rela-tives of Adair, hastily packed their belongings into an ox wagon and traveled eight miles in the night to seek refuge with the Adairs. "But," finished Adair, "these men did not live to carry out their plans. The wicked is taken in his own craftiness." [45]

Charles Robinson, writing almost thirty-six years after the dust had settled on Pottawatomie, charged that Brown's massacre inaugurated an unprecedented "war of murder and pillage," which injured the free-state cause as a whole. Thayer corroborated this assessment of Brown's role when during one of his tirades against the Garrisonians in 1890, he wrote, "their principal stock in trade now is John Brown. They hang to him still and my only regret is that they did not hang with him." However the men associated with the NEEAC may have judged Brown in historical perspective, they appear to have maintained cordial relations with him during his days in Kansas. Brown held a share in the capital stock of the company. According to Edward E. Hale, the old man made the Aid Company office his headquarters in Boston when he came east. Lawrence gave Brown money and a letter of introduction to Robinson when the abolitionist left for Kansas in 1855. Although the Boston Whig did not like Brown's "way of thinking," he thought it "best to keep his goodwill" since he was on the right side of the free-state question. Four months after the Pottawatomie massacre, Robinson commended Brown on his course, which in the former's judgment was such "as to merit the highest praise from every patriot." He went on to offer his "heartfelt thanks" for Brown's "efficient and timely action against the invaders of our rights, and the murderers of our citizens." [46]

In early 1857 Brown traveled east to solicit aid for a plan to defend Kansas with the assistance of a volunteer regular army.[47] It is probable that Thayer, among other prominent New England friends of the free-state cause in Kansas, was amenable to Brown's appeal. In March 1857 the NEEAC founder arranged for Brown to "present his case," which was the "case of mankind," before an antislavery audience in Worcester and in a subsequent letter referred to subscriptions raised for his cause. At Thayer's request, Allen and Wheelock supplied Brown with a large gun, a cannon, rifles, and pistols.[48] Apparently Brown also appealed to Lawrence for aid. The industrialist responded that since he had just contributed fourteen thousand dollars to the cause of education in Kansas, he was unable to advance much cash for the purpose Brown named. He assured the abolitionist, however, that if anything should happen to shorten his life while he was engaged in his "great and good cause," his family would be well provided for. "The family of Captain John Brown of Osawatomie will not be turned out to starve in this country until liberty herself is driven out," Lawrence concluded.[49] Apparently, during the days of Bleeding Kansas, Lawrence paid for weapons dispatched to Brown, a fact that was discovered by the numbers upon the arms when "Brown was taken" and caused the Boston industrialist some embarrassment.[50]

One is tempted to speculate whether the NEEAC officials' endorsement of Brown during his days in Kansas had something to do with their ignorance of his culpability in the Pottawatomie murders. Franklin B. Sanborn, who served on the militant abolitionist Massachusetts State Kansas Committee and became one of John Brown's most ardent supporters, claimed that at a meeting of the Antislavery Society of Lawrence, Kansas, on December 19, 1859, Robinson declared that he had always believed Brown was connected with the Pottawatomie massacre, that "indeed he believed old John Brown had told him so . . . ; that when he first heard of the massacre, he thought it was about right." Robinson apparently added that as long as anarchy reigned, he was pleased with the cooperation of old John Brown but that once the free-state men had gained control of the offices in the territory, the sheriff of the several counties rather than unauthorized individuals like Brown should have been called upon to preserve peace.[51]

William E. Connelley, Secretary of the Kansas State Historical Society and a severe critic of the NEEAC, reported that Sanborn had told him at Hiawatha, Kansas, on April 30, 1903, that at one of the meetings of the company at which Sanborn was present, Thayer had disclosed a plan to redeem Kansas by having Atchison and Stringfellow assassinated. Although no member present encouraged these "murderous designs," Thayer persisted in his "diabolical" scheme, instigating his protégé in Kansas (presumably Robinson) to propose to John Brown that he undertake the assassination of the proslavery leaders. Brown's refusal to comply turned "Thayer and his protégé" into the old man's "bitter and unrelenting enemies," Connelley wrote. Although Robinson did invite Brown to visit Lawrence to discuss Governor Geary and "talk of some other matters" in September 1856, Connelley's charge seems too far-fetched to merit serious attention, especially in view of the generally cautious approach adopted by the Aid Company and its agents in Kansas. Whatever the truth of NEEAC-Brown relations, the immediate reaction of the northeastern evangelicals and entrepreneurs to the Pottawatomie massacres demonstrated, as nothing else did, the growing acceptance of violent means in achieving antislavery ends.[52]

On the other hand, by the time John Brown struck, the Slave Power had changed its tactics in Kansas, Amos Finch wrote the AMA. The clergyman suspected that the approaching presidential election had propelled Southerners away from mob violence, toward attempts at organized emigration. Several men "noted for their wicked deeds of outrage" had gone South as traveling agents for the proslavery party: "We fear that there will be such a flood of southern scarp-gallows into the territory that for many years to come, good and wholesome citizens will be annoyed by them. . . . We hope the North will keep up their emigration to the territory, and send us ten to where they have sent one heretofore, this alone will keep us from being thronged with these miserable characters."[53] Southern attempts at organized emigration through the spring and summer of 1856 did indeed promise to keep the contest in the West lively for some time to come.

6

A Slave State without Masters or Slaves: The South in Kansas—2

Fraudulent capture of the polls was not the only means by which the South sought to win Kansas. Since the territory had opened to white settlement, counties in western Missouri and the Deep South had staged Kansas meetings to raise money and recruit settlers in slavery's behalf. Joint-stock ventures in organized emigration sought to help Southern settlers preempt 160 acres of Kansas lands each on the Yankee model.[1] Nor were such efforts confined to private enterprise. The Texas legislature considered a measure to appropriate some fifty thousand dollars to aid proslavery emigration to Kansas.[2]

Southern colonization projects sought to combine business with politics. They were at once political campaigns for the Southernization of the West and speculative ventures in land investment. The most celebrated sponsor of Southern emigration was Maj. Jefferson Buford, a lawyer of Eufala, Alabama. The "gallant" Major's proposed expedition, funded by the sale of his plantation slaves, assumed a "business-like character" clothed in the familiar rhetoric of white supremacy. As incentives to emigrate, Buford offered prospective settlers forty acres of land, free passage to Kansas, support for a year, and the awful specter of social degradation resulting from universal emancipation. As a return on his investment, Buford expected each emigrant to hand over his preemption claim of 160 acres, of which he would get back only the forty acres promised at the outset, leaving the major the rest. If the plan were successfully implemented, Buford expected to make a tidy profit of fifty thousand dollars on his initial investment. But the issue, Buford assured his fellow public-spirited Alabamians, was not "property" but rather

> a question of races, equally affecting every white skin in the land —
> a question of whether the inferior race, ceasing to be producers and
> tax-payers, shall become drones and eat up the hive; whether the
> stenchy Ethiopian shall sleep with the white man, sit with him in
> church, jostle him in the street, thrust him from the assembly, . . .
> marry his daughters, make and administer his laws, steal his pigs,
> and put him in prison for complaining; a question in which every
> white skin is equally interested.[3]

It is reasonable to speculate that "every white skin" was at least as interested in profit as in preserving white supremacy. The target emigrants were typically young non-slave-holding males of slender means, enticed by the offer of material inducements and long-term prospects to secure their economic future, usually unaccompanied by their families if they had any. Even when Southern efforts at organized emigration included women and children, they did so in very small numbers. Of the forty-six men who accompanied Capt. H. D. Clayton of Alabama in August 1856, for instance, only nine moved their families West.[4] In Abbeyville, South Carolina, recruits were promised two hundred dollars to do their bit for their state in Kansas.[5] Buford's men were expected to be "orderly and temperate, to attend to their reading of the scriptures and prayers. . . , learn to be gentle with females. . . , merciful to slaves and beasts, and just to all men."[6]

A Southern missionary in Kansas complained that "capitalists of the South" seemed to expect "poor young men" with no personal interest in "southern property" to "settle the country, improve the soil, drive back the wolves, and fight their battles, while they enjoy the ease and luxury of their Southern homes."[7] And indeed, masters and slaves were conspicuous by their absence in the "proslavery colonies." As one Southerner put it, "if to make plantations in Kansas, we must leave a desert somewhere else, where is the gain?"[8] At a time when the southeastern states were being "outgrown and politically outweighed," encouraging the exodus of taxpaying citizens and their slaves seemed imprudent. On the other hand, inducing the emigration of indigent non-slaveholders offered distinct possibilities, as a Mississippi politician saw it. Sen. A. G. Brown proposed that if ready-made slaveholders could not be transplanted to Kansas, the South might create masters with slaves on the windswept western prairies. His scheme, to be funded by a tax on slave property, called for each Southern state to purchase slaves and dispatch them to the territory under the charge of government-appointed emigrants: "A young Mississippian, thus made the master of a slave by his state, and sent free of charge to . . . Kansas, would do the necessary voting, and if needs be, the fighting also, required to sustain the acts of his state in the territory."[9]

Such grandiose schemes failed to materialize, with the result that if Kansas was, in law, "as much a slave state as South Carolina or Georgia," as Pres. James Buchanan claimed in the wake of the Supreme Court's ruling in the Dred Scott decision, it was one with a difference.[10] In 1858 it was a slave state largely without slaves by the standards of its Deep South sisters. A dash of black occasionally darkened, ever so slightly, a red or white pocket here and there, but never enough to give Kansas anything resembling the demographic hue of a Southern black belt.

Pre-territorial military posts and Indian missions, where slave-holding had long prevailed, formed the nucleus of Kansas's black belt, populated, according to one estimate, by not more than thirty slaves before 1854.[11] By March 1855 the largest number of bondspeople, not surprisingly, inhabited the Southern-majority Missouri-river Districts Fourteen, Fifteen, Sixteen, and Seventeen in northeastern Kansas, as well as the well-watered Fifth and Sixth Districts south of the Kansas river (see table 11).[12]

The military outpost of Fort Leavenworth, on the right bank of the Missouri in the northeast, had established a well-deserved reputation for being thoroughly "sound on the goose question." Those who made it so included Major Macllin of the Pay Department, a slaveholder from Arkansas; Chaplain Leander Kerr, who lectured the Self-Defensives of Platte City on his favorite subject, "the new faith of gooseology"; and Col. Hiram Rich, formerly of Liberty, Missouri. Likewise, Fort Scott on the south bank of the Marmaton River south of the Kansas had its share of "gooseologists." Further west, skipping over white-settled central districts along the Kansas river, surprisingly colorful pockets nestled amidst the sprawling Smoky River valley and the vast expanse of level prairie north of the Neosho River. In these Indian hunting grounds, designated Districts Eight and Nine, where whites feared to tread, slaves made up between 3.5 percent and 8.6 percent of the sparse population enumerated in the 1855 census. At Fort Riley, army officers owned slaves or hired them from Indian masters as household servants.[13]

Kansas's eastern black belt adjoining the state of Missouri claimed a slave population of no more than 2 to 3 percent in March 1855, with the significant exception of District Seventeen. A tiny sliver of prairie bounded by the Kansas River on the north, this darkest zone was 15 percent enslaved. It was the seat of Shawnee Mission, where a minister had introduced the Southern labor system before Kansas was organized. The slave-holding career of the Shawnee Manual Labor School's principal, Rev. Thomas Johnson, allegedly began in 1837 when, during a temporary sojourn in Fayette, Missouri, he acceded to the entreaties of a young man named Jackson on the auction block and bought him. While in Missouri, Johnson hired out his new slave for labor on the river steamboats. Subsequently, Jackson married a "handsome mulatto woman" from Howard County, Missouri, and served as chief cook of Shawnee Mission, in charge of feeding its nearly two hundred teachers and pupils. His wife became dairymaid. Between them, the slave couple assumed responsibility for the mission's "domestic economy" as well as their owner's children, Master Alec and Miss Annie. During the tumultuous years of Bleeding Kansas, one chronicler notes, "free papers were given them at least twice, and were used by Uncle Jack as pipe lighters." In the meantime, though, Uncle Jack's master had acquired a taste for Southern ways. By the time popular sovereignty had mired Kansas in a national controversy, the good reverend had six slaves at work making improvements on his Johnson County farm. He reportedly emancipated "his people" in 1860.[14]

An analysis of the demographic profile of Kansas slavery based on the census of March 1855 suggests that at that early date when Southern settlers were in the majority, their peculiar institution did not constitute a significant element in the territorial labor system. Sixty-three slaveholders could be identified by sectional affiliation and occupation,

Table 11 Frequency Distribution of Slaves by Electoral Districts, March 1855

District	Total Population	Slaves
1	962	2 (0.2%)
2	519	7 (1.3%)
3	252	6 (2.3%)
4	177	1 (0.5%)
5	1407	26 (1.8%)
6	810	11 (1.3%)
7	118	1 (0.8%)
8	116	10 (8.6%)
9	86	3 (3.5%)
10	151	0 (0%)
11	36	0 (0%)
12	243	7 (2.8%)
13	284	8 (2.8%)
14	1158	33 (2.8%)
15	873	15 (1.7%)
16	1183	33 (2.7%)
17	150	23 (15.3%)
Total	8525	186 (2.2%)

Source: Kansas Territorial Census of March 1855, reprinted in *1855 Territory of Kansas Census*, 2 volumes, transcribed and compiled by Kansas Statistical Publications, Overland Park, Kansas.

owning a total of 146 slaves (see table 12). Information on the ownership of the remaining 40 or so slaves was unclear.[15] Nearly half of all masters and mistresses surveyed (47.6 percent) held only one slave each. The average size of slave-holding was 2.3, compared with 6.1 in Missouri's "Little Dixie," 7.7 in the Upper South, and 12.7 in the Deep South.[16]

Of the sixty-three masters whose sectional identity and occupations could be established, forty-six were from Missouri, about 65 percent of them farmers, and 17 percent merchants. The remaining included a doctor, a lawyer, a hotelkeeper, a carpenter, a millwright, and two Indian agents-traders. Likewise, a majority of the seven border southwestern slaveholders from Kentucky and Tennessee were farmers. On the other hand, only one out of the four Chesapeake masters tilled the soil for a living — the rest included two merchants and a judge. The Lower South's contribution to Kansas's "planter class" included a Georgian farmer and an Arkansan clergyman whose six slaves were all minors. Free Ohio did as well, sending forth a blacksmith and a farmer who attained slave-holding status in their adopted home, as did a New York farmer and an Irish mechanic. Aspiring masters may have viewed the opportunity to own land in Kansas as an avenue to slave-holding status. Carey B. White-head of Missouri traded his farm in Doniphan County for "a family of negroes" and returned to Missouri when Kansas seemed poised for freedom.[17] Kansas slaveholders included a few recent converts to the proslavery persuasion. One "Ganther, . . . a radical antislavery man . . . became equally radical on the other side" when he acquired a slave in some transaction in Missouri.[18]

As late as January 1858, Gen. Benjamin Stringfellow found time, in between his hobnobbing with Yankee entrepreneurs, to write Preston S. Brooks of South Carolina that Kansas held no future for small farmers with no command of labor: "The great staple articles of Kansas must be hemp and tobacco."[19] But as Rev. Charles B. Boynton observed, "no slaveholder . . . has ventured to bring what they call their 'force,' that is, field hands to the territory." The age and sex distribution of the slave population in March 1855 suggests that the bondspeople prob-ably supplemented family labor on the farm, in the shop, and within the household. Of the 110 slaves whose owners could be identified, and ages and sexes determined, 52 were male and 58 female; over half (61) were minors and less than one-third (36) were prime workers in the age group 21 to 40 (see table 13). Judge Rush Elmore was not atypical of the larger slaveholders in Kansas territory. His "family" of 14 slaves, imported from his Alabama home, included a disproportionate share of the aged and the young: Nero, 70; Mike and John, both 30; Fanny, 40; Mary, 18 to 20; Violet, 70 — the hot-tempered "mammy" who had raised the judge; Fanny's five children; and Violet's three charges. The territorial slave community's balanced sex ratio and the high proportion of children suggest the possible importation of bondspeople with their families intact or at least in groups of related individuals. A family of ten

Table 12 Sectional/National Origins of Slaveholders in Kansas, March 1855 *

State(s)/Country	Number of Slaveholders
Missouri	46
Kentucky/Tennessee	7
Virginia/Maryland	4
Ohio	2
Arkansas/Georgia	2
New York	1
Ireland	1
Total	63

* This table is based on 63 slaveholders whose sectional origins could be determined. They owned a total of 146 slaves. The ownership of the rest of the slaves was unclear.

Source: Kansas Territorial Census of March 1855, reprinted in *1855 Territory of Kansas Census*, 2 volumes, transcribed and compiled by Kansas Statistical Publications, Overland Park, Kansas.

slaves, consisting of parents and their eight children, built a log house and did farm work for their Kentuckian master—a certain Bowen, who settled on Washington Creek in Douglas County.[20]

The worlds of the slaves and their masters in Kansas bore little resemblance to those of their counterparts in the more mature slave states.[21] The obvious discrepancies between the stringent provisions of the "bogus" slave code and the reality of the slave regime in the territory were reflected in perceptions of Kansas slavery as relatively "mild." A retired lawyer from New York who, while in Kansas, drew up several wills in which slaves were bequeathed recalled, "There was one fact about slavery in the territory that I never heard disputed, and that was that the slaves were never badly treated by their owners"—a sentiment that occurs in other observations on slavery in Kansas.[22] The travails of frontier life prevented the transplanting of the Old South's hierarchical, organic social system with its intricate etiquette of class and race relations, and blurred the boundaries between the worlds of master and slave. As in pioneer America, owner and owned rubbed shoulders in the daunting task of taming a wild land—breaking the prairie, clearing forests, and building rude cabins. Mrs. Rush Elmore found the transition from "Southern lady" to pioneer woman fraught with difficulties. She

Table 13 Age and Sex Distribution of Slaves in Kansas, March 1855 *

Minor			20s			30s			40s			50+		
M	F	T	M	F	T	M	F	T	M	F	T	M	F	T
28	33	61	14	12	26	4	6	10	4	5	9	2	2	4

* This table is based on 110 slaves from the March 1855 territorial census whose owners, ages, and sex
could be identified (see table 12).
Minor: under 21 years; 20s:21–29; 30s:31–39; 40s:41–49.
M=male; F=female; T=total.

Source: Kansas Territorial Census of March 1855, reprinted in *1855 Territory of Kansas Census*, 2 volumes,
transcribed and compiled by Kansas Statistical Publications, Overland Park, Kansas.

confided to Governor Reeder who had tea with the Elmores in their one-
room cabin one afternoon in May 1856 that she had never cooked a meal
before her arrival in Kansas. Now she had to do housework and "nurse
her [sick] negroes" as well.[23]

John Sedgwick Freeland, who owned a farm adjoining the Elmore
claim six miles southeast of Topeka on Deer Creek, recalled that Mrs.
Elmore "did the sewing for the slaves" and tended them when the bitter Kansas winters froze their fingers and toes. The Judge was "himself
obliged to haul wood and cut it to keep [his bondspeople] warm." Each
slave family lived in a separate log house on the farm. The judge's son,
Nesbit, wrangled with his seven-year-old black playmate, Webster, every
day: "Webster was heavier than Nesbit and used to lick him nearly every
time," much to Mrs. Elmore's disapproval. The judge, however, believed
that "if Nesbit puts himself with a Negro, he must take Negroes' fare."[24]

The variety of slave work contradicted the proslavery vision of a plantation Kansas based on coerced gang labor. Notwithstanding Benjamin
Stringfellow's asseverations that "the great staple articles of Kansas
must be hemp and tobacco," most slaves that we know of appear to have
done almost everything *but* cultivate hemp and tobacco. They plied the
ferry, operated printing presses, cooked and baked in homes and hotels
and on river boats, drove teams and carriages, and fought in the territorial militia. Sol Miller of the *White Cloud Chief* newspaper recalled that
"our first roller boy was a colored lad . . . held as a slave."[25] Fox Booth's
slave woman rowed travelers over "the raging Kaw many a time." Before

long Booth traded her for a white stallion, when he could not get the cows he wanted for her.[26] One young black man served his storekeeper master at Tecumseh as teamster, "hauling goods up from Westport." One of the fugitives whom J. B. Abbott—a leading operator on the Underground Railroad—hid in his house in the fall of 1857 had cooked for the river steamboats. John Speer, editor of the *Kansas Tribune*, "had his horse put up by a one-eyed slave" when he stopped at the house of a Shawnee family in Tecumseh.[27]

A good many slaves were hired out, occasionally with the option to purchase their freedom. The AMA missionary Samuel L. Adair recalled a merchant from Kansas City who hired "a colored boy eight or ten years old" for a summer in Osawatomie.[28] A slave by the name of Buck Scott who labored in Lawrence gave 70 percent of his earnings to his master in Lecompton toward the payment of his purchase price.[29] Judge Rush Elmore hired out at least two of his slaves: one served as cook at the Big Springs Hotel, and John, a thirty-year-old professional baker, worked his way toward freedom in Lecompton.[30]

Like the Elmore slave John, Marcus Linsey Freeman had his master's permission to work out his freedom in Kansas City. Freeman had been born a slave on George Bayne's farm in Kentucky's Bluegrass area. Master George had bequeathed Marcus to his grandson Thomas when both were babies, so that young Marcus and his new master Thomas "grew up together just as if we had been two little puppies," Freeman recalled. "When [Thomas] was big enough to eat at the table, he used to leave a lot of victuals on his plate and some coffee in his cup and bring it out for me to eat. . . . He thought a great deal of me, and once when his stepbrother licked me, he nearly cut him to pieces with a Barlow knife." Bayne was "kind to his slaves," Freeman claimed. "He would buy cloth for himself and me off of the same piece of goods." Before their arrival in Kansas in 1854, the Bayne family moved to Missouri, where they ran a boarding house near Kansas City. There, Freeman learnt to cook. When his master bought a farm in Jefferson County, Kansas, he obtained permission to hire out his time for two hundred dollars a year for seven years, at the end of which time he would be emancipated. During the firing on Fort Sumter, Freeman was working in the printing office of the *Kansas City Journal*. Master Bayne evidently remained in

Kansas throughout the Civil War, helping destitute black refugees by inviting them "to come out to his woodland and carry in all the wood they needed for fuel, free of cost."[31]

One observer who was personally acquainted with "a representative class of the southern people" suggested that some slaveholders brought their slaves into Kansas not to plant the peculiar institution on its prairies, but in order to "shift the responsibility of caring for an undesirable class upon a state."[32] Given the large proportion of nonprime hands in the slave population and the apparently widespread practice of allowing slaves to work out their freedom, it is plausible that some Free-Soil Southerners, thwarted by slave codes prohibiting the unconditional manumission of slaves within their home states, saw Kansas as a possible haven for themselves as well as their prospective emancipated slaves.

Not all slaves attained freedom with their masters' blessings, of course. The presence of a busy underground railroad posed the greatest challenge to the territory's slave code, as a certain Mr. Bourn discovered to his cost. A year's stay at Bloomington, twelve miles southwest of Lawrence, convinced this slaveholder of the wisdom of returning his twelve slaves to his home state of Virginia. His "head slave," Tom Bourn demurred: "No, Massa Bourn, I cum to Kansas wid you to help 'stablish de inst'uton of slavery and I'ze gwine to see it froo." Two weeks later, Tom and his fellow bondspeople had sped away to freedom on the UGRR, whereupon their "massa" returned to Old Virginny alone and apparently died of a broken heart. Likewise, Peter T. Abell's plump, efficient, and seemingly contented house servant Aunt Nancy, especially beloved of the children in her master's household, surprised everyone by her sudden and permanent disappearance in 1859: "Her sprightly figure as she had been wont to go on family errands about the town was seen no more."[33] One exasperated master in pursuit of a slave who had escaped with a valuable horse determined to let his slave go if only he could get his horse back.[34]

One of the more daring flights on the UGRR was that of forty-something Anne, jointly held by two Lecompton slaveholders. Intercepted by reward-hungry proslavery men in 1856, she was taken to a Lecompton hotel where her captors gave themselves up to a round of intoxicated revelry. Taking advantage of their preoccupation, she slipped out of the kitchen, where she had been dispatched in order to tidy up and eat. The fugitive spent the night in a bushy ravine, emerging at dawn at the sight of a man with a book under his arm. "She thot [*sic*] a man with a book must be free state," reminisced John Armstrong, a conductor on the UGRR. Anne was evidently not disappointed. Before long, she lay concealed beneath comforters in a wagon bound for Topeka, where she found refuge at a Mrs. Scales's boarding house. She spent several nights hidden "in a great hogshead in the cellar," and days helping her benefactress in the kitchen. A proslavery boarder who discovered her was sworn to silence. In the last days of February 1857, a closed carriage drawn by mules carried Anne and her conductor, John Armstrong, to Iowa, and thence to Chicago. The contributors to Anne's cause included NEEAC agent Governor Robinson and the preacher Major Abbott, the basement of whose home, screened by curtains from prying eyes, sheltered many a wayfarer to freedom.[35]

Kansas slaves who did not use the UGRR resorted to other means of resistance. Judge Elmore's bondsman Nero, at "70 or 80 [years]," may have been too old to forsake his "patriarch" for a chance at freedom. Nevertheless, the Kansas winters supplied this resourceful old man with an alternate line of defense. Sent out to get some wood one evening, he stayed out in the cold all night so that he "was badly frozen and so disabled that it was necessary to wait on him"—by no less a person than his mistress herself. Pompey, Nero's fifteen-year-old brethren in bondage, followed his senior's example, "as he saw it worked well in Nero's case," recalled a neighbor of the Elmores. Other slaves went so far as to take their own or their masters' lives. One bondswoman rid herself of her hard-drinking, "desperate . . . dangerous" master by throwing herself into a river.[36] When an ordinance sergeant died mysteriously at Fort Riley on suspicion of poisoning, all fingers pointed accusingly at two slave women, Aunt Cely and Patsy. The women pleaded innocence and at least one went on to live in free Kansas to a ripe old age.[37]

While the UGRR divested many slaveholders of their human property, others left with their chattel, either voluntarily, or under duress. The Skaggs family, originally from Kentucky, repaired to Texas with their slaves in 1858–59. By a strange quirk of fate, 1870 saw a financially ruined Skaggs renting a portion of a former slaves's farm between

Parker and Coffeeville, Kansas. The records are frustratingly silent on how this state of affairs transpired. Bowen, a grocer and "doggery" keeper of Lawrence who threatened a New England lady, Miss Sarah Armstrong, for teaching his ten slaves the three Rs, was run out of the territory by free-state men.[38] Bleeding Kansas offered enslaved people unusual opportunities to participate in the struggle for freedom. Two slaves joined John Brown in fighting off the enemy in the Battle of the Spurs with great ferocity. John Speer, editor of the antislavery *Kansas Tribune*, reminisced that in the Wakarusa War "more than half as many slaves . . . as able-bodied free-state men . . . stood up in the ranks of our defense."[39]

Investment in human property was clearly a risky proposition west of Iowa and Missouri. But one must guard against cavalierly dismissing the potential viability of slavery in Kansas. Although the predominantly Southern-settled territory of early 1855, with fewer than two hundred slaves, was only about 2 percent enslaved, the slave population more than doubled during the bloody years of 1856 and 1857. Reliable census returns do not exist for these years, but according to some estimates approximately fifty slaveholders held between four hundred to five hundred bondspeople, suggesting an increase in the average size of slave-holding.[40]

Moreover, the precarious status of slavery may have had little impact on the market value of its victims. In August 1857 James M. and Minta E. Ducker of Illinois sold a thirty-six-year-old woman named Lucinda to a Wiley Patterson of Bourbon County, Kansas, for $500 —a price that compared favorably with the estimated value of $450 to $600 placed on a thirty-eight-year-old slave woman belonging to the Sappington estate in slave Missouri's Saline County. In January 1857 another young mulatto named Sibha Ann, aged twenty-four years, fetched $1,000—considerably more than the $700 estimated for a female slave of the same age at the William Lewis estate in Saline County.[41] These high prices are clearly inconsistent with the picture of Kansas slavery's vulnerability presented by other evidence and may have been an aberration from the norm. On the other hand, the high demand for labor may have enhanced the value of slave property. In Missouri, advertisements seeking to hire slaves occurred repeatedly in several successive issues of local newspapers, suggesting to one historian the high demand for and scarcity of such labor in a society lacking in an adequate supply of free white workers.[42]

Overall, slave-holding hype yielded disappointing results. Not only did slavery remain a highly precarious institution through much of its existence in Kansas, pro-Southern emigrants failed to secure its future in the territory. Much of the money pledged at Kansas meetings did not materialize, and "colonists" who immigrated frequently returned unvictorious, as did a squad of Texas Rangers in 1856. Captain Clayton's Alabamians "lost so much valuable time" in military jaunts that "they had not the means with which to purchase their winter provisions." Thus their sponsor provided them with provisions for six months as well as "one wagon, two yoke of oxen, and three cows and calves for the joint use of the company."[43] To a majority of Buford's men, unschooled in the arts of plowing and sowing, marauding apparently held an excitement unmatched by farming. After serving brief stints in proslavery raids, the "settlers" returned whence they came. On the other hand, those who stayed, like a group of "substantial" farm families from Arkansas, not infrequently reneged on the Southern cause. It is small wonder then that the Texas bill to sponsor proslavery emigration to Kansas came to nought. Similarly, a Georgia legislative proposal to advance state aid to Kansas-bound Southern settlers financed by special taxes on slave property went down in defeat in the face of apprehensions that the emigrants in question, while depopulating the native state, would not prove loyal to its principles in Kansas.[44]

John Byrd noted with satisfaction that the proslavery party had hoped to bring thousands of emigrants to Kansas, but had succeeded in obtaining "a drunken rabble" of a few hundred. Amos Finch concurred: "All the Southern Emigrant Aid Company has as yet sent into the territory are desperate characters, gambling, thieving, and dissipated . . . devoid of human feeling." Having failed to turn the tide of population flowing into Kansas in their favor, the Southern blackguards had established a political quarantine at Lexington, Missouri, to prevent free-state emigrants from entering the territory, Byrd complained.[45] Jim Lane rose to the challenge of proslavery road and river blocks by blazing the famous "Lane trail" through Iowa, which became a bridge to Kansas for emigrant groups dubbed "Lane's Army of the North."[46] Meanwhile, federal forces, impotent against proslavery outrages, had forcibly dispersed the Topeka legislature when it attempted to convene on July 4, 1856.[47]

Whatever slavery's prospects in Kansas, its advocates were not prepared to concede the fight just yet. Indeed, the South's peculiar institution was no longer either Southern or peculiar, warned one Northern minister. Slavery was everywhere, including Washington, D.C., where it was "seated in the President's chair, ruling in the Council chamber, judging on the bench of the Supreme Court, moving to and fro armed among Senators and representatives."[48] Kansas would bleed a little longer before Slavery admitted to losing the day.

7

Kansas Bleeds On

In the early hours of August 30, 1856, Samuel Adair awoke to the report of a rifle. Accompanied by his cousin David Garrison, the clergyman repaired to a spot close to his cabin about a mile west of Osawatomie, where his nephew Frederick Brown lay dead. This eldest son of John Brown had fallen prey to the bullet of an advance guard of Atchison's "Grand Army" of "300 fire-eaters from Missouri," commanded by "General" John W. Reid. By the time Adair and Garrison reached the side of Frederick's body, the advance guard appeared to have retreated, but a moment later, the gleam of bayonets became visible in the light of the rising sun. A squad of Missourian cavalry shot Garrison dead as he attempted to run to the village to arouse John Brown and his troops. Adair "secreted himself in the brush," and escaped.[1] The clergyman relived the harrowing experience in a letter to the AMA: "I shall not attempt to describe my feelings as I lay concealed, much less the feelings I had, when late at night I got help, and with lantern in hand, went to the woods, found the dead body of my cousin, and brought it home on the Sabbath."[2] Having forced a defensive free-state party led by John Brown and others to retreat across the Marais des Cygnes River, the invaders from Missouri proceeded to burn and pillage the town of Osawatomie. On their journey home, they stopped by the Adairs' cabin and prepared to burn it. An officer, upon entering, found five women sick in bed. Exclaiming that he could not burn sick women, he spared the house and the company marched on.[3]

The Pottawatomie massacres had unleashed a reign of unprecedented violence in Kansas marked by vicious savagery on both sides. The letters of the AMA and AHMS missionaries seldom dwelt on the outrages perpetrated by free-state men. Nevertheless, Byrd's cursory comment

marked *private*, that "our men have committed some unjustifiable outrages" spoke volumes for the other side of the Kansas picture. Finch
was "pained" by the conduct of free-soilers who broke into proslavery
homes at night and plundered them, butchering cattle belonging to
members of the rival party and freely distributing the beef among free-
state families, so much so that "there has been great quantities of [beef]
in this settlement and every family as far as I know (excepting ours) has
partaken of it." Such behavior prompted severe strictures from Finch,
much to the annoyance of some free-state men. Some of the "leading blacklegs" called the missionary proslavery and threatened to steal
his pony.[4]

Bleeding Kansas had become the cynosure of a polarized nation's
eyes. The *Herald of Freedom* reported that daily meetings composed
of "hewers of wood and drawers of water, of farmers and mechanics,"
passed resolutions and raised money "all about and for Kansas."[5] In
July 1856, at a national convention of various Kansas aid committees
in Buffalo, the friends of a free Kansas organized the National Kansas
Committee to offer relief to the victims of proslavery crimes. Thaddeus
Hyatt, New York manufacturer and entrepreneur, became president;
Eli Thayer was appointed to organize sympathetic states for relief. Believing that nothing would "strike dread" into the hearts of the enemy
"but the conviction that the free settlers were . . . so well-provisioned,
clothed, and munitioned," that it would be futile to impede "the on-
ward march of liberty, justice, and humanity," the NEEAC threw the
weight of its support behind the relief efforts of the National Kansas
Committee.[6]

Embarrassed by Northern disapproval of its conduct of Kansas affairs, especially its hand in dispersing an attempted meeting of the
Topeka legislature, the Pierce Administration replaced Governor Shannon with Col. John W. Geary, a Mexican War veteran from Pennsylvania.
On his arrival in the territory in September 1856, the new governor
determined to pacify the territory. He did succeed in establishing an uneasy truce by disbanding the territorial militia and armed bands on both
sides. Geary's success in bringing about a temporary truce in Kansas
did little, however, to salvage Pierce's faltering career. Bleeding Kansas
sealed the president's political fate just as surely as it brightened that

of the newborn Republican party. Northern Democrats alienated by Pierce's blundering Kansas policy would foil his chances of renomination in 1856. Democrats in Congress tried to stem the damage done by the Kansas conflict to their collective political fortune by introducing a measure for the early admission of the territory to statehood. Under the Toombs bill, named after Sen. Robert Toombs of Georgia, Kansas voters registered by federal commissioners would elect a constitutional convention immediately. Kansas would enter the Union under the constitution so framed with or without slavery. House Republicans responded to the proposal by demanding that Kansas be admitted as a free state under the Topeka constitution instead. Neither measure passed, and the shadow of Bleeding Kansas hung heavy over the presidential campaign of 1856.[7]

A new two-party system crystallized during the electoral season of 1856. The Know-Nothing party split along sectional lines over a resolution calling for the repeal of the Kansas-Nebraska Act. Antislavery nativists bolted to form the North American party. The remaining delegates nominated former Pres. Millard Fillmore to run on their ticket. Meanwhile, several North American party members engineered the absorption of their movement into Republicanism by having their presidential candidate, Nathaniel Banks, withdraw his candidacy in favor of his Republican counterpart. The Republican party, staging its first national convention, nominated for president the politically uncontroversial explorer of the Far West, John C. Frémont. The Republican platform condemned the Kansas-Nebraska Act and endorsed free soil. It courted Whig support by favoring federal aid to internal improvements and sought to avoid alienating nativist support by calling for freedom of conscience and equal rights "among citizens." The Democrats opted for a "safe" candidate, James Buchanan of Pennsylvania, who, by his recent absence from the country as minister to England, was free of the taint of complicity in the Kansas troubles. The Democratic platform upheld popular sovereignty and states' rights, and rejected federal spending on internal improvements and a national bank.[8]

Kansas supplied the most compelling case for the Republican cry of "free soil, free speech, free men, and Frémont," and the most incriminating evidence of the Democratic party's alleged domination by the

Slave Power. It helped Frémont carry New England, New York, and most of the Northwest. But the specter of disunion it raised drove the rest of the North, including Pennsylvania, New Jersey, Indiana, Illinois, and California into Buchanan's camp. The Democrats prevailed in all of the South except Maryland, which Fillmore won. With 45 percent of the popular vote and 184 electoral votes, James Buchanan was elected president in 1856. The new president would find it hard to forget his political debt to the South. Before his tenure ended in the White House, the Democratic party would assume an immutable Southern complexion, while Republicanism, having consumed the remaining embers of Know-Nothingism, would become the majority party in the North.[9]

Back in Kansas, the pressing call of politics prompted Robinson to resign his office as the agent of the NEEAC, with the blessing of his former employers. He continued to correspond with the company and enjoyed their financial support for six months after his resignation.[10] In his place the company appointed Charles Branscomb permanent agent to work in cooperation with Pomeroy.[11] The frustration of Republican aspirations to the presidency in November 1856 was a major setback to the Topeka government's hopes of an early achievement of statehood for Kansas under a free-state constitution. But all was not lost, believed the NEEAC faction, for as Amos Lawrence wrote an associate, "Governor Geary is steering his course straight on for a free port. He rather hopes to be the first governor of the new state, and our friend Robinson will help him in that. Robinson and Pomeroy are on capital terms with him: he consults them and they him." Evidently so, because soon after the election, Robinson alienated a considerable faction of the free-state party by entering into an arrangement with Geary that provided for the entry of Kansas into the Union under the Topeka constitution. Robinson would step down from the governorship of the territory in favor of Geary, an administration Democrat, and would proceed to Washington to reconcile the Republicans and presumably advance his own senatorial prospects. It was hoped that the Democratic party would fall in with the plan in order to bring the new state into the Democratic fold, while the Republicans would revel in their role as saviors of freedom in Kansas. Accordingly, Robinson resigned as governor under the Topeka constitution in January 1857, but discovered to his dismay that neither political party was amenable to his plan. The free-state settlers of Law-rence and Topeka, moreover, gave vent to their sense of betrayal by censuring the former governor at public meetings. An associate of John Brown wrote the abolitionist, "Dr. Robinson recently made a proposi-tion with some leading proslavery men to compromise. The free-state men won't do it." [12]

Geary had no more luck than Robinson in persuading his party either at Washington or in Kansas to go along with his proposal for pacify-ing Kansas. The proslavery legislature at Lecompton adopted, over the governor's veto, a bill designed to take the free-state-majority territory into the Union as a slave state. The bill provided that voters registered by proslavery county sheriffs would elect a convention to frame a con-stitution that would be adopted without a referendum. Geary, bereft of any support from the Buchanan administration, resigned in protest on March 4, 1857. His successor, Robert J. Walker of Mississippi, chosen by Buchanan to implement popular sovereignty impartially, tried in vain to persuade the free-state faction to vote in the election to the constitutional convention authorized by the territorial legislature. The governor's failure resulted in the election of a proslavery convention in June 1857, chosen by less than 10 percent of the eligible electorate.[13]

Walker found himself in an unenviable situation. His attempts to con-ciliate the free-state party, including his insistence that the forthcom-ing constitution be subjected to a referendum, alienated friends of the South within and outside Kansas without securing any compensatory gain of antislavery confidence. Adair conceded that Governor Walker had some sense of honor and justice, but the clergyman had no doubt that his sympathies were proslavery. The missionary reported having heard from "the lips of some of [Walker's] warm National Democrat friends here" that the governor intended to do as little as possible to en-force the "bogus law" and would throw the weight of his support behind the endeavor to make Kansas a free state, so as to "save the Democracy and ride on it and on the reputation that he [may have gained] by so doing into the Presidency at the next election." [14]

Despite many free-soilers' deep suspicion of his motives, Walker suc-ceeded in securing free-state participation in the October election to a new territorial legislature. Unhappily, recent history repeated itself.

Proslavery fraud at the polls threatened to make a mockery of popular sovereignty once again. Byrd held the governor himself culpable. A gentleman from Platte County, Missouri, apparently claimed that Walker solicited his vote for the proslavery ticket, and when he declined, the governor requested him not to mention the incident. "There is decided corroborating testimony," the missionary claimed, "which I cannot detail, which to my mind leaves his guilt almost beyond a doubt." [15] Subsequent events suggest that Byrd's allegation was rather unfair. Walker threw out the fraudulent election returns from two districts, giving the antislavery faction a majority in the new territorial legislature.

Proslaveryism was far from a spent force, however. It had a mighty tool left in the constitutional convention elected in June. That body met in Lecompton—a "celebrated whiskey-drinking capital," according to the *New York Tribune*—to frame a constitution upholding property rights in slaves already in the territory for eternity.[16] The settlers were not given the option to vote on the constitution as a whole, but simply on the question whether new slaves could be introduced into Kansas: choices misleadingly labeled "the constitution with slavery" and "the constitution without slavery." Buchanan had earlier supported Walker's pledge of a referendum on the constitution. Now the president gave the document his unqualified support. His volte-face prompted a thoroughly frustrated Walker to depart from Kansas forever, discredited the president in the North, fragmented the Democratic party, and unleashed a barrage of indignant protest among free-state people in the territory. "There seems to be but one feeling; *that the proslavery constitution shall not go into effect*," Adair wrote.[17] Free-state men made this sentiment amply clear by rejecting the Lecompton constitution altogether at an election called by the territorial legislature in January 1858. Proslavery men, who boycotted this election, had, a month earlier, decided in favor of the constitution "with slavery." Buchanan, solicitous as ever of Southern opinion, supported them even though as Adair warned, "It is madness in the administration to attempt to force [the Lecompton constitution] upon this people. Every man who would receive office under it, to enforce it, would need a body of U.S. troops around him everywhere in the territory by day and by night." [18]

Northern Democrats understood this sentiment all too well, none better than the controversial champion of popular sovereignty Stephen Douglas. Aghast at the president's flagrant disregard for the majority will, the Little Giant broke with the administration amidst angry charges of treason from the South. Twenty-two Northern Democrats in the House followed suit, joining the Republicans to defeat Lecompton in April 1858. Indiana Democrat William English then proposed a bill to resolve the congressional deadlock over Lecompton. The Buchanan administration, anxious to save face and avoid further party strife, supported the bill. This compromise formula provided that the Lecompton constitution, together with a bribe in the form of a federal land grant, would be subjected to a popular vote. If the voters decided in favor of Lecompton, Kansas would enter the Union with the land grant as a slave state; if not, she would remain a territory till her population reached 93,600.[19] Kansans voted in August 1858 to reject the Lecompton constitution and to defer the admission of their territory to statehood until it reached the stipulated population. Even in Leavenworth, once a proslavery stronghold, 1,610 turned down Lecompton; only 138 voted in its favor.[20]

Byrd was not wide off the mark when he exulted in 1858 that the territory had grown more antislavery than "if it had been received into the Union two years ago under the Topeka Constitution," partly because the ranks of the proslavery faction had been much depleted by the departure of many of its members who sought safety in flight and partly because of the "progress of antislavery opinion among the people." Robinson claimed that the Democrats were as anxious to see Lecompton voted down as the Republicans were, for they knew that "if Lecompton should go into the Union," Kansas would not only send two radical Republicans into the Senate, but also a Republican state government and members of Congress would change the constitution "in the twinkling of an eye." The English bill was "no more and no less than Lecompton." It had passed chiefly with the support of Southerners who did not suppose that Kansas would do "anything else than vote the ordinance down."[21]

Robinson suspected that until the new Congress met in December 1859 the Democratic party intended to administer the territory in an "eminently just and fair" fashion, and take a lead in developing its resources. It would induce old Democrats to return to its fold and make as many new converts as possible from the ranks of Republicans who made antislavery "anywhere except in the territories a secondary consideration" and were primarily concerned with the material interests of the state of their adoption, and as a result were "given the cold shoulder by the more zealous antislavery members of the [Republican] party." The Democrats, Robinson believed, also wished to wean away from Republican ranks another group of men who were "strongly antislavery" but saw the importance of developing the resources of Kansas, of building roads, and planting literary and other institutions, and who attracted the criticism of radical Republicans for their espousal of a conciliatory attitude toward all members of the party. Presumably, Robinson considered himself a member of this group. Referring to the radical element in the Republican party represented by such men as Lane, Robinson wrote, "The Democrats see that the free-state party has an element that will destroy it as soon as permanent peace is established." It was this element that must be reined in, if the Republicans were to win Kansas, according to the former NEEAC agent.[22]

Kansas prepared for statehood as the territorial legislature provided for a new constitutional convention to meet at Wyandotte in 1859. Both major parties set their sights on winning the forthcoming state. A territorial Democratic convention held at Tecumseh in May 1859 adopted a platform opposing congressional intervention in domestic institutions and endorsing popular sovereignty, a homestead law, and the exclusion of free blacks. Democrats also proclaimed that they "recognized no difference between proslavery and free-state men as such."[23] The territorial Republican party, founded at a convention in Osawatomie in May 1859, absorbed many of the former free-staters of both the Lane and Robinson stripes. Friction between the radicals and the moderates continued, a Lane supporter accusing Robinson of working "to destroy the Republican wing of the free-state party in every possible way — the price perhaps for favors at Court."[24] Samuel Pomeroy served as one of the vice presidents of the Republican party, which resolved that freedom was national and slavery sectional. The party was "inflexibly opposed to the

extension of slavery to soil now free" and recommended that the Wyandotte convention incorporate an article in the constitution prohibiting
black bondage.[25]

Byrd seemed disappointed with the initial returns of the territorial
elections held in July 1859, which indicated a small Republican majority
in the constitutional convention. Much to his disillusionment, a great
many free-state people proved to have "very short memories or very
little moral principle," because they were credulous enough to believe
in Democratic professions of support for a free state and "only failed by
a few votes of giving them the control of the Constitutional Convention."
The old "border ruffians," the "body and soul of the Democratic party"
now sought to ingratiate themselves into the favor of free-state men
whom they had "hunted to death" not long ago. "These hunters and the
hunted now join in the chase of the poor black man and if they succeed
in running him down, their political fortunes are assured," Byrd wrote
disgustedly.[26]

The Wyandotte Convention convened on July 5, 1859, and on July 29
adopted a constitution that denied blacks the right to vote, although it
did not exclude them from the territory. The constitution was ratified by
a popular vote in October 1859, thus paving the way for the admission of
Kansas to the Union in 1861. Even before the political resolution of the
Kansas conflict, however, common economic concerns had prompted
the men Byrd characterized as "the hunters and the hunted" to forgive
and forget their old animosities and forge fresh alliances based on new
priorities.

8

A "Rehearsal for Redemption"?

One bright Saturday morning in September 1860, two men in a carriage savored the delights of the town of Atchison, once a legendary bastion of "soundness on the goose question." One of the men was Thaddeus Hyatt, a New York–based free-soil entrepreneur and chairman of the National Kansas Committee established to provide relief to recent drought victims in the territory. His companion was none other than one of the town's founding fathers and David Atchison's former lieutenant, Peter T. Abell. In due course, the two men ascended a "beautiful knoll" that afforded a breathtaking view of the surrounding countryside. Hyatt admired the spectacle. Abell promptly responded with a proposal hard to reject. As Hyatt wrote his wife, "he at once offered it to me as a present if I would come here and live." The New Yorker claimed, "my friends here, the head border ruffians of 1855, offer me almost any spot as a building site that I choose to select, and there are some truly superb ones."[1]

Robert Gaston Elliot, a cofounder of the *Kansas Free State,* reported from Delaware, Kansas, an equally cordial welcome from the erstwhile authors of "ruffianly outrages." He wrote his sister in May 1857 that the very men who had led marauding excursions against free-state settlers in the town the previous season, were the first to "take us by hand," and appeared most anxious to induce "Northern Vagabonds" and "Nigger Thieves" to settle in their midst. For the "Tory party" knew "from experience," that "[free-staters] were the class of settlers to enhance the value of their property." The contrast between the growth and prosperity of the free-state towns and the stagnation of "Tory" towns, which had become "about as worthless as a dead horse a hundred miles from a button factory," afforded a practical demonstration of the benefits of

Northern emigration and free institutions. Elliot claimed that before the so-called "Lawrence paupers" bought out the greater part of the town of Delaware, it had consisted of 25 or 30 unimproved, weather-beaten shanties, 3 whiskey shops, and a population of about a "dozen very respectable proslavery men, a score or two of bloated ruffians loafing about the whiskey shops to sponge a glass of grog off some liberal tippler, . . . about fifty hungry sheep-killing looking dogs, and about a half Dozen [sic] ragged thick-lipped niggers." As soon as the Yankees took over, "everything took an upward tendency." The new company had set in motion the work of "grading the levee and a portion of the streets" for thirty thousand to forty thousand dollars, and "hundreds of tons of freight" were landed in the town for Lawrence and points in the interior. Small wonder, then, that "proslavery men are as anxious to see Free-State men settle here as we are." Indeed, several of them, including one who led the destruction of the *Free State* press in 1856, had subscribed to numerous copies of the paper, believing it would attract the right sort of emigration to their town.[2]

Likewise, the Planter's House hotel of Leavenworth, established under proslavery auspices in 1855, saw no point in mixing political principle with business forever. In 1857 by-laws that decreed the hotel should be governed according to "exclusive southern principles" fell by the boards. Soon thereafter, the hotel attracted a number of distinguished guests, among them Abraham Lincoln, William T. Sherman, and William H. Seward. D. R. Anthony, a New York insurance agent in Leavenworth, reported to his father that his business was doing very well, thanks to proslavery patronage: "Although there are four other insurance agents, yet somehow the 'damned Yankee' does the business — best proslavery men give me their business." [3]

Clearly, even before the curtain closed officially on the clash over slavery, a significant realignment of interests rooted in commerce was taking place west of the Missouri river. Once despised as the scum of eastern cities, the Yankees, or at any rate those of them that had some capital, received a warm welcome from Southern town boosters.[4] Northern men of progress too, were discovering that they had more in common with their "ruffianly adversaries" than the gory events in Bleeding Kansas indicated. A composite biography of prominent champions of the South in Kansas suggests that key figures in the proslavery camp, whatever their party affiliations, bore perhaps greater resemblance to the bourgeois Yankees they professed to despise than to the Southern patriarchs whose idealized slave-holding world they so vigorously defended.

In the case of many friends of slavery, of course, their brief careers in Kansas ended with the death of their cause, so that a researcher on their trail is apt to find her path disappear abruptly into the wilderness of oblivion. Nevertheless, several others stayed. The following profiles, representing six of the more prominent and historically retrievable leaders on the side of the losers, united by their participation in the 1857 proslavery Lecompton constitutional convention, suggest that the South's champions were hardly a monolithic crowd of "drunken, bellowing, bloodthirsty demons" of Missourian nativity.[5] Several, like associate judge Rush Elmore, descended from an illustrious Old South bloodline, were no less sensitive to the business opportunities their new home had to offer than their Yankee brothers.

The Elmore family tree, rooted in colonial Virginia, was liberally sprinkled with Revolutionary War veterans, Indian fighters, Alabama pioneers and politicians, and a South Carolina bank president. The Alabama-born Rush was himself a Mexican War veteran who opened a law partnership with his older brother, John A. Elmore, and the infamous fire-eater William C. Yancey in Montgomery, Alabama. Appointed to the Kansas Supreme Court in 1854, Elmore joined hands with Governor Reeder, among others, in founding the town of Tecumseh in Shawnee County, where he settled. The Judge's "courtly and chivalrous" manner endeared him to many free-state sympathizers, including Reeder. Indeed, Elmore's friendship and business association with the governor cost him his job in the fall of 1855, when President Pierce dismissed both men on the grounds that they had illegally contracted for the purchase of Indian lands. In 1857 Pres. James Buchanan restored Elmore to the court, where he served until 1861. Thereafter he practiced law in Topeka until his death in 1864. During his lifetime, Elmore continued to delight the Kansas "gentry"—both free-state and proslavery—with his many social qualities, including his love of hunting. One Monday morning, on his way to court in Lecompton, the judge was "inoculated with the spirit of the chase by the sight of a herd of six deer that crossed the road in front of him." He immediately adjourned court, sent for the fine dogs he had brought with him from his Southern home, and went on a deer hunt, which territorial governor Wilson Shannon joined with gusto. Although Elmore, master of fourteen bondspeople, was one of the largest slaveholders in the territory, his love of the Union prevailed over his loyalty to the peculiar institution when Kansans defeated the Lecompton constitution he had helped frame.[6]

In contrast to the judge, his fellow Lecompton architect, the fiery and irascible Jim Adkins, conformed more closely to the "border ruffian" image. A former proslavery Kickapoo Ranger turned respectable Platte County granger, "Old Jim," like his mentor Atchison, had emigrated to Missouri from Kentucky. After a brief stint at the gold digs in California, he took a claim in Port William, Atchison County, where he lived in a secluded house up against the heavily timbered bluffs bordering the valley of Little Walnut Creek. His contemporaries described Adkins as a man of violent temper and "undoubted nerve," quick to draw a rifle, who rode day and night clad in "a belt with two pistols in it, buckled around the outside of his coat." Unlike the high-born Elmore, this "wolf of the border" eventually left free Kansas for slave Missouri.[7]

Not every Southern rights advocate who left Kansas at the end of the territorial period, however, retreated into the South. At least one proslavery trail leads, surprisingly enough, into the heart of Yankeedom. Journalist Alfred W. Jones left for Kansas at the head of a company of colonists from Petersburg, Virginia, in 1855. If 1857 saw this editor of the *Lecompton (Kansas) Union and National Democrat* doing his bit for the Old Dominion at the Lecompton constitutional convention, 1868 found him representing Middlesex County interests in the New Jersey state legislature. Jones even donated a memento of his Kansas days to the New Brunswick Historical Club in 1875—the proslavery Lecompton constitution itself.[8]

Not every man "of the wrong stripe" had been born on the wrong side of the Mason-Dixon line. Ironically enough, one of the most notorious "villains" of the Kansas drama was neither rabidly proslavery nor a Southerner by birth or residence. The very name of Lecompton constitutional convention president John Calhoun became synonymous with proslavery abomination. Every free-stater excoriated the "border ruffi-ans" who persisted in perpetuating "Calhoun frauds" at the polls, as they did the "Calhoun Convention" in Lecompton, which was attempt-ing to fasten slavery around the unwilling neck of Kansas. Yet this "chief rowdy of Lecompton" apparently favored a constitution after the pattern of Massachusetts, which was perhaps not surprising coming as it did from the Boston-born son of a successful merchant-turned-gentleman-farmer. As a youth, Calhoun had been working on his father's farm in Mohawk Valley, New York, besides burning the midnight oil over his law books, when he felt the frontier beckon. Moving west, he put down stakes in Springfield, Illinois, home to two influential future friends. A Douglas Democrat in politics, Calhoun shared warm vibes with the Little Giant as well as with the future Great Emancipator. Indeed, Abra-ham Lincoln served as his deputy when he became the surveyor of San-gamon County, Illinois. Elected to the Illinois state legislature in 1838, Calhoun denied the right of Congress to prohibit slavery in the territo-ries. The Pierce administration dispatched him to Kansas as surveyor-general with instructions to establish a Democratic stronghold in the ter-ritory — a responsibility that led him to blunder into proslavery politics as the only alternative to "Black Republicanism." Although he eschewed the politics of Black Republicanism, he embraced its economics.[9]

Like Calhoun, Indian agent and Lecompton father Daniel Vanderslice was born a Yankee. A Pennsylvanian by birth and Jacksonian Democrat in politics, his eventful career had, by 1854, spanned several decades, diverse states, and myriad professions. Vanderslice had manufactured paper in his native state, worked lead mines in northwestern Illinois, taught school and edited a newspaper in Kentucky before arriving in Kansas Territory in April 1853 as government agent for the Kickapoos, the Iowas, the Sacs, and the Foxes living within the Great Nemaha Agency in Doniphan County. Vanderslice's commitment to the Union overcame his sympathies for slavery before long. Indeed, he contrib-uted a son to Kansas's effort to beat back the murderous Sterling Price in 1864.[10]

The Southern contingent contained its fair share of pragmatists who knew when to stop touting a lost cause. Proslavery territorial chief jus-tice Samuel D. Lecompte, a lawyer originally from Maryland, arrived in

Kansas with his wife, five children, and two Negro women in 1854. In
1857 the judge did all he could for slavery at Lecompton—a town he
had helped found. When the people of Kansas spoke on the resultant
constitution, he bowed to the popular will by eventually becoming a Republican politician. Even before his political transformation, however,
he did not balk at entering into lucrative business alliances with his
political enemies.[11]

Not all high-profile proslavery activists in Kansas served in the Lecompton convention. Among those that defended Southern institutions
in other ways were the former Missouri senator David Atchison and the
physician John Stringfellow, both of whom remained loyal to the South.
The same cannot be said for their associates: Benjamin Stringfellow, who
owned all of one female slave, and his Whig law partner, Peter T. Abell,
whose slave-holding status likewise rested on the possession of a sole
Aunt Nancy. Both men were particularly active in promoting the territory's—and their own—economic prosperity from the start.[12] Stringfellow and Abell were among those Whiggish and unionist proslavery
entrepreneurs who, like many of their Northern opponents, threw themselves into railroad promotion and town-boosterism with abandon, even
though many of their projects did not progress beyond incorporation. A
host of "paper" enterprises—the Central Gulf Railway Company, Eastern Kansas and Gulf Railroad Company, the Kansas Central Railroad
Company, the Kansas Valley Railroad Company, the Leavenworth and
Lecompton Railroad Company, the Marysville and Denver City Railroad Company, the Marysville and Roseport Railroad Company, and the
Mine Hill Railroad and Mining Company—bore prominent proslavery
names in their catalogs of directors and incorporators. Had they suc-
ceeded, Kansas would have early been traversed by an intricate network
of railroads linking the continent's heart with the Gulf coast and the
Pacific.[13]

In the intensely competitive economic environment of pioneer Kansas, however, several pro-Southern business enterprises discovered that
sectional politics did not always mix well with commercial success. At
the height of the Kansas wars in November 1856, a group of proslavery
leaders including Luther Challis, Isaac Hascall, John Stringfellow, and
Peter Abell issued a circular to the general public, particularly those

living north of the Kansas River inviting settlement, pledging to protect their families and property, no matter what their sentiments on
slavery—certainly a far cry from earlier threats to clear all Yankee abolitionists from Missouri's neighborhood. What was more, the assurance
was published in the *Squatter Sovereign*, that most reliable of Southern
organs.[14]

On the other side of the slavery question, NEEAC agents Robinson
and Pomeroy combined their commitment to free-state politics with a
Whiggish concern for the business development of their adopted home.
In this context, their support of Robert P. Flenneken for territorial
delegate to Congress in November 1854 is instructive. The three candidates for delegate on that occasion consisted of the proslavery favorite
John W. Whitfield of Missouri, the independent candidate Flenneken of
Pennsylvania, and free-state candidate John A. Wakefield, a Republican
judge from Illinois. According to Kansas historian William E. Connelley, NEEAC emigrants "did not support the free-state candidate, but
were in favor of the election of Mr. Flenneken on the ground that his
election would be in the interest of business development." A committee
of men on both sides of the slavery question called upon voters to elect
Flenneken for "he will make a most useful . . . delegate . . . to whom we
may confidently look for procuring the appropriations for military roads
and bridges, public buildings . . . the modification of Indian treaties. . . .
We cannot see the necessity or propriety of agitating the [slavery] question at this time. A delegate in Congress . . . should be elected only with
an eye to his value, efficiency, and influence in procuring the legislation
we so much need to advance the prosperity . . . of this territory." The
committeemen added that the "best evidence" of their sincerity was that
they were themselves "divided in opinion on the [slavery] question—
some of us being antislavery men and some proslavery."[15]

The free-state vote divided between Wakefield and Flenneken. Amos
Finch was no doubt not alone among the AMA missionaries in voting for
the more progressive Illinois Republican. NEEAC agent Charles Robinson and AHMS missionary Samuel Lum, on the other hand, voted for
Flenneken, whom the Ohio abolitionist S. N. Wood described as being "a
rabid pro slavery man in private, taking the extreme hunker side of the
question." In an acrimonious exchange with Robinson through the col-

umns of the *Herald of Freedom*, Wood accused the Flenneken supporter of saying at a meeting in Lawrence before the election that a delegate to Congress had nothing to do with the question of slavery.[16]

It is not entirely surprising that even before free-statism became a fait accompli in Kansas, sectional partisans realigned into interest groups based on commercial concerns and united by the canker of negrophobia. A torrent of speculative capitalism swept away all vestiges of sectional animosities over slavery in some business circles. Land was, of course, a particularly attractive article of commercial exploitation. The California gold rush, along with the Crimean War, rising foreign demand for American wheat, high commodity prices, an enormous expansion in immigration, and the movement of native white Americans westward to preempt government land, greatly inflated land values in the West and unleashed an orgy of speculative activity.[17]

If Kansas proved particularly prone to land jobbing, it was because the situation in that territory was complicated by the congressional blunder in opening to white settlement territory that legally belonged to the Indians. As of May 30, 1854, none of the treaties providing for land cessions by Indians dislodged from their native states in the east and established on reservations along the Kansas-Missouri border had been ratified, nor had arrangements been made to survey the public lands. On July 22, 1854, Congress, under pressure from land reformers, recognized squatters' rights to unsurveyed public lands to which all Indian titles had been extinguished. These included the Missouri cessions of the Sac and the Fox; the Kickapoo cession in Northwestern Kansas, the boundaries of which were not clearly delineated; and the cessions of the Pottawatomies, the Shawnees, and the Delaware Outlet in the interior. Scattered among these tracts were Indian cessions held in trust, allotments, diminished reserves, and original reserves to which various Indian tribes held titles, so that squatters on the public domain of Kansas extending westward from the Missouri border were "in danger of finding when the survey lines were run that their improvements were on lands retained by the Indians."[18]

Conflicting land disposal policies by the land-administering agencies only contributed to the confusion of the settlers, which the various immigrant guides did nothing to alleviate.[19] Under such circumstances, the settlers were not allowed to use land claims as collateral for loans, prompting many prospective farmers to engage in land speculation instead.[20] This line of business proved to be a fruitful instrument for the dissolution of ideological barriers between the friends and foes of slavery. Proslavery leaders adopted supposedly bourgeois Northern attitudes and appeared willing to mingle their fortunes with that of their former adversaries with an alacrity that anticipated the reconciliation between the business interests of the North and the South after Reconstruction.

Likewise, the "iron horse" prompted economic alliances across sectional lines in a common endeavor to bring Kansas into the mainstream of national economic life and fulfill its destiny as the commercial emporium of the North American continent. Arguments in favor of a transcontinental railroad to tie the Pacific coast securely to the nation combined with the local transportation and commercial needs of the West to create a strong case for railroad building in the territory. The opportunity to tap the highly profitable commerce with New Mexico over the Santa Fe Trail, the heavy westward flow of people and provisions over Kansas following the discovery of gold in Pike's Peak, Colorado, the transportation demands of cattle drivers from Texas to Kansas City and beyond after 1857, and the necessity to provide the large local population of sodbusters with access to markets for their produce in the absence of navigable waterways in the territory made railroad promotion a highly attractive proposition to Kansas entrepreneurs.[21]

Burgeoning towns, even those on the same side of the slavery question, did not necessarily balk at a little healthy competition with one another. Lawrence and Council City, for instance became embroiled in a controversy over an article published in the *New York Independent* claiming that the American Settlement Company had founded "a very prosperous town in a most advantageous locality — Council City, where there are said to be 1,500 inhabitants." Believing that "the tendency of the article" was to injure the free-state cause in Kansas by "conveying a wrong impression," the *Herald* proceeded to place the size and prospects of the settlement in what it believed to be a true perspective by reporting that "there was but one house on the city site." The American Settlement Company disagreed with the *Herald*'s perspective. Its president, J. M. Winchell, proclaimed in a subsequent rejoinder that the American Settlement Company had never aspired to be a rival of the New England Emigrant Aid Company, and had never made "grand promises" that it could not fulfill.[22]

The *Herald* also undertook to refute the proslavery *Leavenworth Herald*'s claim that Leavenworth had a larger population and greater promise to develop into the territory's principal commercial center than Lawrence. The NEEAC organ drew prospective emigrants' attention to the fact that the town of Lawrence had forty more residences than Leavenworth and was "far in advance" of the latter town "in population and improvements."[23] Irked by Pomeroy's disparaging portrayal of Leavenworth in the *New York Tribune*, Reverend Byrd, who had taken a claim near the proslavery town, wrote the AMA that it was natural that the NEEAC agents should wish to draw attention to their towns, but that in strength of population, extent of business, and "indications of growth," Lawrence and Topeka combined compared unfavorably with Leavenworth. Through the pages of the *American Missionary*, the clergyman invited "businessmen and Christians" to take advantage of the ready availability of valuable claims in the "fertile and unsurpassingly beautiful country" surrounding his adopted hometown and build there a "rampart against the aggressions of slavery."[24]

In 1860, when Thaddeus Hyatt and Samuel C. Pomeroy spearheaded a relief campaign to aid the victims of a protracted drought in Kansas, a group of Leavenworth citizens issued a manifesto alleging that Hyatt had grossly exaggerated the extent of suffering in the territory. In retaliation, Hyatt addressed a series of circulars to the eastern public, which, in essence, charged that all denials of Kansas's sorry plight stemmed from the "jealousy of a rival city" that entertained "a stupid idea that to tell the whole truth about this Kansas Famine" would "destroy land values and trade, and prevent immigration to the new state." In one of his "Letters from Kansas" he wrote, "As I read [the Leavenworth Manifesto], an instructive feeling came over me that an old fashioned border ruffian lie of the '56 type lay curled up somewhere inside of that telegram; . . . I find on entering the territory that while the terrible drought has baked everything else to a 'cup,' the owners of corner lots remain as green as ever."[25]

The quest for commercial supremacy frequently prompted ambitious proslavery towns to solicit Yankee enterprise and capital. In 1857 the proslavery fathers of Atchison sold a controlling interest in their town to NEEAC agent Pomeroy and a Cincinnati-based emigrant company agent Robert McBratney. The NEEAC, unable to bear the expenses involved in making improvements, confined its investments in Atchison to one hundred lots at five dollars each, and a three-story frame hotel, including its site at three thousand dollars. It also agreed to finance a flour mill in the town.[26] Pomeroy in his private capacity, however, plunged into the promotion of Atchison with all the zeal he could muster. To advance his new project, the NEEAC agent entered into a business relationship with Thaddeus Hyatt of New York, whom Abell was so anxious to have settle in their town. In May 1857 Pomeroy wrote Hyatt, "You and I have every alternate lot upon 330 acres adjoining the present town plot [of Atchison], . . . some few lots and buildings in the town . . . one half of the *Squatter Sovereign* (Stringfellow again) — Mr. McBratney of Ohio owns the other half — we have hoisted a free-state flag." Sure enough, in February 1858 the formerly virulent proslavery newspaper assumed a new name, *Freedom's Champion*.[27]

Pomeroy and his Atchison associates strove to make their town the pivot of a network of railroads extending to the north, the west, and the southwest. In this endeavor, they sought the cooperation of that wing of the Republican party that favored high tariff rates, the import of contract labor, the grant of profitable contracts to industry, and the promotion of transcontinental railroads through land grants and bond subsidies.[28] As early as July 1857, the Atchison promoters sought to forge railroad connections with the east by building a road from Atchison to St. Joseph, Missouri, the western terminus of the Hannibal and St. Joseph Railroad. Accordingly, President Pomeroy and Secretary Abell announced a meeting of stockholders at Atchison on Saturday, August 8, 1857, to select a board of directors and officers for the projected line — to be known as the Atchison and St. Joseph Railroad. A new city charter issued in February 1858 authorized the issue of up to two hundred thousand dollars worth of bonds for the railroad project, in which, incidentally, the former "chief rowdy of Lecompton," Surveyor-General Calhoun, took a healthy interest.[29]

Meanwhile Pomeroy, Hyatt, and others envisioned a related source of profit: a town opposite Atchison as the Missouri terminus of the railroad. A party from Kentucky evidently had the same idea. When they discovered that Pomeroy had bought "the best 200 acres," they offered to buy him out on terms that were "quite good." Pomeroy wrote, "I tell them two things are sure. First, if a town is made opposite us, *I am to control it* and second, I let no parties in who will not consent to let me have and cut off all the timber that I choose. These men are willing to consent to that." Pomeroy planned to "harmonize the streets [of the proposed town] with the railroad track, and sell lots to mechanics and all sorts of laborers. . . . If the railroad can be put through next season, we can sell lots enough to make such sinners as we are, rich, as sinners ought to be. . . . I tell my Kentucky friends that when the time comes I will let them have shares very reasonably, always keeping a majority." [30]

Cooperation with the Platte Valley Railroad did not materialize, and a railroad construction contract was awarded to local contractors. The projected town opposite Atchison, however, did take shape. Winthrop, by name, it sprawled over six hundred acres of land on the east bank of the Missouri. Until the railroad was completed, Pomeroy and Hyatt arranged for the "splendid steamer *Lightfoot*" to transport Atchison travelers to St. Joseph, where they could catch connecting trains on the Hannibal and St. Joseph. When the Atchison railroad project ran into financial trouble, Pomeroy sold it to a Missouri consortium, which completed it in 1860. [31]

In 1859 the Atchison interests obtained charters for the construction of three railroads west from Atchison to Topeka, Fort Riley, and Pikes Peak. [32] Pomeroy's favorite venture was the Pikes Peak Line, of which he was president. He wrote Hyatt that he intended to visit Boston to see how he could "marry our Road with the Hannibal and St. Joseph Railroad." [33] Apparently he did so by buying off the opposition of St. Joseph interests to a treaty providing for the cession of surplus lands in the Kickapoo Reserve to the Pike's Peak Line in 1863. The squatters who had made improvements on the Kickapoo lands reluctantly acceded to the sale, but expressed their disapproval of the treaty by delaying the purchase of their claims as long as possible and by despoiling the unoccupied railroad lands of their timber. [34] Pomeroy also participated in the incorporation of the Atchison and Topeka Railroad Company, chartered in 1859, and renamed the Atchison, Topeka, and Santa Fe Railroad by charter amendment in 1863. A brainchild of the free-state Topeka town-company president Cyrus K. Holliday, the line's incorporators included, besides Pomeroy and Abell, the New Jersey–born proslavery merchant and banker Luther C. Challis.[35]

Pomeroy's reconstruction of the town of Atchison included the resuscitation of a moribund banking project begun by John Stringfellow and J. C. Walker of Weston, Missouri, among others. One of six banks to be chartered by the "bogus" territorial legislature in February 1857, the Kansas Valley Bank of Atchison failed to get off the ground thanks to opposition from the apparently hard money Jacksonian Democrat governor Robert J. Walker. Its original incorporators sold their interest in the charter to Pomeroy.[36] The shrewd business operator immediately saw, as he later acknowledged, that there were "splendid chances to make money with money."[37] For while the territory was reeling under the effects of the panic of 1857, the government, in a bid to maximize its returns from the public domain, ordered millions of acres of land into the market, forcing the squatters to secure loans at exorbitant interest rates to pay for their claims. Eastern creditors circumvented the problem of security arising from the fact that claims could not be mortgaged before their sale by agreeing with the squatter to enter the property, take the title in their own name, and sign a contract providing for the transfer of the land to the debtor on condition that the latter pay the principal, a premium, plus legal interest.[38] Pomeroy's former NEEAC colleague Charles Robinson admitted to his wife that he was strongly tempted to engage in no other business than to buy and sell property, and loan money: "I can make as much that way as any. Just think of 5% a month or 60% a year for money."[39]

At a time when "no money was to be had," Pomeroy and his associates raised $26,300 in specie and obtained Gov. James W. Denver's approval of the Kansas Valley Bank, only to confront a fresh hurdle. As Pomeroy wrote Hyatt:

when the concern was ready to go into operation, the legislature at Lawrence repealed the charter! I heard of it three days before the adjournment, and by riding all night, I got there in [time] to see them. I found them—or such of them as were opposed to me of easy virtue and ready to be seduced. So I got a bill excepting our bank from the provisions of their act—got it through both branches, and got the governor's signature, four hours before the adjournment! . . . The bankers and merchants here and all the towns upon the river had an hour of rejoicing![40]

In February 1858, the Kansas Valley Bank opened its doors to the public, but not until its reorganization in July with the aid of eastern capital supplied by freighting and railroad firms, did it begin to prosper. Its business associates included the Bank of St. Louis and the Importers and Traders Bank of New York; its patrons were such Atchison pioneers as Peter T. Abell and George M. Million. As Pomeroy informed Thaddeus Hyatt, he had promised various parties bank loans at 5 percent interest per month. The securities, he assured his partner, were all within ten miles of Atchison.[41]

Like Pomeroy, Robinson combined his political and cultural pursuits with an active interest in speculation and railroad promotion, often in collaboration with prominent Kansas Democrats. In concert with Abelard Guthrie, a Wyandotte Indian, he founded in 1856 the town of Quindaro on Wyandotte land bordering the Missouri river, envisioning the new town as the free-state port of entry into the territory. The NEEAC and the Kansas Land Trust of Boston, of which Amos Lawrence was a trustee and Robinson the Kansas agent, acquired interests in the town. Robinson sought to put Quindaro in the center of the railroad map through the vehicle of the Missouri River and Rocky Mountain Railroad Company. His project entailed a road extending westward from Quindaro, or Wyandotte. In this enterprise, he enjoyed the support of prominent Kansas Democrat Robert S. Stevens. In 1858 he tried in vain to acquire a portion of the Delaware Reserve to realize his iron-horse ambition. Two other Kansas-based railroad groups vied for the same Delaware Trust lands. The Pomeroy-led Atchison faction comprised one group. More powerful, however, was the Leavenworth, Pawnee, and Western Railroad (LP&W) incorporated in 1855 by such strange bedfellows as the banker and trucking company partner William H. Russell;

the Ewing brothers, Hugh Boyle and Thomas Jr., sons of former Whig Secretary of the Interior and Ohio senator Thomas Ewing; and the proslavery judge Samuel D. Lecompte of Kansas. The LP&W was to extend from Leavenworth to Lawrence and beyond to Pawnee, and subsequently to Fort Riley along the north bank of the Kansas River.[42]

Meanwhile, the leaders of Lawrence became disgruntled at what they feared would be a betrayal of their town's interests. Robinson learned that the Lawrence interests were "tired of hearing of the Missouri River and Rocky Mountain Railroad" and preferred a railroad on the south side of the Kansas River for fear that if the road ran up the north side Lawrence would be superseded by a new town built to its north. The governor responded impatiently that any railroad on the south side of the Kansas river below Lawrence would have to rely on stock subscriptions alone and "need not wait for land grants. . . . Certainly the Delawares will part with none of their lands for a road that does not go up the north side of the river. Lawrence and Douglas County may pass resolutions from now till the judgment day for such a road, and it will not interfere with our project, as we are only endeavoring to build such roads as can be built with lands granted for the purpose." He went on in the same letter to assert that free-state men, most of them residents of Lawrence, controlled the stock of his enterprise, the Missouri and Rocky Mountain Railroad Company: "No border ruffian has a dollar's worth of stock in the road so far as I know. . . . The directors of the company are honorable gentlemen . . . and have the confidence of both the Republican and Democratic parties, and this is necessary to success, as no grant of land can be got through Congress without both Republican and Democratic votes." [43]

In Washington, however, where the various railroad interests had assembled to further their respective causes but soon agreed to join forces for mutual benefit, Robinson found that he had to "fight the Lawrence battle entirely alone." The Leavenworth men were unwilling to make Lawrence a point on the road south, although Robinson's group intended to make it a point west.[44] Before long, Russell's influential LP&W gained a commanding lead over its rivals in the race for federal support. Leavenworth town booster Thomas Ewing Jr. sought Robinson's aid in requisitioning Lawrence property worth ten thousand to fifteen thousand dollars to help secure the passage of a land grant bill favorable to the Leavenworth interests. Even though the desired bill did not materialize, the LP&W inveigled the government into concluding a treaty with the Delawares in May 1860 providing eighty-acre allotments to tribe members and authorizing the LP&W to purchase surplus lands for not less than $1.25 an acre. Subsequently, the railroad manipulated an agreement to make payments in company bonds rather than specie. For his role in the deal, Robinson received a handsome land grant. In 1864 the LP&W, now known as the Union Pacific, Eastern Division, built a road from Kansas City to Lawrence, which became a point of transfer for westward-bound freight trains. The railroad came to blows with squatters who had spread over the Delaware Reserve and had organized themselves into a squatter association to protect their rights. Many turned down the railroad's offer to let the settlers pay for their lands with labor on the company's construction crews, prompting the railroad to enlist the aid of federal troops to drive out the "trespassers."[45]

Less than a generation after the Kansas conflict, the most serious threat to the small commercial farmer and entrepreneur was coming no longer from the advocates of slave labor but from a new intersectional coalition of land jobbers, railroad interests, and moneylenders, which included former leaders of the "border ruffians" on the one hand and those of "Yankee abolitionists" on the other.

A decade later, events in the nation at large suggested that the aftermath of Bleeding Kansas may have represented, in microcosm, the economic and political patterns of the post-Reconstruction era. In postbellum North America, a lack of understanding of the cultural implications of slavery for the black "work ethic" and the relentless tide of economic change rendered the social vision of free labor ideology obsolete, and enlisted the collaboration of the business interests of the North and the South in a joint program of economic integration at the expense of the Negro.[46] At the outset of Reconstruction, Northern free labor ideologues, whether school teachers or prospective planters who went south during Reconstruction to facilitate the vanquished section's transition to wage labor and to inculcate the Protestant ethic among the emancipated blacks, had not bargained for the blacks' own definition of the meaning of freedom and proved ready converts to the Southern planters' view of the Negro's incapacity to function as a productive worker in a free labor market system. The rapid expansion of industrial capitalism in the North and the attendant emergence of a wage-earning class reinforced the growing awareness of the reality of conflict between capital and labor, and further undermined the assumptions of the free labor ideology.[47]

The free labor experiment in the West differed fundamentally from that in the post-Reconstruction South in that there were few blacks on the prairies of Kansas to make over in the image of efficient wage workers. The success of the western experiment as conceived by the NEEAC and its evangelical allies depended on the creation of a world of small commercial farmers imbued with the culture of New England. Yet the fate of the free labor experiment in Kansas was not unlike that in the rest of the country. The very steam engine that was eroding the social underpinnings of the free labor ideology in the North was also straining the ideal of the independent small entrepreneur upon which that ideology rested in Kansas. Furthermore, as in the nation at large, men who had been on opposite sides of the battle line over slavery not long ago joined forces in promoting that railroad, which, as Henry Nash Smith has put so well, subordinated the homesteader to the banker and the merchant of the urban West, and eventually transformed him into a producer of staple crops, thus subjecting him to the vagaries of freight rates and international commodity prices.[48]

The story of Bleeding Kansas unfolded along two channels, not always in close correspondence with each other. On one level, Yankee confrontations with the allegedly parallel unprogressive forces of slavery, rum, and to a lesser extent "Romanism," evoked compelling public images of civilization and vulgarism, independence and vassalage that resonated deeply in the culture of the Victorian North and facilitated the emergence of antislavery politics. It is true that the Northeast did not contribute a substantial proportion of the population in territorial Kansas. Although NEEAC agents Charles Robinson and Samuel Pomeroy rose to prominence in free-state politics, the company aided fewer than two thousand emigrants, a third of whom may have returned east.[49] As for the evangelical foes of slavery, their exertions in behalf

of racial justice and "true religion" collided head-on with widespread
negrophobia, a popular obsession with "earthly claims," political anarchy, and the settlers' ready resort to whiskey, profanity, and Sabbath
desecration, not to mention the bowie knife and the Sharps rifle. A typical abolitionist congregation, for instance, claimed no more than thirty
members.[50]

Nevertheless, if historian David Potter was right in arguing that for
the rest of the country the Kansas conflict was a propaganda war that
the South had lost by 1857, the northeastern evangelicals and entrepreneurs certainly played a large role in determining that outcome.[51]
Shaped by their experiences and perceptions, the crusade for a free West
emerged as a larger struggle to implant the progressive values of Northern society on the frontier. This broad definition of Yankee goals was
consistent with an evolving Republican worldview that juxtaposed the
dynamism and humanism of the free labor North with the economic
stagnation and cultural inferiority of the slave South in a compelling indictment of Dixie's peculiar institution. Kansas became a symbol of the
contest to decide whether the western social order would be modeled
after that of the North or the South—a decision pregnant with profound
implications for the American republic's future. The conjunction of religious and secular antislavery that covered a wide range of opinion on
black bondage but spoke the common language of middle-class Northern society helped invest the Kansas crusade with that larger meaning.
Thus Bleeding Kansas became a potent stepping stone to the creation
of a Republican North on the eve of sectional conflict.

On the other hand, the neat moral polarities of antislavery discourse
blurred broad areas of agreement that rendered Northerner and Southerner less than perfect mirror images of each other in territorial Kansas.
On occasion, polemicists on both sides of the slavery issue resorted to
nativist as well as racist appeals to broaden their constituencies. Business, of course, provided the most effective remedy in healing the great
sectional divide. The willingness on the part of some free labor ideologues and proslavery entrepreneurs to forgive and forget old scores may
elicit an impression of déjà vu from students who have followed the fortunes of free labor experiments below the Potomac in the postbellum
era. Historian Lawrence Powell has unraveled the story of Northern cot-

ton planters who went South after the Civil War to make money and re-juvenate the devastated region through the vehicle of free labor.[52] Powell found that his protagonists received the same cordial welcome from the capital-starved "masters without slaves" in the South that the proslavery town boosters and railroad enthusiasts—engaged in "healthy" business rivalry with each other as well as with their free-state counterparts—accorded the "Yankee abolitionists" even before slavery was doomed in Kansas. Many of the South's friends in the territory who were so solicitous of Yankee money and enterprise exhibited the same Whiggish predilections for economic growth along national lines that C. Vann Woodward found to be a prominent element in the post-Reconstruction Southern Democratic Party. The numerous instances of economic co-operation between the erstwhile friends and foes of slavery are reminiscent of the Woodwardian thesis of an alliance between the business interests of the North and South at the Negro's expense embodied in the Compromise of 1877.[53]

If the Kansas affair, by reinforcing the perception of irreconcilable differences between North and South, made fratricidal conflict inevitable, it also contained the key to understanding the impulses that reconciled Americans deeply divided by the bitterest of all wars in their history less than a quarter-century before. If the gory sectional encounters of Bleeding Kansas provided a foretaste of the impending crisis of the Union, their aftermath may have represented, in microcosm, the larger history of sectional reunion and national reaction following Reconstruction.

Notes

Introduction

1. Eli Thayer, *A History of the Kansas Crusade: Its Friends and Its Foes* (New York, 1889), 69.

2. Edward E. Hale, "New England in the Colonization of Kansas," manuscript, New England Emigrant Aid Company Papers (microfilm edition), Manuscript Division, Kansas State Historical Society, Topeka, 83; hereinafter cited as NEEAC Papers. On the New England Emigrant Aid Company, see Samuel A. Johnson, *The Battle Cry of Freedom: The New England Emigrant Aid Company in the Kansas Crusade* (1954; reprint, Westport, 1977); Horace Andrews Jr., "Kansas Crusade: Eli Thayer and the New England Emigrant Aid Company," *New England Quarterly* 35 (December 1962): 497–514. On Amos Lawrence, a key figure within the NEEAC, see Thomas H. O'Connor, "Cotton Whigs in Kansas," *Kansas Historical Quarterly* 26 (spring 1960): 34–58; Richard H. Abbott, *Cotton and Capital: Boston Businessmen and Antislavery Reform, 1854–1868* (Amherst, 1991).

3. Information on Finch taken from Finch to Simeon Smith Jocelyn, March 16, 1855; *Ninth Annual Report of the AMA* (New York, 1855), p. 52, both in Archives of the American Missionary Association, Amistad Research Center at Tulane University, New Orleans; hereinafter cited as AMA Archives. On the American Missionary Association, see Clifton H. Johnson, "The American Missionary Association, 1846–1861: A Study in Christian Abolitionism" (Ph.D. diss., University of North Carolina, 1959); Clara Merritt DeBoer, *Be Jubilant My Feet: African American Abolitionists in the American Missionary Association, 1839–1861* (Hamden, 1994); Joe M. Richardson, *Christian Reconstruction: The American Missionary Association and Southern Blacks, 1861–1890* (Athens, 1986). On an event that had a significant bearing on the founding of the AMA, see Howard Jones, *Mutiny on the Amistad: The Saga of a Slave Revolt and its Impact on American Abolition, Law and Diplomacy* (New York, 1987). On a key

figure within the AMA, see Bertram Wyatt-Brown, *Lewis Tappan and the Evangelical War against Slavery* (Cleveland, 1969); Lawrence J. Friedman, "Confidence and Pertinacity in Evangelical Abolitionism: Lewis Tappan's Circle," *American Quarterly* 31 (spring 1979): 81–106, and *Gregarious Saints: Self and Community in American Abolitionism, 1830–1870* (New York, 1982). On the AHMS see Colin B. Goodykoontz, *Home Missions on the American Frontier with Particular Reference to the American Home Missionary Society* (1939; reprint, New York, 1971). On the Northern churches and slavery, see John R. McKivigan, *The War against Proslavery Religion* (Ithaca, 1984); Victor B. Howard, *Conscience and Slavery: The Evangelistic Calvinist Domestic Missions, 1837–1861* (Kent, Ohio, 1990).

4. My overall interpretation of the way in which religious and economic arguments against slavery, working together, facilitated the emergence of antislavery politics has been most influenced by the theoretical insights of Howard Temperley, "Antislavery as a Form of Cultural Imperialism," in *Antislavery, Religion and Reform: Essays in Memory of Roger Anstey,* ed. Christine Bolt and Seymour Drescher (Folkestone, Eng., 1980), 335–49; David Brion Davis, *The Problem of Slavery in Western Culture* (Ithaca, 1966), and *The Problem of Slavery in the Age of Revolution* (Ithaca, 1975); the discussions among Davis, Thomas L. Haskell, and John Ashworth in *The Antislavery Debate: Capitalism and Abolitionism as a Problem in Historical Interpretation,* ed. Thomas Bender (Berkeley, 1992); and Eric Foner, *Free Soil, Free Labor, Free Men: The Ideology of the Republican Party before the Civil War* (New York, 1970), and *Politics and Ideology in the Age of the Civil War* (New York, 1980).

James L. Huston, in "The Experiential Basis of the Northern Antislavery Impulse," *Journal of Southern History* 56 (November 1990): 609–40, makes the valid point that the recent historiographic tendency to place abolitionism in a Northern rather than national context by linking it with "social environmental" conditions within Northern society has, in effect, led us to neglect the crucial connection between abolitionism and the actual functioning of Southern slavery. Merton L. Dillon makes a similar point in a different context in "Gilbert Barnes and Dwight L. Dumond: An Appraisal," in *Reviews in American History* 21 (September 1993): 539–52. As Dillon has noted, his own wide-ranging study, *Slavery Attacked: Southern Slaves and Their Allies, 1619–1865* (Baton Rouge, 1990), and Herbert Aptheker's *Abolitionism: A Revolutionary Movement* (Boston, 1989) view antislavery as a response to slavery rather than to transformations within Northern society.

The temporal coexistence in the 1840s and 1850s of a staggeringly diverse range of motivations, strategies, appeals and goals within the "movement of movements" that was antislavery suggests that whether one believes the opposition to slavery was an experiential response to the cruel realities of slavery, or was rooted in broad economic and cultural changes within Northern society, or for that matter prompted by introspective forays on the part of individual reformers, or a combination of these factors depends on which antislavery individual or group one is talking about. For that same reason, it seems equally hard to make generalizations about the reasons for the growing acceptance of antislavery doctrines among Northerners. It is well known, for instance, that although NEEAC founder Eli Thayer opposed slavery, he was not an abolitionist, in the sense of one morally outraged by slavery and committed to immediate abolition and racial egalitarianism. He was, in fact, vociferously anti-abolitionist. His reasons for opposing slavery were clearly rather different from those of a Harriet Tubman. I am persuaded by Huston's argument that hitherto neglected factors played a role in the advent of antislavery and the spread of its influence in Northern society, especially the rise of a youthful generation of Northerners unaccustomed to the presence of slavery in their midst and a growing revulsion against the violence and coercion of slavery in a society relying increasingly on contractual mechanisms to settle disputes. Nevertheless, my evidence, based on the appeals of three diverse groups of free-state people in Kansas — only one of which qualified as "abolitionist" — bears out what Huston calls the "middle-class synthesis" in antislavery historiography, organized in this book around the principle of progress in an emerging wage-labor-based capitalist culture. I suggest, therefore, that the appeal to middle-class values buttressed the impact of the factors Huston mentions in broadening the antislavery constituency in the free North on the eve of the Civil War.

My understanding of the complex history of Northern antislavery has been shaped by too many excellent works to name in full here. A fraction of those not already mentioned include Gilbert H. Barnes, *The Antislavery Impulse, 1830–1844* (New York, 1933); Stanley Elkins, *Slavery: A Problem in American Institutional and Intellectual Life* (Chicago, 1959); Louis Filler, *The Crusade against Slavery, 1830–1860* (New York, 1960); Dwight L. Dumond, *Antislavery: The Crusade for Freedom in America* (Ann Arbor, 1961); Larry Gara, *The Liberty Line: The Legend of the Underground Railroad* (Lexington, 1961); Russell B. Nye, *Fettered Freedom: Civil Liberties and the Slavery Controversy, 1830–1860* (East Lansing, Mich., 1963); Louis Ruchames, *The Abolitionists: A Collection of Their Writings* (New York, 1963); James M. McPherson, *The Struggle for Equality: The Abolitionists and the Negro in the Civil War and Recon-*

struction (Princeton, 1964); Richard O. Curry, ed., *The Abolitionists: Reformers or Fanatics?* (New York, 1965); Martin B. Duberman, ed., *The Antislavery Vanguard: New Essays on the Abolitionists* (Princeton, 1965); William H. Pease and Jane H. Pease, eds., *The Antislavery Argument* (New York, 1965); Gerda Lerner, *The Grimké Sisters from South Carolina: Rebels against Slavery* (Boston, 1967); Alma Lutz, *Crusade for Freedom: Women of the Antislavery Movement* (Boston, 1968); Staughton Lynd, *The Intellectual Origins of American Radicalism* (New York, 1968); Betty Fladeland, *James Gillespie Birney: Slaveholder to Abolitionist* (Westport, 1969); Aileen S. Kraditor, *Means and Ends in American Abolitionism: Garrison and His Critics on Strategy and Tactics, 1834–1850* (New York, 1969); Benjamin Quarles, *Black Abolitionists* (New York, 1969); Gerald Sorin, *Abolitionism: A New Perspective* (New York, 1972); Lewis Perry, *Radical Abolitionism: Anarchy and the Government of God in Antislavery Thought* (Ithaca, 1973); Jane H. Pease and William H. Pease, *They Who Would Be Free: Blacks' Search For Freedom, 1830–1861* (New York, 1974); Merton L. Dillon, *The Abolitionists: The Growth of a Dissenting Minority* (De Kalb, Ill., 1976); James B. Stewart, *Holy Warriors: The Abolitionists and American Slavery* (New York, 1976); Ronald G. Walters, *The Antislavery Appeal: American Abolitionism after 1830* (Baltimore, 1976); Joel Schor, *Henry Highland Garnet: A Voice of Black Radicalism in the Nineteenth Century* (Westport, Conn., 1977); Blanche Hersh, *The Slavery of Sex: Feminist Abolitionists in Nineteenth-Century America* (Urbana, 1978); Peter F. Walker, *Moral Choices: Memory, Desire, and Imagination in Nineteenth-Century American Abolitionism* (Baton Rouge, 1978); Lewis Perry and Michael Fellman, eds., *Antislavery Reconsidered: New Perspectives on the Abolitionists* (Baton Rouge, 1979); Robert Abzug, *Passionate Liberator: Theodore Dwight Weld and the Dilemma of Reform* (New York, 1980); Nathan Irvin Huggins, *Slave and Citizen: The Life of Frederick Douglass* (Boston, 1980); Lewis Perry, *Childhood, Marriage, and Reform: Henry Clarke Wright 1797–1870* (Chicago, 1980); R. J. M. Blackett, *Building an Antislavery Wall: Black Americans in the Atlantic Abolitionist Movement, 1830–1860* (Baton Rouge, 1983); Alan M. Kraut, ed., *Crusaders and Compromisers: Essays on the Relationship of the Antislavery Struggle to the Antebellum Party System* (Westport, Conn., 1983); Edward Magdol, *The Antislavery Rank and File: A Social Profile of the Abolitionists' Constituency* (Westport, Conn., 1986); Louis S. Gerteis, *Morality and Utility in American Antislavery Reform* (Chapel Hill, 1987); William Cheek and Aimee Lee Cheek, *John Mercer Langston and the Fight for Black Freedom, 1829–65* (Urbana, 1989); David E. Swift, *Black Prophets of Justice: Activist Clergy before the Civil War* (Baton Rouge, 1989); Jean Fagan Yellin, *Women and Sisters: The Antislavery Feminists in American Culture* (New Haven, 1989); Lawrence B. Goodheart, *Abolitionist, Actuary, Atheist: Elizur Wright and the Reform Impulse* (Kent, Ohio, 1990); William S. McFeely, *Frederick Douglass* (New York, 1991); John W. Blassingame et al., eds., *The Frederick Douglass Papers*, 5 vols. (New Haven, 1979-92); C. Peter Ripley et al., eds., *The Black Abolitionist Papers*, 5 vols. (Chapel Hill, 1985-92); Stewart, *William Lloyd Garrison and the Challenge of Emancipation* (Arlington Heights, Ill., 1992); Shirley J. Yee, *Black Women Abolitionists: A Study in Activism, 1828-1860* (Knoxville, 1992); Debra Gold Hansen, *Strained Sisterhood: Gender and Class in the Boston Female Antislavery Society* (Amherst, 1993); Donald M. Jacobs, ed., *Courage and Conscience: Black and White Abolitionists in Boston* (Bloomington, 1993); Carlton Mabee, *Sojourner Truth: Slave, Prophet, Legend* (New York, 1993); Jean Fagan Yellin and John C. Van Horne, *The Abolitionist Sisterhood: Women's Political Culture in Antebellum America* (Ithaca, 1994).

On antislavery historiography, see Merton L. Dillon, "The Abolitionists: A Decade of Historiography, 1959-1969," *Journal of Southern History* 35 (November 1969): 500-522; Ronald G. Walters, "The Boundaries of Abolitionism," in *Antislavery Reconsidered: New Perspectives on the Abolitionists*, 3-23; Lawrence J. Friedman, "Historical Topics Sometimes Run Dry: The State of Abolitionist Studies," *Historian* 43 (February 1981): 177-94; Kraut, introduction to *Crusaders and Compromisers*, 1-22; Richard O. Curry and Lawrence B. Goodheart, " 'Knives in Their Heads': Passionate Self-Analysis and the Search for Identity in Recent Abolitionist Historiography," *Canadian Review of American Studies* 14 (winter 1983): 401-14; James L. Huston, "The Experiential Basis of the Northern Antislavery Impulse"; Dillon, "Gilbert Barnes and Dwight L. Dumond."

5. Jean Baker, "From Belief into Culture: Republicanism in the Antebellum North," *American Quarterly* 37 (fall 1985): 532-50. On Revolutionary America's attempt to reconcile individual rights and private interest with the public good on an ideological level, see Cathy Matson, "Toward a Republican Empire: Interest and Ideology in Revolutionary America," *American Quarterly* 37 (fall 1985): 496-531. My understanding of revolutionary and early American republicanism has been most influenced by Bernard Bailyn, *The Ideological Origins of the American Revolution* (Cambridge, 1967); Gordon S. Wood, *The Creation of the American Republic, 1776-1787* (Chapel Hill, 1969), and *The Radicalism of the American Revolution* (New York, 1992); Joyce Appleby, *Capitalism and a New Social Order: The Republican Vision of the 1790s* (New York, 1984); and Robert E. Shalhope, *The Roots of Democracy: American Thought and*

Culture, 1760–1800 (Boston, 1990). J. G. A. Pocock, *The Machiavellian Moment: Florentine Political Thought and the Atlantic Republican Tradition* (Princeton, 1975), places republicanism within the larger context of all Western civilization. Richard C. Sinopoli, in *The Foundations of American Citizenship: Liberalism, the Constitution, and Civic Virtue* (New York, 1992), makes the point that liberalism and civic virtue are not necessarily incompatible. On republican politics in antebellum America, see also Lloyd E. Ambrosius, ed., *A Crisis of Republicanism: American Politics in the Civil War Era* (Lincoln, 1990), and Harry L. Watson, *Liberty and Power: The Politics of Jacksonian America* (New York, 1990). I found a few historiographical essays on the republican synthesis in American history especially useful: Robert E. Shalhope, "Toward a Republican Synthesis: The Emergence of an Understanding of Republicanism in Early American Historiography," *William and Mary Quarterly* 29 (January 1972): 49–80, and "Republicanism and Early American Historiography," *William and Mary Quarterly* 39 (April 1982): 334–56; Joyce Appleby, "Republicanism and Ideology," *American Quarterly* 37 (fall 1985): 461–73; Daniel T. Rogers, "Republicanism: The Career of a Concept," *Journal of American History* 79 (June 1992): 11–38.

6. On martial patriotism as public service see Jean Baker, "From Belief into Culture," 542.

7. The only systematic analysis of the proslavery argument in Kansas that I know of is Bill Cecil-Fronsman, " 'Death to All Yankees and Traitors in Kansas': The *Squatter Sovereign* and the Defense of Slavery in Kansas," *Kansas History* 16 (spring 1993): 22–33.

George M. Frederickson applied Pierre L. van den Berghe's term "herrenvolk democracy" to Southern white society. See van den Berghe, *Race and Racism: A Comparative Perspective* (New York, 1967); and Frederickson, *The Black Image in the White Mind: The Debate on Afro-American Character and Destiny, 1817–1914* (New York, 1971).

8. Drew Gilpin Faust, "The Peculiar South Revisited," in *Interpreting Southern History: Historiographical Essays in Honor of Sanford W. Higginbotham*, ed. John B. Boles and Evelyn Thomas Nolen (Baton Rouge, 1987), 114. The literature on Southern republicanism is voluminous. A fraction of the key works—several of which challenge the theory that Southern-style "herrenvolk democracy" was grounded in true socioeconomic equality—include: J. Mills Thornton III, *Politics and Power in a Slave Society: Alabama, 1800–1860* (Baton Rouge, 1978); Steven Hahn, *The Roots of Southern Populism: Yeomen Farmers and the Transformation of the Georgia Upcountry, 1850–1890* (New York, 1983); Kenneth S. Greenberg, *Masters and Statesmen: The Political Culture of American*

Slavery (Baltimore, 1985); J. William Harris, *Plain Folk and Gentry in a Slave Society: White Liberty and Black Slavery in Augusta's Hinterlands* (Middletown, 1985); James Oakes, "From Republicanism to Liberalism: Ideological Change and the Crisis of the Old South," *American Quarterly* 37 (fall 1985): 551–71; Lacy K. Ford Jr., *Origins of Southern Radicalism: The South Carolina Upcountry, 1800–1860* (New York, 1988); Michael Wayne, "An Old South Morality Play: Reconsidering the Social Underpinnings of the Proslavery Ideology," *Journal of American History* 77 (December 1990): 838–63; Stephanie McCurry, "The Two Faces of Republicanism: Gender and Proslavery Politics in Antebellum South Carolina," *Journal of American History* 78 (March 1992): 1,245–64; Eugene D. Genovese, *The Slaveholders' Dilemma: Freedom and Progress in Southern Conservative Thought, 1820–1860* (Columbia, 1992).

9. On concern for republican virtue and honor as components of Kansas proslavery, see Cecil-Fronsman, " 'Death to All Yankees'," 28, 30–31. For an interpretation of "honor" as the central theme of Southern culture, see Bertram Wyatt-Brown, *Southern Honor: Ethics and Behavior in the Old South* (New York, 1982). On "the unity of life and work" in Missouri's traditional order, see David Thelen, *Paths of Resistance: Tradition and Democracy in Industrializing Missouri* (New York, 1986), 11–24. On slavery in Missouri, see R. Douglas Hurt, *Agriculture and Slavery in Missouri's Little Dixie* (Columbia, 1992).

10. Whether the antebellum South was prebourgeois or capitalist is the subject of a well-known and lively scholarly debate, shaped to some extent by varying definitions of capitalism as characterized by the market-oriented pursuit of profit on the one hand, and free labor on the other. Eugene D. Genovese's work on the pre-capitalist world-view of a hegemonic planter-elite has established the framework for much of that discussion. See Genovese, *The Political Economy of Slavery: Studies in the Economy and Society of the Slave South* (New York, 1965), *The World the Slaveholders Made: Two Essays in Interpretation* (New York, 1969), *Roll Jordan Roll: The World the Slaves Made* (New York, 1974), and Elizabeth Fox Genovese and Eugene D. Genovese, *Fruits of Merchant Capital: Slavery and Bourgeois Property in the Rise and Expansion of Capitalism* (New York, 1983). More recently, in *The Slaveholders' Dilemma*, Genovese has argued that slaveholders reconciled their commitment to freedom and progress with slavery by proclaiming that slavery did a better job of harmonizing the interests of capital and labor than did the capitalist wage system. For a more liberal, capitalist portrayal of the antebellum ruling class, see James Oakes, *The Ruling Race: A History of American Slaveholders* (New York, 1982), and *Slavery and Freedom: An Interpretation of the Old South* (New York, 1990); Shearer Davis

Bowman, *Masters and Lords: Mid-Nineteenth-Century U.S. Planters and Prussian Junkers* (New York, 1993). On the argument that Southern planters made essentially rational economic choices, see Robert W. Fogel and Stanley L. Engerman, *Time on the Cross: The Economics of American Negro Slavery* (Boston, 1974) and more recently Fogel, *Without Consent or Contract: The Rise and Fall of American Slavery* (New York, 1990); Gavin Wright, *The Political Economy of the Cotton South: Households, Markets, and Wealth in the Nineteenth-Century* (New York, 1978) and "Prosperity, Progress and American Slavery," in *Reckoning with Slavery: A Critical Study in the Quantitative History of American Negro Slavery*, ed. Paul A. David et al. (New York, 1976), 302–36. A few responses to the cliometricians include Genovese, "Commentary: A Historian's View," *Agricultural History* 45 (January 1970): 143–47; Harold D. Woodman, "Economic History and Economic Theory: The New Economic History in America," *Journal of Interdisciplinary History* 3 (autumn 1972): 323–50; Herbert G. Gutman, *Slavery and the Numbers Game: A Critique of Time on the Cross* (Urbana, 1975); and Peter Kolchin, "More Time on the Cross? An Evaluation of Robert William Fogel's *Without Consent or Contract*," *Journal of Southern History* 58 (August 1992): 491–502.

I have to admit that I am wary of speculating on the implications of my whiggish portrayal of prominent pro-Southern Kansans who sought material profit at the same time that they criticized wage labor, for the debate over whether the antebellum South was capitalist or pre-capitalist. My evidence base is too narrow to make generalizations about the nature of the Southern elite, resting as it does on the behavior of pro-Southern folks who remained in Kansas *after* 1858. Moreover, as I point out in the course of my narrative, most of my proslavery subjects—however vigorously they may have defended the right to carry slaves to Kansas—owned few bondspeople themselves.

11. Edward Pessen, "How Different From Each Other Were the Antebellum North and South?" *American Historical Review* 85 (December 1980): 1119–49.

12. Select works on expansionism, the Mexican War, and various interpretations of national and sectional politics before and during the crises of the 1850s include Allan Nevins, *The Ordeal of the Union*, 2 vols. (New York, 1947); Roy F. Nichols, *The Disruption of American Democracy* (New York, 1948); Charles S. Sydnor, *The Development of Southern Sectionalism, 1819–1848* (Baton Rouge, 1948); Henry Nash Smith, *Virgin Land* (Cambridge, 1950); Charles M. Wiltse, *John C. Calhoun: Sectionalist, 1840–1850* (Indianapolis, 1951); Harry V. Jaffa, *The Crisis of the House Divided: An Interpretation of the Lincoln-Douglas Debates* (Chicago, 1959); Frederick W. Merk, *Manifest Destiny and Mission in American*

History (New York, 1963); Hans L. Trefousse, *Benjamin Franklin Wade: Radical Republican from Ohio* (New York, 1963); Holman Hamilton, *Prologue to Conflict: The Crisis and Compromise of 1850* (Lexington, 1964); Richard H. Sewell, *John P. Hale and the Politics of Abolition* (Cambridge, 1965); Merk, *The Monroe Doctrine and American Expansionism, 1843–1849* (New York, 1966); Thomas B. Alexander, *Sectional Stress and Party Struggle: A Study of Roll-Call Voting Patterns in the United States House of Representatives, 1831–1860* (Nashville, 1967); Edward Magdol, *Owen Lovejoy: Abolitionist in Congress* (New Brunswick, 1967); Joel Silbey, *The Shrine of Party: Congressional Voting Behavior, 1841–1852* (Pittsburgh, 1967); James A. Rawley, *Race and Politics: "Bleeding Kansas" and the Coming of the Civil War* (Philadelphia, 1969); Steven A. Channing, *Crisis of Fear: Secession in South Carolina* (New York, 1970); Merk, *Slavery and the Annexation of Texas* (New York, 1972); Robert F. Dalzell Jr., *Daniel Webster and the Trial of American Nationalism, 1843–1852* (Boston, 1973); Robert W. Johannsen, *Stephen A. Douglas* (New York, 1973); David M. Pletcher, *The Diplomacy of Annexation: Texas, Oregon, and the Mexican War, 1846–1848* (Columbia, 1973); William L. Barney, *The Secessionist Impulse: Alabama and Mississippi in 1860* (Princeton, 1974); Ray Allen Billington, *Westward Expansion,* revised edition (New York, 1974); David Potter, *The Impending Crisis* (New York, 1976); Sewell, *Ballots For Freedom: Antislavery Politics in the United States, 1837–1860* (New York, 1976); James B. Stewart, *Holy Warriors;* Michael P. Johnson, *Toward a Patriarchal Republic: The Secession of Georgia* (Baton Rouge, 1977); William J. Cooper, *The South and the Politics of Slavery, 1828–1856* (Baton Rouge, 1978); Michael F. Holt, *The Political Crisis of the 1850s* (New York, 1978); J. Mills Thornton III, *Politics and Power in a Slave Society;* William R. Brock, *Parties and Political Conscience: American Dilemmas, 1840–1850* (Millwood, 1979); Perry and Fellman, eds., *Antislavery Reconsidered;* Don E. Fehrenbacher, *The South and Three Sectional Crises* (Baton Rouge, 1980); Daniel W. Howe, *The Political Culture of the American Whigs* (Chicago, 1980); John Mayfield, *Rehearsal for Republicanism: Free Soil and the Politics of Antislavery* (New York, 1980); Stephen E. Maizlish and John J. Kushma, eds., *Essays on Antebellum American Politics, 1840–1860* (College Station, Tex., 1982); Wyatt-Brown, *Southern Honor;* John Ashworth, *'Agrarians' and 'Aristocrats': Party Political Ideology in the United States, 1837–1846* (London, 1983); Joel H. Silbey, *The Partisan Imperative: The Dynamics of American Politics Before the Civil War* (New York, 1985); William E. Gienapp, *Origins of the Republican Party, 1852–1856* (New York, 1987); James M. McPherson, *Battle Cry of Freedom: The Civil War Era* (New York, 1988); John Niven, *John C. Calhoun and the Price of Union:*

A Biography (Baton Rouge, 1988); Sewell, *A House Divided: Sectionalism and Civil War, 1848–1865* (Baltimore, 1988); Johannsen, *The Frontier, the Union and Stephen A. Douglas* (Urbana, 1989); Norma Peterson, *The Presidencies of William Henry Harrison and John Tyler* (Lawrence, 1989); William W. Freehling, *The Road to Disunion: Secessionists at Bay, 1776–1854* (New York, 1990); Vernon Volpe, *Forlorn Hope of Freedom: The Liberty Party in the Old Northwest, 1838–1848* (Kent, Ohio, 1990); David Zarefsky, *Lincoln, Douglas, and Slavery: In the Crucible of Public Debate* (Chicago, 1990); Peter B. Knupfer, *The Union As It Is: Constitutional Unionism and Sectional Compromise, 1787–1861* (Chapel Hill, 1991); Tyler G. Anbinder, *Nativism and Slavery: The Northern Know-Nothings and the Politics of Slavery* (New York, 1992); Holt, *Political Parties and American Political Development From the Age of Jackson to the Age of Lincoln* (Baton Rouge, 1992).

13. McPherson, *Battle Cry,* 121–23; Freehling, *The Road to Disunion,* 536–60; Rawley, *Race and Politics,* 26–38; Johnson, *The Battle Cry,* 92–96. The option of popular sovereignty had emerged in 1848 as a possible solution to the explosive question of the Congressional role in legislating on slavery in the territories. As James McPherson has observed, the idea had "the political charm of ambiguity," since it did not specify when settlers might vote on slavery—whether during the territorial stage or when adopting a state constitution. See McPherson, *Battle Cry,* 58. On the circumstances surrounding the passage of the Kansas-Nebraska Act, see also Roy F. Nichols, "The Kansas-Nebraska Act: A Century of Historiography," *Mississippi Valley Historical Review* 43 (September 1956): 187–212; Frank H. Hodder, "The Railroad Background of the Kansas-Nebraska Act," *Mississippi Valley Historical Review* 12 (June 1925): 3–22; James C. Malin, *The Nebraska Question* (Lawrence, 1953); Jaffa, *Crisis of the House Divided,* 104–80; Johannsen, *Stephen A. Douglas;* Potter, *The Impending Crisis,* 145–76; Gerald Wolff, *The Kansas-Nebraska Bill: Party, Section, and the Origin of the Civil War* (New York, 1980); Joan E. Lampton, "The Kansas-Nebraska Act Reconsidered: An Analysis of Men, Methods and Motives" (Ph.D. diss., Illinois State University, 1979). On the Atchison-Benton conflict, see also William E. Parrish, *David Rice Atchison of Missouri: Border Politician* (Columbia, 1961); Clarence Henry McClure, *Opposition in Missouri to Thomas Hart Benton* (Nashville, 1927). On Benton see William M. Meigs, *The Life of Thomas Hart Benton* (1904; reprint, New York, 1970); William Nisbet Chambers, *Old Bullion Benton: Senator from the New West, 1782–1858* (Boston, 1956); Elbert B. Smith, *Magnificent Missourian: The Life of Thomas Hart Benton* (Philadelphia, 1957).

14. Nichols, "The Kansas-Nebraska Act," 187–88.

15. McPherson, *Battle Cry*, 124–25; Dick Johnson has examined the historiography of "The Appeal of the Independent Democrats in Congress to the People of the United States," which proposed the "conspiracy theory" of the Nebraska bill in "Along the Twisted Road to Civil War: Historians and the Appeal of the Independent Democrats," *Old Northwest* 4 (June 1978): 119–41.

16. Johnson, *The Battle Cry*, 93–95.

17. On Benjamin Stringfellow, see Lester Baltimore, "Benjamin Stringfellow: The Fight for Slavery on the Missouri Border," *Missouri Historical Review* 62 (October 1967): 14–29. On Peter T. Abell's politics, see H. Everett to Abiel Leonard, October 9, 1854, Abiel Leonard Collection, Joint Collection, 1769–1928, Western Historical Manuscript Collection, State Historical Society of Missouri Manuscripts, Kansas City and the University of Missouri-Kansas City Archives; hereinafter cited as WHMC.

1 Appeal to the Census versus Appeal to the Conscience

1. The poem by John Greenleaf Whittier was sung by members of the second NEEAC party on the eve of their departure to Kansas on August 29, 1854. Cited in Alfred T. Andreas, *History of the State of Kansas*, vol. 1 (1883; reprint, Topeka, 1976), 313. On Whittier, see Charles A. Jarvis, "Admission to Abolition: The Case of John Greenleaf Whittier," *Journal of the Early Republic* 4 (summer 1984): 161–76.

David Brion Davis, *The Problem of Slavery in Western Culture* and *The Problem of Slavery in the Age of Revolution;* Thomas L. Haskell, "Capitalism and the Origins of Humanitarian Sensibility," part 1, *American Historical Review* 90 (April 1985): 339–61, and part 2, ibid., 90 (June 1985): 547–66; Davis, "Reflections on Abolitionism and Ideological Hegemony," *American Historical Review* 92 (October 1987): 797–812; Bender, ed., *The Antislavery Debate: Capitalism and Abolitionism as a Problem in Historical Interpretation;* Foner, *Politics and Ideology*, and *Free Soil, Free Labor.*

See note 4 to the introduction for a discussion of the debate over whether antislavery was an experiential response to slavery or grounded in Northern economic and cultural changes. See the same note for a definition of "abolitionism" as distinct from "antislavery," which I use in this book as an umbrella term to encompass the diverse array of movements against slavery.

2. Quotation from James B. Stewart, *Holy Warriors*, 14. See also Barnes, *The Antislavery Impulse;* David Brion Davis, "The Emergence of Immediatism in British and American Antislavery Thought," *Mississippi Valley Histori-*

cal Review 49 (September 1962): 209–30; Anne C. Loveland, "Evangelicalism and 'Immediate Emancipation' in American Antislavery Thought," *Journal of Southern History* 32 (May 1966): 172–88; John R. Bodo, *The Protestant Clergy and Public Issues, 1812–1848* (Philadelphia, 1980). On a key figure in evangelical abolitionism, see Abzug, *Passionate Liberator: Theodore Dwight Weld and the Dilemma of Reform.* On the AMA see Clifton H. Johnson, "The American Missionary Association, 1846–1861," and Wyatt-Brown, *Lewis Tappan.* On the American Home Missionary Society, see Colin B. Goodykoontz, *Home Missions on the American Frontier.* On religious antislavery in the North, see James D. Essig, *The Bonds of Wickedness: American Evangelicals against Slavery* (Philadelphia, 1982); McKivigan, *The War against Proslavery Religion;* Victor B. Howard, *Conscience and Slavery;* and Richard M. Lawless, "To Do Right to God and Man: Northern Protestants and the Kansas Struggle, 1854–1859" (Ph.D. diss., Graduate Theological Union, 1974).

3. Quotation from David A. Hollinger and Charles Capper eds., *The American Intellectual Tradition,* vol. 1 (New York, 1989, 1993), 189. On the relationship between evangelicalism and the rise of a new socioeconomic order in the antebellum North, see Paul E. Johnson, *A Shopkeeper's Millennium: Society and Revivals in Rochester, New York, 1815–1837* (New York, 1978).

Foner, *Politics and Ideology,* 23, and *Free Soil, Free Labor.* On the diverse perspectives of antebellum writers on free labor, see Jonathan A. Glickstein, *Concepts of Free Labor in Antebellum America* (New Haven, 1991).

4. Davis, *The Problem of Slavery in the Age of Revolution,* 358.

5. Foner, *Free Soil, Free Labor,* 13.

6. Ibid., 54–56.

7. Quotation from Temperley, "Antislavery as a Form of Cultural Imperialism," 345. McPherson, *Battle Cry,* 6–24. See also Thomas C. Cochran, *Frontiers of Change: Early Industrialism in America* (New York, 1981), and David A. Hounshell, *From the American System to Mass Production, 1800–1932: The Development of Manufacturing Technology in the United States* (Baltimore, 1984). Charles Sellers, *The Market Revolution: Jacksonian America, 1815–1846* (New York, 1991), explores the far-reaching ramifications of the market revolution in all spheres of life.

8. Temperley, "Antislavery as a Form of Cultural Imperialism," 346.

9. *Kansas Herald of Freedom,* March 31, 1855; hereinafter referred to as *Herald of Freedom.*

10. Eli Thayer, *A History,* 2–3, 25, 31.

11. Ibid., 30; Johnson, *The Battle Cry of Freedom*, 17–19; Hale, "New England," NEEAC Papers, 79, 82.

12. Johnson, *The Battle Cry of Freedom*, 53; Thayer, *A History*, 32–33; Hale, "New England," NEEAC Papers, 82–83. On Robinson see Don W. Wilson, *Governor Charles Robinson of Kansas* (Lawrence, Kans., 1975), and Homer E. Socolofsky, *Kansas Governors* (Lawrence, Kans., 1990), 81–85.

13. Thayer, *A History*, 52; Johnson, *The Battle Cry of Freedom*, 25–28; Thomas Webb, *Information for Kansas Emigrants* (Boston, 1855–57), 17.

14. *Herald of Freedom*, October 21, 1854, March 3, 10, 24, 1855, April 14, 21, 28, 1855. My analysis of the demographic profile of rank and file NEEAC emigrants reveals that more than half were artisans who may have moved west in order to avoid descent into permanent wage labor dependence (see chap. 3). The debate over the connection between capitalism and the rise of humanitarian reform especially as articulated in the theory that antislavery may have served to stifle radical dissent within the antislavery proponents' own industrializing societies, opened the way for fresh perspectives on relations between the antislavery and labor movements. I am persuaded by the argument that antislavery discourse may have served to deflect attention from the traumas of transition to wage labor at home, although it may not have been *consciously intended* to serve that function. As David Brion Davis has observed, "At issue are not conscious intentions but the social functions of ideology; not individual motives but shifting patterns of thought and value which focussed attention on new problems" (cited in *The Antislavery Debate*, 5). John Ashworth has pointed out that opponents of slavery emphasized that the interests of capital and labor could be harmonized under capitalism, while those of masters and slaves were irreconcilable (*The Antislavery Debate*, 184). On the abolitionists' contradictory positions on economic competition, poverty and free labor, see Jonathan A. Glickstein, " 'Poverty Is Not Slavery': American Abolitionists and the Competitive Labor Market," in *Antislavery Reconsidered*, 195–218. A more favorable portrayal of abolitionist attitudes toward labor occurs in Betty Fladeland, *Abolitionists and Working-Class Problems in the Age of Industrialization* (London, 1984). Fladeland's work, which focuses on Britain, argues that the abolitionists espoused a humane capitalism responsive to the grievances of labor as well as those of slaves. Gilbert Osofsky, "Abolitionists, Irish Immigrants, and the Dilemmas of Romantic Nationalism," *American Historical Review* 80 (October 1975): 889–912, contends that Garrisonian abolitionists did reach out to Irish immigrants but that the individualist, egalitarian assumptions of Garrisonian

abolitionist ideology prevented an adequate response to the economic conditions of the immigrants and militated against a fruitful alliance with them. Clearly, labor's relations with segments of the antislavery movement were uneasy. On the argument that the anti-abolitionism of Northern white laborers stemmed from their fear of black competition for jobs in the North, see Leon Litwack, *North of Slavery: The Negro in the Free States, 1790–1860* (Chicago, 1961); Lorman Ratner, *Powder Keg: Northern Opposition to the Antislavery Movement, 1831–1840* (New York, 1968). In the light of the findings of such works as Alan Dawley, *Class and Community: The Industrial Revolution in Lynn* (Cambridge, 1976); Leonard Richards, *Gentlemen of Property and Standing: Anti-Abolition Mobs in Jacksonian America* (New York, 1970); and John B. Jentz, "Artisans, Evangelicals, and the City: A Social History of Abolition and Labor Reform in Jacksonian New York" (Ph.D. diss., City University of New York, 1977), Eric Foner underscored the distinction between the labor movement's response to abolitionism or even to competition from emancipated slaves on the one hand, and its attitude toward slavery on the other. In *Politics and Ideology* Foner drew attention to a relatively neglected portion of the antislavery constituency—a class of radical artisans who drew their antislavery sentiments from Enlightenment rationalism and republican notions of equality and liberty and opposed the evangelical campaign for its perceived drive for special privileges (60–65).

15. Hale, "New England," NEEAC Papers, 81; Report by Committee of Operations submitted to a meeting of the corporators of the Massachusetts Emigrant Aid Company, May 12, 1854, in "Massachusetts Emigrant Aid Company," A History by Eli Thayer, manuscript, NEEAC Papers, 1–5.

16. Lawrence to Robinson, August 9, 1854, Samuel C. Pomeroy, "The Plan of the Emigrant Aid Company," both in NEEAC Papers; *Herald of Freedom*, April 14, 1855, March 22, 1856.

17. See Thomas H. O'Connor, "Cotton Whigs in Kansas." Ironically, as James B. Stewart has argued in *William Lloyd Garrison and the Challenge of Emancipation*, Garrison was no enemy of liberal capitalism.

18. Thayer, *A History*, 83; O'Connor, "Cotton Whigs in Kansas," 57. On anti-abolitionism among Northern industrialists, see Philip S. Foner, *Business and Slavery* (Chapel Hill, 1941), and Richards, *Gentlemen of Property and Standing*. Historians have not always been kind to the Garrisonians either, as Betty Fladeland documented in "Revisionists versus Abolitionists: The Historiographical Cold War of the 1930s and 1940s," *Journal of the Early Republic* 6 (spring 1986): 1–21. As Fladeland pointed out, the portrayal of Garrison in Barnes,

The Antislavery Impulse, as well as the publication of *Letters of Theodore Dwight Weld, Angelina Grimké Weld, and Sarah Grimké, 1822–1844,* ed. Barnes and Dwight L. Dumond, 2 vols. (1934; reprint, Gloucester, 1965), and *Letters of James Gillespie Birney, 1831–1857,* ed. Dumond, 2 vols. (New York, 1938), were used to buttress the case of an allegedly needless Civil War, which revisionists such as Avery Craven, *The Repressible Conflict, 1830–1861* (Baton Rouge, 1939), and George Fort Milton, *The Eve of Conflict: Stephen A. Douglas and the Needless War* (New York, 1934), blamed principally on "meddlesome [abolitionist] fanatics." As Fladeland noted, however, the revisionists missed the point that Barnes and Dumond had tried to convey: the qualitative distinction between the radical Garrisonian wing of the antislavery movement on the one hand and the "moderate, mainstream" Theodore Dwight Weld-Lewis Tappan-James Gillespie Birney faction of evangelical and political abolitionists on the other, as well as the relative insignificance of the former. The recourse by some historians to the insights of the behavioral sciences in an attempt to explain abolitionist mentality and behavior in sociopsychological terms helped fuel the fire of revisionist onslaughts against the abolitionists. See for instance, Hazel C. Wolf, *On Freedom's Altar: The Martyr Complex in the Abolition Movement* (Madison, 1952); Stanley M. Elkins, *Slavery;* David Donald, *Lincoln Reconsidered: Essays on the Civil War Era* (New York, 1956), and *Charles Sumner and the Coming of the Civil War* (New York, 1960).

The 1960s witnessed a historiographical volte-face on abolitionism, especially in the hands of New Left historians who restored the despised fanatics of the revisionist era to their exalted post-emancipation stature as moral heroes. Some of these "neo-abolitionist" works, as well as more detached scholarship in the 1970s and 1980s, have prompted an appreciation of the antislavery movement's diversity in terms of motivations, means, ends, and constituencies; the ambiguity of its position on race and relationship with labor; the role of women and African Americans in the crusade; a search for the origins of antislavery and reasons for its growing influence in the changing economic, cultural, and political world of the antebellum North; and psychohistorical explorations of abolitionist "inner histories" — "the search for personal identity and the quest for community in a hostile world," in the words of Richard O. Curry and Lawrence B. Goodheart (" 'Knives in Their Heads,' " 402). More recently, some scholars have reacted against the focus on the *Northern* context of antislavery, calling attention to the vicious reality of slavery as the key factor in spurring antislavery. See note 4 to the introduction for select works and historiographical essays on antislavery.

19. Cunningham to Hale, June 10, 1854, NEEAC Papers. In the mid-1960s, when black protest in the urban North drew attention to the fact that racial injustice was not the exclusive domain of the South (see Merton Dillon, "The Abolitionists," 518), two trends became discernible in antislavery scholarship. While some scholars called into question the egalitarian credentials of the abolitionists on the race question, others emphasized the anti-abolitionist bias of a Northern society pervaded with racism. On antislavery ambivalence on the race issue, see Leon Litwack, "The Emancipation of the Negro Abolitionist," in *The Antislavery Vanguard*, 137–55; and Foner, "The Racial Attitudes of the New York Free Soilers," in *Politics and Ideology*, 77–93. On racism as an underpinning of antislavery, see Eugene H. Berwanger, *Frontier against Slavery: Western Anti-Negro Prejudice and the Slavery Extension Controversy* (Urbana, 1967); William Westfall, "Antislavery as a Racist Outlet: A Hypothesis," *International Social Science Review* 61 (winter 1986): 3–11. On the pervasive racism in Northern society, see Litwack, *North of Slavery;* and James A. Rawley, *Race and Politics.* On Northern anti-abolitionism, see Linda K. Kerber, "Abolitionists and Amalgamators: The New York City Race Riots of 1834," *New York History* 48 (January 1967): 28–39; Robert Trendel, "The Expurgation of Antislavery Materials by American Presses," *Journal of Negro History* 57 (July 1973): 271–90; Howard A. Morrison, "Gentlemen of Proper Standing," *New York History* 62 (January 1981): 61–82. Of course, anti-abolitionism stemmed from other causes besides racism. See for instance, Lorman Ratner, "Northern Concern for Social Order as Cause for Rejecting Antislavery," *Historian* 28 (November 1965): 1–18; and John M. McFaul, "Expedience versus Morality: Jacksonian Politics and Slavery," *Journal of American History* 62 (June 1975): 24–39. On the anti-abolitionism of labor and business, see notes 14 and 18 to this chapter.

20. G. W. Brown to E. E. Hale, December 27, 1854, NEEAC Papers; *Herald of Freedom*, May 12, 1855.

21. Cited in *Herald of Freedom*, June 23, 1855.

22. The organization of the AHMS represented an effort to establish a missionary body on a national scale to evangelize America. The first step in this direction had been taken in 1822 with the formation of the predominantly Presbyterian United Domestic Missionary Society (UDMS) by the merger of local missionary bodies including the Young Men's Missionary Society of New York and the New York Evangelical Missionary Society. At a New York City convention in May 1826, the UDMS merged with the American Home Missionary Society formed at the same convention by members of the Congregational, Presbyterian, Dutch Reformed, and Associate Reformed churches from thir-

teen states and territories. Under the Plan of Union designed by the General Assembly of the Presbyterian Church and the General Association of Connecticut to provide for cooperation between the Presbyterians and the Congregationalists, the AHMS was able to hire missionaries from both denominations, and tap both sources financially. See Goodykoontz, *Home Missions*, 290–91.

23. In 1834, students at Cincinnati's Lane Seminary rebelled against the institution's ban on immediatist abolitionist activism and ultimately joined Oberlin College, Ohio. See Robert S. Fletcher, *A History of Oberlin College* (Oberlin, 1943); Wyatt-Brown, *Lewis Tappan*, 127–32; and Lawrence Lesick, *The Lane Rebels: Evangelicalism and Antislavery in Antebellum America* (Metuchen, N.J., 1980).

24. Johnson, "The American Missionary Association, 1846–1861," 94–117.

25. On the anti-institutionalism of the Garrisonian abolitionists, see Elkins, *Slavery*. For a critique of the Elkins thesis see Bertram Wyatt-Brown, "Stanley Elkins' *Slavery:* The Antislavery Interpretation Reexamined," *American Quarterly* 25 (May 1973): 154–76. *Tenth Annual Report of the AMA* (1856), p. 83, AMA Archives. *American Missionary* 2 (September 1858): 226. See also Johnson, "The American Missionary Association, 1846–1861," 8–12.

26. Quotation from Foner, *Politics and Ideology*, 48. On the differences between the radicals and the moderates within the abolitionist movement, see Kraditor, *Means and Ends in American Abolitionism*. Schisms within abolitionism continued during the Civil War and Reconstruction, and centered on divergent visions of the future of antislavery societies. See McPherson, *The Struggle for Equality*. I discuss the congruence between evangelical and free labor goals in chapter 4.

For an alternative interpretation of religious-humanitarian reform motivation and its critique, see Clifford S. Griffin, "Religious Benevolence as Social Control, 1815–1860," *Mississippi Valley Historical Review* 44 (December 1957): 423–44; Lois W. Banner, "Religious Benevolence as Social Control: A Critique of an Interpretation," *Journal of American History* 60 (June 1973): 23–41. On social conservatism among evangelical reformers, see Louis Gerteis, *Morality and Utility in American Antislavery Reform*, and Hugh Davis, *Joshua Leavitt: Evangelical Abolitionist* (Baton Rouge, 1990). Other scholars have seen in the crusade against slavery a desire to impose order and morality on a rapidly changing society and opined that abolitionism spoke the language of the middle class. For instance, see Griffin, *Their Brothers' Keepers: Moral Stewardship in the United States, 1800–1865* (New Brunswick, 1960); Ronald G. Walters, "The Erotic South: Civilization and Sexuality in American Abolitionism," *American*

Quarterly 25 (May 1973): 177–210, and *The Antislavery Appeal;* Lewis Perry, *Radical Abolitionism,* and *Childhood, Marriage and Reform;* Peter Walker, *Moral Choices;* George M. Frederickson, *The Arrogance of Race: Historical Perspectives on Slavery, Racism and Social Inequality* (Middletown, 1988), 73–93.

27. *American Missionary* 7 (April 1853): 45–47.

28. Ibid., 9 (November 1854): 5.

29. *Home Missionary* 25 (August 1853): 100–103.

30. *American Missionary* 7 (November 1852): 1.

31. *American Missionary* 8 (July 1854): 77; *Seventh Annual Report of the AMA* (1853), p. 75, AMA Archives; *Thirteenth Annual Report of the AMA* (1859), AMA Archives; *Thirty-third Annual Report of the AHMS* (May 1859), 65, Archives of the American Home Missionary Society, the Amistad Research Center at Tulane University, New Orleans; hereinafter cited as AHMS Archives. On the idea of the West as the "Garden of the World," see Henry Nash Smith, *Virgin Land,* 123–32.

32. *American Missionary* 8 (October 1854): 102. See also Cora Bolbee ed., "The Second Book on Kansas; An Account of C. B. Boynton and T. B. Mason's 'A Journey Through Kansas'," *Kansas Historical Quarterly* 4 (May 1935): 115–48.

33. *Home Missionary* 28 (September 1855): 218; *Herald of Freedom,* January 27, 1855.

34. Adair to Simeon S. Jocelyn, June 24, September 19, 1854, Finch to George Whipple, June 17, 1854, and *Ninth Annual Report of the AMA* (1855), p. 52, all in AMA Archives.

35. Adair to Jocelyn, August 25, September 19, 1854, AMA Archives.

36. In August 1854 the company appointed two other general agents for Kansas Territory besides Robinson. One was Samuel C. Pomeroy; the other was Charles H. Branscomb, a lawyer from Holyoke, Massachusetts. See Johnson, *The Battle Cry,* 58.

37. Adair to Jocelyn, October 21, 1854, AMA Archives.

38. *American Missionary* 8 (October 1854): 102.

39. Introduction to *The Letters of the Reverend Samuel Young Lum, Pioneer Kansas Missionary, 1854–1858,* ed. Emory Lindquist (Topeka, 1959).

40. Johnson, *The Battle Cry of Freedom,* 59.

41. Ibid., 56.

42. *Herald of Freedom,* January 20, 1855.

2 "Wolves of the Border" and Other Men of the "Wrong Stripe": The South in Kansas—1

The expression "Wolves of the Border" is taken from John Greenleaf Whittier's poem "Le Marais du Cygne," published in *Atlantic Monthly*, September 1858, and cited in Daniel W. Wilder, *Annals of Kansas* (1886; reprint, New York, 1975), 235.

1. On the establishment of Lawrence, see the introduction to this book. The town of Topeka astride the Kansas River was another major free-state stronghold. It was founded by Pennsylvanian entrepreneur Cyrus K. Holliday in consultation with NEEAC agent Charles Robinson.

2. Quotation from W. W. Boyce in *Winnsboro Register*, cited in Elmer LeRoy Craik, "Southern Interest in Territorial Kansas, 1854–1858," *Kansas Historical Collections* 15 (1919–21): 342.

3. Craik, "Southern Interest," 426. On the proslavery interest in Kansas, see also James C. Malin, "The Proslavery Background of the Kansas Struggle," *Mississippi Valley Historical Review* 10 (December 1923): 285–305.

4. Andreas, "Leavenworth County," in *History*, 418–20. Under the treaty of May 1854, the Delawares gave up all their lands except for a tract along the northern bank of the Kansas River known as the Delaware Reserve. Proceeds from the sale of the Delaware lands were to be held in trust by the government for the Delawares. These lands were known as the Delaware Trust lands.

5. Ibid., 420.

6. "Territorial Legislature of 1857–58," in *Transactions of the Kansas State Historical Society*, ed. Geo Martin, 10 (1907–8): 212–13; hereinafter cited as *Transactions*.

7. Andreas, "Leavenworth County," *History*, 421.

8. Cited in Craik, "Southern Interest," 349.

9. Frederick Starr to Father, August 21, 1854, Frederick Starr Papers, 1850–1863, WHMC; Peter Beckman, "The Overland Trade and Atchison's Beginnings," in *Territorial Kansas* (Lawrence, 1954), 149–51; "The Pioneer Merchants of Atchison County," *Atchison Daily Globe*, June 17, 1910, in "Scrapbook," vol. 1, p. 237, comp. G. J. Remsburg, Kansas State Historical Society Library, Topeka, Kansas.

10. Parrish, *David Rice Atchison*, suggests that the Softs deliberately instigated rumors of an Atchison-Benton split in a failed attempt to deflect enough Democratic votes to keep Benton from the Senate in 1844 (31–36). On Atchi-

son's identification with the Softs, see McClure, *Opposition in Missouri*, 49, 65, 67. On "Bourbon Dave," see Freehling, *The Road to Disunion*, 545.

11. "Sketch of the Life of Dr. John Gano Bryan, 1788–1860," typescript, n.d., John Gano Bryan Papers, 1788–1860, WHMC, 31, 48–49.

For someone apparently convinced of slavery's "positive good," Atchison appears to have given his sister Beck [Rebecca] a rather uncharacteristic piece of advice at the height of the Kansas conflict: "I wish you would set [two slaves] free; you have a tender conscience; if you will set them free I will bind myself to pay you fifty dollars a year for five or ten years. . . . You would rid your conscience of a heavy load." See Atchison to Beck, May 23, 1855, David Rice Atchison Papers, 1837–1953, WHMC. Although I could not find a signature on the letter, the handwriting was Atchison's.

12. A. S. Mitchell to Leonard, November 20, 1854, Leonard to Samuel Glover, October 25, 1854, Glover to Leonard, October 30, 1854, I. C. Richardson to Leonard, October 30, 1854, Lindley to Leonard, December 7, 1854, all in Leonard Collection, WHMC. On the role of Yankee capital in spurring the rise of St. Louis as a commercial entrepot, see Jeffrey S. Adler, *Yankee Merchants and the Making of the Urban West: The Rise and Fall of Antebellum St. Louis* (Cambridge, England, 1991).

13. J. S. Rollins to Leonard, November 29, 1854, Leonard Collection, WHMC. Another Whig corroborated this charge: "Benton's friends will thwart the St. Louis Whigs in their trade with the antis going for a bank and the interest law" (Lindley to Leonard, December 7, 1854, Leonard Collection, WHMC).

14. Parrish, *David Rice Atchison*, 156–159.

15. After the passage of the Kansas-Nebraska Bill, one Missouri Whig, referring to the growing influence of the American Party in his state, wrote that no man would be elected to the Senate who was not a Know-Nothing, adding that Atchison was "one of 'em already" (Abram S. Mitchell to Abiel Leonard, November 20, 1854, Abiel Leonard Collection, WHMC). Atchison's reputation as an apologist for nativism rested on his support of the Clayton Amendment — a proviso in the original Kansas-Nebraska Bill but excluded from its final version — which disenfranchised foreigners. The senator evidently shared the proslavery Whig apprehension that in the absence of nativist safeguards, a flood of antislavery German immigration to the new lands would tip the balance of popular power away from his constituency. The foreigners were not pioneers but rather "paupers and peddlers" in large part, claimed this border politician before the Senate while on the subject of alien suffrage in the territory. See Craik, "Southern Interest," 357.

16. McHolland cited in Newspaper Clippings, Starr Papers, WHMC. These and most subsequent news clippings from the Starr collection that I have used came from the Weston *Platte Argus* and the Weston *Reporter;* the complete series of neither newspaper is extant. Only three issues of the *Reporter* are available at the State Historical Society of Missouri, Columbia. Other quotations from Starr to Father, September 19, 1854, WHMC. See also Lester Baltimore, "Benjamin Stringfellow," 17.

17. Oliver Diefendorf to the Editor, the Weston *Platte Argus* July 21, 1854, and James H. McHolland to the Public, August 1854, Newspaper Clippings, Starr Papers, WHMC. The hostility of many German immigrants to slavery did not endear the newcomers to slavery's friends. On German immigrant antislavery, see Bruce Levine, *The Spirit of 1848: German Immigrants, Labor Conflict, and the Coming of the Civil War* (Urbana, 1992).

18. "Platte County Self-Defensive Association" and "Negro Slavery and Its Effects on the Social Position of the White Laborer," Newspaper Clippings, Starr Papers, WHMC. On Kansas proslavery, see Cecil-Fronsman, " 'Death to all Yankees.' " On the Self-Defensives, see Johnson, *The Battle Cry of Freedom,* 97, and Parrish, *David Rice Atchison,* 162–63. On "herrenvolk democracy" in the South, see George Frederickson, *The Black Image in the White Mind,* and Michael Wayne, "An Old South Morality Play." Works that emphasize the primacy of race in Southern social relations include Winthrop D. Jordan, *White over Black: American Attitudes toward the Negro, 1550–1812* (Chapel Hill, 1968), and Carl N. Degler, *Place over Time: The Continuity of Southern Distinctiveness* (Baton Rouge, 1977). Scholars have, of course, long recognized that racism was not peculiar to the American South (see note 19 to chapter 1). On the centrality of race in American culture, see Ronald Takaki, *Iron Cages: Race and Culture in Nineteenth-Century America* (New York, 1979).

Eugene Genovese, on the other hand, has interpreted slavery in terms of class relations, arguing in *The World the Slaveholders Made* that George Fitzhugh's defense of slavery as more humane than capitalist "wage slavery" for all workers irrespective of race, reflected the prebourgeois mentality of the South's planter-elite. In *The Slaveholders' Dilemma,* Genovese contended that the Fitzhugh defense represented an attempt to reconcile slavery with the slaveholders' commitment to progress. Another class analysis of slavery occurs in Barbara J. Fields, "Slavery, Race, and Ideology in the United States of America," *New Left Review* 181 (May–June 1990): 95–118. William Freehling has pointed out that the predominance of class or race varied according to time and place in the Old South. See his *Road to Disunion,* 572. The literature on Southern proslavery is rich, multifaceted, and too vast to summarize here. For an overview, see Drew Gilpin Faust, ed., *The Ideology of Slavery: Proslavery Thought in the Antebellum South, 1830–1860* (Baton Rouge, 1981), 1–20. A tiny sample of the excellent literature on the evangelical defense of slavery and its motives, which my proslavery Kansas subjects rarely invoked, includes Donald G. Mathews, "Charles Colcock Jones and the Southern Evangelical Crusade to Form a Biracial Community," *Journal of Southern History* 41 (August 1975): 299–320; Bertram Wyatt-Brown, "Modernizing Southern Slavery: The Proslavery Argument Reinterpreted," in *Region, Race, and Reconstruction: Essays in Honor of C. Vann Woodward*, ed. J. Morgan Kousser and James M. McPherson (New York, 1982), 27–49; Jack P. Maddex, " 'The Southern Apostasy' Revisited: The Significance of Proslavery Christianity," *Marxist Perspectives* 2 (fall 1979): 132–41; Anne C. Loveland, *Southern Evangelicals and the Social Order, 1800–1860* (Baton Rouge, 1980); David T. Bailey, *Southwestern Evangelical Religion and the Issue of Slavery, 1783–1860* (Ithaca, 1985); Larry Tise, *Proslavery: A History of the Defense of Slavery in America, 1701–1840* (Athens, 1987); Clarence L. Mohr, "Slaves and White Churches in Confederate Georgia," in *Masters and Slaves in the House of the Lord: Race and Religion in the American South, 1740–1870*, ed. John B. Boles (Lexington, 1988), 153–72.

19. *History of Clay and Platte Counties, Missouri* (St. Louis, 1885), 636–37; "Citizen's Meeting," Broadside, Starr Papers, WHMC.

20. Starr to Father, March 19, 1855; "Abolitionists in Weston," Newspaper Clippings, Starr Papers, WHMC.

21. Moore to Stringfellow, *Weston Reporter*, August 2, 1854, Moore, " 'An Abolitionist Trick Exposed!' Eh?" both in Newspaper Clippings, Starr Papers, WHMC.

22. Stringfellow, "An Abolitionist Trick Exposed!" Newspaper Clippings, Starr Papers, WHMC.

23. Moore, " 'An Abolitionist Trick Exposed!' Eh?" Newspaper Clippings, Starr Papers, WHMC.

24. Thelen, *Paths of Resistance*, 24; "Sketch of the Life of John Gano Bryan," Gano papers, WHMC, 48.

25. Testimony of Amos Reese, "Report of the Special Committee to Investigate the Troubles in Kansas with the Views of the Minority of Said Committee" (Washington, 1856), 34th Cong., 1st sess., H. Rept. 200, 929; hereinafter cited as Howard Committee Report.

26. *Squatter Sovereign*, May 1, 1855; Craik, "Southern Interest," 343; cited in *Herald of Freedom*, March 3, 1855.

27. *Squatter Sovereign*, March 6, May 1, 1855.

28. Ibid., May 8, June 19, 1855.

29. "The Meeting at Platte City—Hon. D. R. Atchison's Speech," March 24, 1855, Newspaper Clippings, "Kansas—Slavery," Letter from B. F. Stringfellow, March 1855, both in Starr Papers, WHMC.

30. Russell K. Hickman, "The Reeder Administration Inaugurated," part 1, *Kansas Historical Quarterly* 36 (autumn 1970): 305–40, and part 2, ibid., 36 (winter 1970): 424–55; on Reeder as well as the other governors of Kansas Territory, see Homer E. Socolofsky, *Kansas Governors*, 31–78. On Missourians in the election of March 1855, see Sara T. D. Robinson, "On Early Days in Lawrence, Kansas," March 23, 1896, in the Charles and Sara T. D. Robinson Collection (microfilm edition), Manuscript Division, Kansas State Historical Society, Topeka, Kansas (hereinafter cited as Robinson Collection); James A. Rawley, *Race and Politics*, 89.

31. Wilder, *Annals of Kansas*, 66–68.

32. Byrd to Jocelyn, July 7, 1855, AMA Archives. McPherson, *Battle Cry*, 147.

33. Andreas, "Leavenworth," *History*, 422; *History of Clay and Platte Counties, Missouri*, 176–77.

3 From the Pulpit and the Plow to the Sharps Rifle: Pioneer Life in the "Eden of the World"

1. Tables 1 through 8 show the occupational distribution of free males in electoral districts One through Seventeen from foreign countries as well as from all sections and states in the United States, with the exception of California. The figure 2,979, however, includes a lone settler—a farmer from California. This demographic profile is based on the Kansas Territorial Census of March 1855 reprinted in *1855 Territory of Kansas Census*, 2 vols., transcribed and compiled by Kansas Statistical Publications, Overland Park, Kans,; Andreas, *History*, and a map of electoral districts in Russell Hickman, "The Reeder Administration Inaugurated," part 1, 314.

2. T. F. Robley, *History of Bourbon County, Kansas, to the Close of 1865* (Fort Scott, Kans., 1894), 51–53.

3. "Trials of Our Pioneers: Story of the History of Douglas County Giving Personal Reminiscences and Many Hitherto Unpublished Incidents," *Lawrence Jeffersonian Gazette*, February 8, 1900, in Clippings Volume, 1899–1901, Kansas State Historical Society Library, Topeka, 95; Trego to wife, Decem-

ber 11, 1857, in Edgar Langsdorf, ed., "The Letters of Joseph H. Trego, 1857–1864, Linn County Pioneer," *Kansas Historical Quarterly* 19 (May 1951): 113–32.

4. *History and Statistics of Brown County, Kansas, from its Earliest Settlement to the Present Time*, compiled by Maj. E. N. Morrill (Hiawatha, Kans., July 4, 1876), 17–27.

5. Craik, "Southern Interest," 406.

6. Ibid., 423–25.

7. On one immigrant group in territorial Kansas, see Eleanor Turk, "The Germans of Atchison, 1854–1859: Development of an Ethnic Community," *Kansas History* 2 (autumn 1979): 146–56.

8. Occupational profile of NEEAC emigrants based on lists of settlers in the first (March 13, 1855), second (March 20, 1855), and third (March 27, 1855) spring parties to Kansas, NEEAC Papers; original copy certified by Thomas Webb on June 26, 1856, reproduced in Howard Committee Report, 886–92; *Herald of Freedom*, January 27, 1855. Scholarship on labor's ambiguous relationship with the antislavery movement in an emerging capitalist order has produced some interesting insights. On this point, see note 14 to chapter 1. On American industrialism and its impact on workers, see Alan Dawley, *Class and Community;* Herbert G. Gutman, *Work, Culture, and Society in Industrializing America: Essays in American Working-Class and Social History* (New York, 1976); Susan E. Hirsch, *Roots of the American Working Class: The Industrialization of Crafts in Newark, 1800–1860* (Philadelphia, 1978); Paul Johnson, *A Shopkeeper's Millennium;* Bruce Laurie, *Working People of Philadelphia, 1800–1850* (Philadelphia, 1980); Thomas C. Cochran, *Frontiers of Change: Early Industrialism in America;* Alice Kessler-Harris, *Out to Work: A History of Wage-Earning Women in the United States* (New York, 1982); Jonathan Prude, *The Coming of Industrial Order: Town and Factory Life in Rural Massachusetts, 1810–1860* (Cambridge, Eng., 1983); David A. Hounshell, *From the American System to Mass Production;* Sean Wilentz, *Chants Democratic: New York City and the Rise of the American Working Class, 1788–1850* (New York, 1984); Steven J. Ross, *Workers on the Edge: Work, Leisure, and Politics in Industrializing Cincinnati, 1788–1890* (New York, 1985); W. J. Rorabaugh, *The Craft Apprentice: From Franklin to the Machine Age* (New York, 1986); Christine Stansell, *City of Women: Sex and Class in New York, 1789–1860* (New York, 1986); Mary H. Blewett, *Men, Women, and Work: Class, Gender, and Protest in the New England Shoe Industry, 1780–1910* (Urbana, 1988).

9. On pioneer women in Kansas during and after the territorial period, see

Joanna Stratton, *Pioneer Women: Voices from the Kansas Frontier* (New York, 1981); and M. Evangeline Thomas, "The Role of Women Religious in Kansas History, 1841–1981," *Kansas History* 4 (spring 1981): 53–63.

10. Adair to Jocelyn, October 21 and November 16, 1854, AMA Archives.

11. Ibid., December 8, 1854, January 20, March 7, March 13, 1855.

12. *Kansas: A Guide to the Sunflower State,* compiled and written by the Federal Writers' Project of the Works Projects Administration for the State of Kansas (New York, 1939), 266–67.

13. Finch to Jocelyn, March 16, 1855, Adair to Jocelyn, January 20, 1855, AMA Archives.

14. Narrative of John E. Stewart, manuscript, Stewart Papers, Thaddeus Hyatt Collection (microfilm edition), Manuscript Division, Kansas State Historical Society, Topeka; hereinafter cited as Hyatt Collection.

15. *Herald of Freedom,* March 24, 1855.

16. Ibid.

17. Ibid; narrative of John E. Stewart, Hyatt Collection.

18. Sara T. D. Robinson, *Kansas: Its Interior and Exterior Life* (Boston, 1856); Robinson, "On Early Days in Lawrence, Kansas," typescript, Robinson Collection.

19. Johnson, *The Battle Cry of Freedom,* 82.

20. Adair to Jocelyn, March 31, 1855, Finch to Jocelyn, December 14, 1854 and March 16, 1855, both in AMA Archives.

21. On Wabaunsee and Council City, see Johnson, *The Battle Cry of Freedom,* 84–85.

22. *Ninth Annual Report of the AMA* (1855), pp. 52–55, AMA Archives.

23. S. S. Scofield, "Obituary of Reverend H. N. Norton," September 1857, Copeland to Jocelyn, September 28, 1857, and Schuyler to Jocelyn, March 15, 1857, all in AMA Archives.

24. *Eleventh Annual Report of the AMA* (1857), p. 71, AMA Archives. In 1857 Samuel C. Pomeroy, acting on behalf of the NEEAC, bought a controlling interest in the town of Atchison, together with a Cincinnati-based emigrant company. See Johnson, *The Battle Cry of Freedom,* 246; Kenneth Stampp, *America in 1857: A Nation on the Brink* (New York, 1990), 148.

25. *American Missionary* 8 (June 1854): 58.

26. Jones to Jocelyn, April 2, 1856, AMA Archives.

27. *Eleventh Annual Report of the AMA,* p. 72, AMA Archives.

28. *American Missionary* 9 (October 1855): 93.

29. Ibid., 10 (November 1855): 4.

30. Byrd to Jocelyn, January 20, 1859, August 3, 1855, July 7, 1855, December 27, 1859, November 16, 1855, AMA Archives.

31. Ibid., November 16, 1855.

32. Missouri newspaper cited in *American Missionary* 10 (October 1856): 93; Finch to Jocelyn, July 3, 1855, AMA Archives.

33. Byrd to Jocelyn, November 16, 1855, AMA Archives. On free-state racism, see Rawley, *Race and Politics;* Eugene Berwanger, *Frontier against Slavery: Western Anti-Negro Prejudice and the Slavery Extension Controversy.* "Black law" feeling referred to the support of Negro exclusion from Kansas.

34. *American Missionary* 9 (October 1855): 93.

35. Ibid., 1 (January 1857): 17.

36. Finch to Jocelyn, July 3, 1855, Lowry to Jocelyn, July 5, 1855, Byrd to Jocelyn, April 23, 1858, July 22, 1859, all in AMA Archives. On the education of African Americans in territorial Kansas, see John C. Carper, "The Popular Ideology of Segregated Schooling: Attitudes toward the Education of Blacks in Kansas, 1854–1900," *Kansas History* 1 (winter 1978): 254–65.

37. Stephen B. Oates, *To Purge This Land with Blood: A Biography of John Brown* (New York, 1970), 259. The influx of slaves from Missouri into Kansas increased greatly with the outbreak of the Civil War. See Richard B. Sheridan, "From Slavery in Missouri to Freedom in Kansas: The Influx of Black Fugitives and Contrabands into Kansas, 1854–1865," *Kansas History* 12 (spring 1989): 28–47.

38. Oates, *To Purge This Land,* 84–85. On John Brown, see also James C. Malin, *John Brown and the Legend of the Fifty-Six* (Philadelphia, 1942); and Louis Ruchames, ed., *A John Brown Reader* (London and New York, 1959).

39. W. S. Jenks, "Some Unwritten History," Newspaper Clippings, Robinson Collection.

40. Isaac Maris to F. G. Adams, July 27, 1895, Zu Adams, "Slaves in Kansas," typescript, p. 7, both in History—Slavery Collection, Kansas State Historical Society Library, Topeka, Kansas (hereinafter cited as Slavery Collection); Byrd to Jocelyn, December 27, 1859, AMA Archives.

41. Finch to Jocelyn, March 16, 1855, AMA Archives; *Leavenworth Herald* quotation cited in *Herald of Freedom,* April 14, 1855.

42. *Herald of Freedom,* May 12, 1855; *Letters of the Reverend Samuel Young Lum,* ed. Lindquist, 2–5.

43. Finch to Jocelyn, February 28, 1855, AMA Archives.

44. Blood to Badger, May 1 and August 4, 1855, AHMS Archives; *Home Missionary* 29 (December 1856): 191.

45. *Home Missionary* 28 (April 1856): 390, 29 (June 1856): 48.

46. Ibid., 29 (March 1857): 265.

47. Ibid., 30 (March 1858): 268.

48. Lum to Badger, March 8, 1858, October 5, 1857, AHMS Archives (emphasis in original); Goodykoontz, *Home Missions on the American Frontier*, 297.

49. *Home Missionary* 31 (November 1858): 164, 30 (December 1857): 197, 30 (February 1858): 251.

50. Lum to Badger, November 16, 1857, AHMS Archives.

51. *Home Missionary* 31 (November 1858): 166.

52. *Thirty-third Annual Report of the AHMS* (May 1859), pp. 13–65, AHMS Archives.

53. Lum to Badger, January 15, 1857, December 6, 1854, Lum to David B. Coe, February 28, 1855, Lum to Badger, November 16, 1857, all in AHMS Archives.

54. Lum to Badger, December 6, 1854, AHMS Archives.

55. *Home Missionary* 31 (June 1858): 30, 31 (April 1859): 281.

56. Adair to Jocelyn, June 30, 1859, AMA Archives.

57. Lum to the editor of the *Home Missionary*, in *Letters of the Reverend Samuel Young Lum*, ed. Lindquist, 65; *Home Missionary* 31 (November 1858): 164.

58. *Home Missionary* 31 (June 1858): 30.

59. Ibid., 29 (January 1857): 241, 29 (June 1856): 48.

60. Ibid., 27 (April 1855): 285, 30 (March 1858): 270.

61. *Tenth Annual Report of the AMA* (1856), p. 79, Elizabeth Byrd to George Whipple, August 28, 1856, both in AMA Archives.

62. See Edmund Morgan, *Puritan Dilemma: The Story of John Winthrop* (Boston, 1958), 7–8.

63. *Home Missionary* 31 (August 1858): 94.

64. John Hawley to Jocelyn, February 24, 1858, Finch to Jocelyn, April 20, 1858, August 25, 1858 and October 24, 1859, Adair to Jocelyn, March 31, 1858, all in AMA Archives.

65. Blood to Badger, September 27, 1855, AHMS Archives.

66. Jones to Jocelyn, July 3, 1858, AMA Archives.

67. *Home Missionary* 30 (April 1858): 292–93, 32 (January 1860): 210.

68. Lum to Milton Badger, Dec 6, 1854, AHMS Archives; Lowry to Jocelyn, July 5, 1855, AMA Archives.

69. *American Missionary* 9 (July 1855): 67.

70. Norton to Jocelyn, August 6, 1856 and October 10, 1856, AMA Archives.

71. "Statements concerning the conduct of National Kansas Committee agents in Kansas: Kansas Experiences of James B. Abbott, Lemuel Knapp, and Samuel Anderson," Hyatt Collection. On the National Kansas Committee, see Johnson, *The Battle Cry of Freedom*, 194, 212–16.

72. Narrative of John E. Stewart, "Statements concerning the conduct of National Kansas Committee agents in Kansas," both in Hyatt Collection.

4 "A Model New England State"

1. Clifford E. Clark, *Henry Ward Beecher: Spokesman For a Middle-Class America* (Urbana, 1978); William G. McLoughlin, *The Meaning of Henry Ward Beecher: An Essay on the Shifting Values of Mid-Victorian America, 1840–1870* (New York, 1976).

2. *Herald of Freedom*, March 29, 1856.

3. Ibid; Gladstone's observations are cited in Wilder, *Annals of Kansas*, 163.

4. *Herald of Freedom*, January 13, 1855; "Samuel C. Pomeroy," in *United States Biographical Dictionary*, Kansas Volume (Chicago, 1879), 743.

5. *Herald of Freedom*, March 3, 1855; Hale, "New England," NEEAC Papers, 81, 85.

6. Eric Foner, *Free Soil, Free Labor*, 13.

7. *Herald of Freedom*, April 5, 1856.

8. Ibid., July 7, 1855.

9. Ibid.

10. Johnson, *The Battle Cry of Freedom*, 87; Don W. Wilson, *Governor Charles Robinson of Kansas*, 129.

11. Lawrence to Robinson, November 28, 1854, and April 28, 1859, NEEAC Papers.

12. On the relationship between capitalism, the middle-class family in the nineteenth-century, and antislavery, see John Ashworth, "The Relationship between Capitalism and Humanitarianism," in *The Antislavery Debate*, 180–99. On the doctrine of separate spheres and the cult of domesticity, see Barbara Welter, "The Cult of True Womanhood: 1820–1860," *American Quarterly* 18 (summer 1966): 151–74; Katherine Kish Sklar, *Catherine Beecher: A Study in American Domesticity* (New Haven, 1973); Nancy F. Cott, *The Bonds of Womanhood: "Woman's Sphere" in New England, 1780–1835* (New Haven, 1977); Mary P. Ryan, *Cradle of the Middle Class: The Family in Oneida County, New York, 1790–1865* (Cambridge, Eng., 1981); Carroll Smith-Rosenberg, *Disorderly Conduct: Visions of Gender in Victorian America* (New York, 1985).

13. *Herald of Freedom*, January 27, 1855.

14. Ibid., December 15, 1855.

15. Ibid., January 27, 1855.

16. Wilson, *Governor Charles Robinson*, 131; Lawrence to Rev. Ephraim Nute, December 16, 1856, NEEAC Papers.

17. Lawrence to Nute, February 11, 1857, NEEAC Papers.

18. Lawrence to the Hon. G. S. Boutwell, February 19, 1857, Lawrence to Samuel Reynolds, January 23, 1857, Lawrence to Geary, February 5, 1857, all in NEEAC Papers; *Herald of Freedom*, February 23, 1856.

19. Andreas, "Douglas County," in *History*, 325–26; *Herald of Freedom*, April 5, 1856.

20. Johnson, "The American Missionary Association, 1846–1861," 94–117.

21. Paul Johnson, *A Shopkeeper's Millennium*, 140–41. Johnson has shown how the New York revivals legitimated wage-earning free labor by promoting "visions of a perfect moral order based on individual freedom and self-government." As John Ashworth has pointed out, Johnson does not doubt the sincerity of the industrialist reformers, recognizing instead that their class interest was "mediated . . . through the prism of religion" (*The Antislavery Debate*, 279).

22. *Herald of Freedom*, February 23, 1856, and March 8, 1856.

23. Ibid., February 16, 1856.

24. Ibid., March 8, 1856.

25. "Circular of the Committee of Clergymen," NEEAC Papers.

26. Johnson, *The Battle Cry of Freedom*, 114.

27. Lawrence to Webb, June 12, 1855, NEEAC Papers.

28. The expression "bourgeois Christian" is taken from James B. Stewart, "Politics and Belief in Abolitionism: Stanley Elkins' Concept of Anti-institutionalism and Recent Interpretations of American Antislavery," *South Atlantic Quarterly* 75 (winter 1976): 85; Amos Finch to Jocelyn, March 16, 1855, John Lowry to Jocelyn, July 5, 1855, John Byrd to Jocelyn, April 23, 1858, July 22, 1859, and December 27, 1859, Jonathan Copeland to Jocelyn, March 20, 1860, all in AMA Archives.

29. Byrd to Jocelyn, July 7, 1855, AMA Archives.

30. Foner, *Politics and Ideology*, 105–06.

31. See Jacqueline Jones, *Soldiers of Light and Love: Northern Teachers and Georgia Blacks, 1865–1873* (Chapel Hill, 1980); Joe M. Richardson, *Christian Reconstruction*.

32. *Herald of Freedom*, April 5, 1856.

33. Ibid., March 3, 1855, April 28, 1855.

34. Temperley, "Antislavery," 348.

35. *Home Missionary* 30 (April 1858): 292–293.

36. Adair to Jocelyn, March 13, 1856, AMA Archives.

37. *Herald of Freedom,* April 7, 1855, April 21, 1855, October 6, 1855, October 13, 1855, April 28, 1855.

38. Ibid., May 12, 1855.

39. Ibid., October 13, 1855, October 27, 1855.

40. Ibid., May 19, 1855.

41. "Trials of Our Pioneers: Story of the History of Douglas County Giving Personal Reminiscences and Many Hitherto Unpublished Incidents," *Lawrence Jeffersonian Gazette,* February 8, 1900. On the cultural stereotypes perpetuated by the friends and foes of slavery, see Michael Fellman, "Rehearsal for the Civil War: Antislavery and Proslavery at the Fighting Point in Kansas, 1854–1856," in *Antislavery Reconsidered,* 294. On the role of "cultural federalism" in determining voting behavior, see Roy F. Nichols, *The Disruption of American Democracy* (New York, 1948), 20–40.

42. *Free State,* March 3, 1855, and February 7, 1855; Johnson, *The Battle Cry of Freedom,* 76–77.

43. On the association of antislavery with nativism and temperance, see McPherson, *Battle Cry,* 130–44; William E. Gienapp, "Nativism and the Creation of a Republican Majority in the North Before the Civil War," *Journal of American History* 72 (December 1985): 529–59. On the American party, see Anbinder, *Nativism and Slavery.*

44. The *New York Independent* cited in *Home Missionary* 25 (March 1853): 264–65; *Seventh Annual Report of the AMA* (1853), p. 75, AMA Archives.

45. *Herald of Freedom,* May 12, 1855; D. R. Anthony to Sister Susan, September 10, 1858, in Leavenworth County Clippings, vol. 5 (1950–61), Kansas State Historical Society Library, Topeka, Kansas, 189–229.

46. *Squatter Sovereign,* March 27, 1855, and June 26, 1855. The NEEAC declared itself willing to aid all prospective emigrants to Kansas irrespective of their sectional or national origins. The *Herald of Freedom,* April 14, 1855, claimed that the company knew "neither North, South, East or West to the exclusion of the remainder." Indeed the company would protect westward-bound foreign immigrants whose "complete ignorance of our customs . . . and language" rendered them especially vulnerable to fraud by unscrupulous agents of transportation companies. See Report by Committee of Operations submitted to a meeting of the Corporators of the Massachusetts Emigrant Aid Company,

May 12, 1854, NEEAC Papers. Thayer hoped to convince Southerners and others of the superiority of free labor.

5 "White Men Can Never Be Slaves"

1. Robinson to Thayer, July 26, 1855, Robinson Collection; Lawrence to Thomas Webb, July 20, 1855, NEEAC Papers. On the NEEAC's involvement in providing guns to free-state Kansans, see Phillip R. Rutherford, "The Arabia Incident," *Kansas History* 1 (spring 1978): 39–47.

2. *Herald of Freedom,* July 7, September 8, 1855.

3. Bernard Bailyn, *The Ideological Origins of the American Revolution.* On the North's desire to protect democratic government and civil liberties as a factor in shaping sectional conflict, see Russell B. Nye, *Fettered Freedom.*

4. On military service as civic virtue, see Jean Baker, "From Belief into Culture," 542.

5. Johnson, *The Battle Cry of Freedom,* 146, 172.

6. *American Missionary* 9 (November 1854): 3.

7. Quotation from "A North-Side View of Slavery," A Sermon on the Crime against Freedom in Kansas and Washington, Preached at Henniker, New Hampshire, August 31, 1856, by Eden B. Foster, in Slavery, a Collection of Pamphlets, New York Public Library.

8. Byrd to Jocelyn, November 16, 1855, Adair to Jocelyn, January 2, 1858, and March 31, 1858, all in AMA Archives.

9. *Herald of Freedom,* February 10, 1855.

10. Robinson to unknown addressee, August 27, 1855, Robinson Collection.

11. Adair to Jocelyn, May 16, 1856, AMA Archives.

12. Rawley, *Race and Politics,* 93.

13. *Herald of Freedom,* September 8, 1855.

14. Wilder, *Annals of Kansas,* 76; *Herald of Freedom,* September 8, 1855; Byrd to Jocelyn, November 16, 1855, AMA Archives.

15. Potter, *Impending Crisis,* 204; Rawley, *Race and Politics,* 95.

16. These votes were cast at Easton. The poll books at Leavenworth were destroyed. See Wilder, *Annals of Kansas,* 90.

17. Voting data taken from Wilder, *Annals of Kansas,* 90.

18. On the backgrounds of candidates fielded by the Free-State party, see *Herald of Freedom,* December 29, 1855.

19. Potter, *The Impending Crisis,* 204.

20. In the course of the congressional debates on the Kansas troubles, the Emigrant Aid Company was alternately subjected to lengthy diatribes and defenses by its opponents and supporters in Congress, suggesting that the enterprise had achieved recognition as a factor in Kansas affairs. As a result of this controversy, its stock subscriptions skyrocketed. See Johnson, *The Battle Cry of Freedom*, 149–54.

21. Narrative of John E. Stewart, Hyatt Collection; *Herald of Freedom*, December 15, 1855.

22. *Herald of Freedom*, July 14, 1855.

23. Ibid., May 12, 1855.

24. Kickapoo *Kansas Pioneer* citation and *Herald of Freedom*'s response in ibid., January 13, 1855.

25. Narrative of John E. Stewart, Hyatt Collection.

26. Ibid.

27. Sara Robinson, "Notes Prepared for the Second Edition of *Kansas: Its Interior and Exterior Life*," Robinson Collection.

28. Byrd to Jocelyn, December 7, 1855, AMA Archives; Sara Robinson, "Notes Prepared for the Second Edition of *Kansas*," Robinson Collection.

29. Byrd to Jocelyn, December 7, 1855, AMA Archives.

30. *Herald of Freedom*, December 15, 1855.

31. Ibid.; Sara Robinson, "Notes Prepared for the Second Edition of *Kansas*," Robinson Collection.

32. Sara Robinson, "On Early Days in Lawrence, Kansas," Robinson Collection.

33. Adair to Jocelyn, December 9 and December 14, 1855, AMA Archives.

34. Cited in *Herald of Freedom*, December 22, 1855.

35. *Herald of Freedom*, December 15, 1855; Johnson, *The Battle Cry of Freedom*, 142; last quotation from Rawley, *Race and Politics*, 97.

36. *Herald of Freedom*, December 15, 1855.

37. Pomeroy to Webb, December 19, 1855, NEEAC Papers. Pomeroy underlined the part about the Missourians feeling "sold out."

38. Rawley, *Race and Politics*, 130–31; Johnson, *The Battle Cry of Freedom*, 156–58.

39. Atchison's speech reported by the *New York Tribune*, June 5, 1856, and cited in Wilder, *Annals of Kansas*, 118–19, 121. Bernard A. Weisberger, "Newspaper Reporters and the Kansas Embroglio," *Mississippi Valley Historical Review* 36 (March 1950): 633–56; quotation from Weisberger, 646.

40. Pomeroy to Mrs. Rebecca B. Spring, January 16, 1860, John Brown

Collection (microfilm edition), Manuscripts Division, Kansas State Historical Society, Topeka, Kansas; hereinafter cited as Brown Collection; Adair to Jocelyn, May 23, 1856, AMA Archives. The *Herald of Freedom* resumed publication in November 1856 with financial help from Northern supporters.

41. Rawley, *Race and Politics*, 125–26; McPherson, *Battle Cry*, 149–50.

42. "The Last Signs," A Sermon Preached at the Unitarian Church at Jersey City by O. B. Frothingham on June 1, 1856 (New York, 1856), in Slavery—A Collection of Pamphlets, New York Public Library, 10–13.

43. Ruchames, *John Brown Reader*. On Brown see also Oates, *To Purge This Land with Blood;* and James Malin, *John Brown and the Legend of the Fifty-Six*.

44. Memorandum of a statement made by Jason Brown, April 2, 1884, to F. G. Adams, Topeka, Brown Collection.

45. Adair to Jocelyn, July 10, 1856, AMA Archives.

46. Robinson, *The Kansas Conflict* (New York, 1892), 294; Thayer to Sara Robinson, February 2, 1890, Robinson Collection; Copy of Share Certificate, Boston, January 15, 1856, Brown Collection; Hale, "New England," NEEAC Papers, 85–86; Lawrence to Robinson, November 21, 1884, Robinson Collection.; Robinson to Brown, September 14, 1856, Brown Collection.

47. Oates, *To Purge This Land with Blood*, 183.

48. Thayer to Brown, March 19 and March 30, 1857, Thayer to Messrs. Allen and Wheelock, April 4, 1857, Thayer to Brown, April 17, 1857, Allen and Wheelock to Brown, April 20, 1857, all in Brown Collection.

49. Lawrence to Brown, March 20, 1857, Brown Collection.

50. Lawrence to Robinson, December 14, 1883, Robinson Collection.

51. Sanborn, "John Brown in Kansas," typescript, 1859, Brown Collection.

52. William E. Connelley, "John Brown: Never in Breckenridge County, Kansas Territory," Robinson to Brown, September 13, 1856, both in Brown Collection.

53. Finch to Jocelyn, July 10, 1856, AMA Archives.

6 A Slave State without Masters or Slaves: The South in Kansas—2

1. Missouri-based emigrant aid companies included the Kansas Emigration Society of Lafayette County, the Platte County Emigrant Aid Society of Platte City, and the Proslavery Emigrant Aid Society of Weston. See Craik, "Southern Interest," 376–95.

2. Ibid., 422–23.

3. Quotation from *Herald of Freedom*, February 2, 1856; see also *Boston Daily Advertiser*, April 7, 1856; Johnson, *The Battle Cry of Freedom*, 208–9; Walter L. Fleming, "Buford Expedition to Kansas," *American Historical Review* 6 (October 1900): 38–48.

4. Clayton's Report to the Kansas Executive Committee of Bourbon County, Alabama (Eufala, 1856), in Kansas Historical Pamphlets, vol. 1, Kansas State Historical Society Library, Topeka, Kansas, 8.

5. Craik, "Southern Interest," 414.

6. Milton Tabor, "This Day in Kansas History," *Topeka Capital*, January 21, 1856, in Clippings Volume, Kansas State Historical Society Library, Topeka, Kansas, 215.

7. William O. Lynch, "Population Movements in Relation to the Struggle For Kansas," Pamphlet Reprinted from Indiana University Studies in American History, June 1926, Kansas State Historical Society Library, Topeka, Kansas, 394.

8. Craik, "Southern Interest," 438.

9. Ibid., 412.

10. "Slavery in Kansas," an address by C. E. Cory before the Twenty-sixth Annual Kansas State Historical Society Meeting January 21, 1902, *Kansas Historical Collection* 7 (1901–2), 232.

11. Zu Adams, "Slaves in Kansas," typescript, Slavery Collection, 2. I use the term "black belt" to denote the demographic profile rather than soil conditions of a particular region.

12. The following discussion on the frequency distribution of slaves in Kansas by electoral district as of March 1855 is based on *1855 Territory of Kansas Census.*

13. Henry Shindler, "When Slaves Were Owned in Kansas by Army Officers," *Leavenworth Times*, October 13, 1912, Clippings Volume, Kansas State Historical Society Library, 100; statistics based on *1855 Territory of Kansas Census.*

14. Zu Adams, "Slaves in Kansas," 5; Lydia A. Haag, "Slavery Agitation and Its Influence on the State of Kansas" (master's thesis, Kansas State College of Agriculture and Applied Science, Manhattan, 1934), 43.

15. The census takers of 1855 were instructed not to include in their lists U.S. military personnel temporarily stationed in the territory, or "persons of Indian blood." Thus my analysis does not take account of slaveholders belonging to either of the above categories. Although according to some accounts, the first census recorded 193 slaves, I counted 186. On slavery among the Native Ameri-

cans see Charles M. Hudson, ed., *Red, White, and Black: Symposium on Indians in the Old South* (Athens, 1971); R. Halliburton Jr., *Red over Black: Black Slavery among the Cherokee Indians* (Westport, Conn., 1977); Theda Perdue, *Slavery and the Evolution of Cherokee Society, 1540–1866* (Knoxville, 1977).

16. Hurt, *Agriculture and Slavery*, 219.

17. B. Harding to Zu Adams, September 9, 1895, Zu Adams Collection of Letters, Slavery Collection. Whitehead, incidentally, was not destined to enjoy his newfound slaveholding status for long. During the Civil War years, he removed his slaves to Texas, bringing them back later to tend his rented farm near St. Joseph, Missouri. Much to his surprise, his "loyal" servants "planted a big crop, then left it for him to tend himself without a dollar."

18. Cory, "Slavery in Kansas," 238.

19. Ibid., 232.

20. John Sedgwick Freeland, "The Slaves of Judge Rush Elmore," John Armstrong, "Reminiscences of Slave Days in Kansas," and Zu Adams, "Slavery in Kansas," 9, all in Slavery Collection.

21. The historical literature on Southern slavery and slave society is highly sophisticated and too vast to discuss fully here. See notes 8 and 10 to the introduction. In addition, select works on Southern slavery before 1860 include Oscar Handlin and Mary F. Handlin, "Origins of the Southern Labor System," *William and Mary Quarterly* 7 (April 1950): 199–222; Kenneth Stampp, *The Peculiar Institution: Slavery in the Antebellum South* (New York, 1956); Elkins, *Slavery;* Richard C. Wade, *Slavery in the Cities: The South, 1820–1860* (New York, 1964); Philip D. Curtin, *The Atlantic Slave Trade: A Census* (Madison, 1969); Laura Foner and Eugene D. Genovese, *Slavery in the New World: A Reader in Comparative History* (Englewood Cliffs, N.J., 1969); Robert S. Starobin, *Industrial Slavery in the Old South* (New York, 1970); John W. Blassingame, *The Slave Community: Plantation Life in the Antebellum South* (New York, 1972; revised, 1979); Clarence L. Mohr, "Slavery in Oglethorpe County, Georgia, 1773–1865," *Phylon* 33 (spring 1972): 4–21; Gerald W. Mullin, *Flight and Rebellion: Slave Resistance in Eighteenth-Century Virginia* (New York, 1972); George P. Rawick, *From Sundown to Sunup: The Making of the Black Community* (Westport, Conn., 1972); Ira Berlin, *Slaves without Masters: The Free Negro in the Antebellum South* (New York, 1974); Fogel and Engerman, *Time on the Cross;* Eugene D. Genovese, *Roll Jordan Roll;* Peter H. Wood, *Black Majority: Negroes in Colonial South Carolina from 1670 through the Stono Rebellion* (New York, 1974); Edmund S. Morgan, *American Slavery–American Freedom: The Ordeal of Colonial Virginia* (New York, 1975); C. Duncan Rice, *The Rise and Fall of Black*

Slavery (New York, 1975); Claudia Dale Goldin, *Urban Slavery in the American South, 1820–1860: A Quantitative History* (Chicago, 1976); Herbert G. Gutman, *The Black Family in Slavery and Freedom, 1750–1925* (New York, 1976); Leslie Howard Owens, *This Species of Property: Slave Life and Culture in the Old South* (New York, 1976); Willie Lee Rose, ed., *A Documentary History of Slavery in North America* (New York, 1976); Blassingame, ed., *Slave Testimony: Two Centuries of Letters, Speeches, Interviews, and Autobiographies* (Baton Rouge, 1977); Nathan Irvin Huggins, *Black Odyssey: The Afro-American Ordeal in Slavery* (New York, 1977); Lawrence W. Levine, *Black Culture and Black Consciousness: Afro-American Folk Thought from Slavery to Freedom* (New York, 1977); Allan Kulikoff, "The Origins of Afro-American Society in Tidewater Maryland and Virginia, 1700–1790," *William and Mary Quarterly* 35 (April 1978): 226–59; Albert J. Raboteau, *Slave Religion: The "Invisible Institution" in the Antebellum South* (New York, 1978); Thomas L. Webber, *Deep Like Rivers: Education in the Slave Quarter Community, 1831–1865* (New York, 1978); Genovese, *From Rebellion to Revolution: Afro-American Slave Revolts in the Making of the Modern World* (Baton Rouge, 1979); Ira Berlin, "Time, Space, and the Evolution of Afro-American Society in British Mainland North America," *American Historical Review* 85 (February 1980): 44–78; T. H. Breen and Stephen Innes, *"Myne Own Ground": Race and Freedom in Virginia's Eastern Shore, 1640–1676* (New York, 1980); Mark V. Tushnet, *The American Law of Slavery, 1810–1860: Considerations of Humanity and Interest* (Princeton, 1981); Philip D. Morgan, "Work and Culture: The Task System and the World of Lowcountry Blacks, 1770–1880," *William and Mary Quarterly* 39 (July 1982): 563–99; Orlando Patterson, *Slavery and Social Death: A Comparative Study* (Cambridge, 1982); Willie Lee Rose, *Slavery and Freedom* (New York, 1982); Ira Berlin and Ronald Hoffman, eds., *Slavery and Freedom in the Age of the American Revolution* (Urbana, 1983); John B. Boles, *Black Southerners, 1619–1869* (Lexington, 1983); Michael P. Johnson and James L. Roark, *Black Masters: A Free Family of Color in the Old South* (New York, 1984); Charles Joyner, *Down by the Riverside: A South Carolina Slave Community* (Urbana, 1984); Betty Wood, *Slavery in Colonial Georgia, 1730–1775* (Athens, 1984); Barbara J. Fields, *Slavery and Freedom on the Middle Ground: Maryland during the Nineteenth Century* (New Haven, 1985); Jacqueline Jones, *Labor of Love, Labor of Sorrow: Black Women, Work, and the Family from Slavery to the Present* (New York, 1985); Deborah Gray White, *Ar'n't I a Woman: Female Slaves in the Plantation South* (New York, 1985); Elizabeth Fox-Genovese, *Within the Plantation Household: Black and White Women of the Old South* (Chapel Hill, 1988); Peter J. Parish, *Slavery: History and Historians* (New York, 1989); Norrence T. Jones Jr., *Born a Child of Freedom, Yet a Slave: Mechanism of Control and Strategies of Resistance in Antebellum South Carolina* (Hanover, 1990).

22. "Slavery in Kansas," *Topeka Journal*, January 10, 1903, in Negroes—Clippings Volume, 29, Kansas State Historical Society Library; John Armstrong, "Reminiscences"; Testimonial of Marcus Linsey Freeman, typed manuscript, Slavery Collection, 1–3.

23. Governor Reeder, Diary, May 6, 1856, cited in Zu Adams, "Slaves," 17.

24. Mrs. E. E. Winchell to F. G. Adams, September 26, 1896; John Sedgwick Freeland, "The Slaves of Judge Rush Elmore," both in Zu Adams Collection of Letters, Slavery Collection. The Elmore slaves reportedly turned down tickets to freedom on the underground railroad in 1857–58, at the behest of Violet, only to be sent South with Mrs. Elmore in the spring of 1859. The Elmores, however, returned to their new home in Kansas.

25. Zu Adams, "Slaves," 9; "Negro Slavery in Douglas County," *Lawrence Journal-World*, March 13, 1933, in Negroes—Clippings Volume, Kansas State Historical Society Library, Topeka, Kansas, 36–38.

26. W. H. Mackey to George, March 26, 1902, Zu Adams Collection of Letters, Slavery Collection.

27. Reminiscences of Mrs. J. B. Abbott, DeSoto, September 1, 1895, Slavery Collection; "Slaves in Kansas," *Topeka Capital*, February 1897, in Negroes—Clippings Volume, Kansas State Historical Society Library, Topeka, Kansas, 217–18.

28. S. L. Adair to Zu Adams, September 16, 1895, and John Speer to Zu Adams, July 1895, both in Zu Adams Collection of Letters, Slavery Collection.

29. Zu Adams, "Slaves," 12, 16; Haag, "Slavery Agitation," 56.

30. John Speer to Zu Adams, July 1895, Zu Adams Collection of Letters, Slavery Collection; Zu Adams, "Slaves," 16; Haag, "Slavery Agitation," 56.

31. Testimonial of Marcus Linsey Freeman, 1–3.

32. R. G. Elliott, "Grasshopper Falls Convention and the Legislature of 1857," *Transactions* 10 (1907–8): 184.

33. Zu Adams, "Slaves," 8; Cory, "Slavery in Kansas," 236, "Negro Slavery in Douglas County," Slavery Collection.

34. Olive Owen, "Underground Railroad," Slavery Collection.

35. Armstrong, "Reminiscences," Slavery Collection, and Zu Adams, "Slaves," 10–11.

36. John Sedgwick Freeland, "The Slaves of Judge Rush Elmore," Slavery Collection; Zu Adams, "Slaves," 8.

37. Cory, "Slavery in Kansas," 241.

38. John Speer's Reminiscences of Jas Skaggs, July 13, 1895, Slavery Collection; Zu Adams, "Slaves," 9; "Negro Slavery in Douglas County," Slavery Collection.

39. Cory, "Slavery in Kansas," 236.

40. "Slavery in Kansas," *Topeka Journal,* January 10, 1903; "Negro Slavery in Douglas County," *Lawrence Journal-World,* March 13, 1933; Lydia Haag, "Slavery Agitation," 58.

41. Cory, "Slavery in Kansas," 236; Hurt, *Agriculture and Slavery,* 225–28; Bill of Sale dated January 1, 1857, in Zu Adams Collection of Letters, Slavery Collection.

42. Hurt, *Agriculture and Slavery,* 239.

43. Clayton's Report, 5.

44. Craik, "Southern Interest," 348, 398, 401.

45. Byrd to Jocelyn, July 5, 1856, and Finch to Jocelyn, July 10, 1856, both in AMA Archives.

46. Rawley, *Race and Politics,* 159.

47. Johnson, *The Battle Cry of Freedom,* 188–89.

48. Frothingham, "The Last Signs," 16.

7 Kansas Bleeds On

1. W. S. Jenks, "Some Unwritten History," Newspaper Clippings, Robinson Collection.

2. *American Missionary* 10 (October 1856): 94.

3. Jenks, "Some Unwritten History," Newspaper Clippings, Robinson Collection.

4. Byrd to Jocelyn, September 10, 1856, Finch to Jocelyn, September 15, 1856, both in AMA Archives.

5. *Herald of Freedom,* February 23, 1856.

6. Webb to Hyatt, September 24, 1856, Hyatt Collection.

7. Stampp, *America in 1857,* 147.

8. McPherson, *Battle Cry,* 155–57.

9. McPherson, *Battle Cry,* 157–62; Rawley, *Race and Politics,* 168–72.

10. Wilson, *Governor Charles Robinson,* 48.

11. Johnson, *The Battle Cry of Freedom,* 234–35.

12. Lawrence to S. G. Howe, December 22, 1856, NEEAC Papers; James H. Holmes to Brown, April 30, 1857, Brown Collection. See also Johnson, *The Battle Cry of Freedom*, 233–34.

13. Potter, *Impending Crisis*, 300–302; Stampp, *America in 1857*, 168; McPherson, *Battle Cry*, 162–64.

14. Adair to Jocelyn, July 2, 1857, AMA Archives.

15. Byrd to Jocelyn, October 16, 1857, AMA Archives.

16. Quotation taken from Robert W. Johannsen, "The Lecompton Constitutional Convention: An Analysis of its Membership," *Kansas Historical Quarterly* 33 (autumn 1957): 231.

17. Adair to Jocelyn, December 4, 1857, AMA Archives; emphasis in original.

18. Adair to Jocelyn, February 9, 1858, AMA Archives. On the Lecompton controversy, see Stampp, *America in 1857*, 266–94; McPherson, *Battle Cry*, 164–66; Rawley, *Race and Politics*, 214–17.

19. Rawley, *Race and Politics*, 248–52; McPherson, *Battle Cry*, 166–69.

20. Wilder, *Annals of Kansas*, 238.

21. Byrd to Jocelyn, April 6, 1858, AMA Archives; Robinson to Henry Wilson, May 12, 1858, Robinson Collection.

22. Robinson to Henry Wilson, May 12, 1858, Robinson Collection.

23. William Frank Zornow, *Kansas: A History of the Jayhawk State* (Norman, 1957), 82.

24. M. F. Conway to George L. Stearns, June 13, 1858, Brown Collection.

25. Wilder, *Annals of Kansas*, 257.

26. Byrd to Jocelyn, June 16 and August 13, 1859, AMA Archives.

8 A "Rehearsal for Redemption"?

1. Lawrence N. Powell, in his *New Masters: Northern Planters during the Civil War and Reconstruction* (New Haven, 1980), suggested that the experience of free labor experiments in the South after the Civil War may have served as a "rehearsal for redemption" (p. 150). Hyatt to [wife] Lilly, September 25 and 26, 1860, Hyatt Collection.

2. Cited in Carolyn Berneking, ed., "A Look at Early Lawrence: Letters from Robert Gaston Elliot," *Kansas Historical Quarterly* 43 (autumn 1977): 284–85.

3. *Topeka Journal*, April 1910, Leavenworth County Clippings, vol. 2 (1856–1921), and Anthony to Father, November 7, 1857, in vol. 5 (1950–61), 189–229, both in Kansas State Historical Society Library, Topeka, Kansas.

4. Northern planters who went South after the Civil War met with a somewhat similar reception from capital-starved planters. See Powell, *New Masters,*
35–39.

5. Quotation from Gladstone's description of those guilty of the Sack of Lawrence in May 1856, cited in Wilder, *Annals,* 163. Some of the choicest samples of
free-state descriptions of the Lecompton convention delegates occur in Johannsen, "The Lecompton Constitutional Convention." In that article, Johannsen's
collective portrait of the sixty convention members suggests that thirty-seven
were below the age of forty; forty-eight had been born in the slave states;
native Kentuckians outnumbered everyone else; thirty-four were Democrats;
and twenty had been Whigs in their pre-Kansas days.

6. "Incidents in the Life of Rush Elmore," manuscript compiled by Mildred
E. Duncan, Montgomery, Alabama, 1949, in the Kansas State Historical So-
ciety Library, Topeka, Kansas; John Martin, "Biographical Sketch of Judge
Rush Elmore," *Transactions* 8 (1903–4): 435–36.

7. "Kickapoo Ranger and Platte Granger," *Atchison Daily Globe,* July 10,
1909, in G. J. Remsburg Compiled Scrapbook, vol. 1, Kansas State Historical
Society Library, Topeka, Kansas, 235–36.

8. L. Ethan Ellis, "The Lecompton Constitution," *Journal of the Rutgers University Library* 3 (June 1940): 60–61. The New Brunswick Historical Club of
New Brunswick, N.J., returned the original constitution to the Kansas State
Historical Society in September 1957. See Johannsen, "The Lecompton Constitutional Convention," 244.

9. Robert W. Johannsen, "John Calhoun: The Villain of Territorial Kansas?"
Trail Guide 3 (September 1958): 1–19; Vindication by brother, A. H. Calhoun,
cited in *Transactions* 8 (1903–4): 1–2; *Dictionary of American Biography,* ed.
Allen Johnson, vol. 3 (New York, 1929), 411.

10. John H. Monnet, "Daniel Vanderslice: Kansas Territorial Indian Agent,"
Westport Historical Quarterly 2 (May 1966): 10–23; P. L. Gray, *Gray's Doniphan County History* (Bendena, Kans., 1905), part 2, 41; *Transactions* 10 (1907–
8): 278.

11. "Defense by Samuel D. Lecompte," *Transactions* 8 (1903–4): 389. See
also William E. Treadway, "The Gilded Age in Kansas," *Kansas Historical
Quarterly* 40 (spring 1974): 4–5.

12. Baltimore, "Benjamin Stringfellow: The Fight for Slavery on the Missouri Border," 16; Treadway, "The Gilded Age in Kansas," 1–37.

13. Names and list of incorporators/directors of the projects cited can be
found in the Lela E. Barnes Railroad Collection, 1855–1959 (microfilm edi-

tion), Manuscripts Division, Kansas State Historical Society, Topeka, Kansas; hereinafter cited as Barnes Collection.

14. *Squatter Sovereign,* November 22, 1856.

15. William E. Connelley, *A Standard History of Kansas and Kansans,* vol. 1 (Chicago, 1918), 378–83.

16. Finch to Jocelyn, February 28, 1855, AMA Archives; *Herald of Freedom,* January 13 and 6, 1855.

17. Paul W. Gates, *Fifty Million Acres: Conflicts over Kansas Land Policy, 1854–1890* (Ithaca, 1954), 50.

18. Ibid., 19–22.

19. Ibid., 22–23.

20. Wilson, *Governor Charles Robinson,* 56.

21. L. L. Waters, *Steel Rails to Santa Fe* (Lawrence, Kans., 1950), 9–24.

22. *Herald of Freedom,* October 6, 1855.

23. Ibid., February 24, 1855.

24. Byrd to Jocelyn, July 7, 1855, AMA Archives.

25. Hyatt, "Thaddeus Hyatt's Reply to the Leavenworth Manifesto," August 1860; "Hyatt's Letters from Kansas: An Appeal and an Apology, No 1," Hyatt Collection.

26. Johnson, *The Battle Cry for Freedom,* 246.

27. Pomeroy to Thaddeus Hyatt, May 18, 1857, Hyatt Collection; Beckman, "The Overland Trade," 152.

28. Gates, *Fifty Million Acres,* 133.

29. Beckman, "Atchison's First Railroad," *Kansas Historical Quarterly* 31 (autumn 1954): 153–65.

30. Pomeroy to Hyatt, August 6, 1857, Hyatt Collection.

31. Beckman, "Atchison's First Railroad," 153–65; untitled announcement in Barnes Railroad Collection.

32. Gates, *Fifty Million Acres,* 115.

33. Pomeroy to Hyatt, February 17, 1859, Hyatt Collection.

34. Gates, *Fifty Million Acres,* 133–139.

35. Treadway, "The Gilded Age in Kansas," 10–11; Waters, *Steel Trails to Santa Fe,* 26–27.

36. George L. Anderson, *The Widening Stream: The Exchange National Bank of Atchison, 1858–1968* (Atchison, 1968), 8–9.

37. Pomeroy to Hyatt, February 17 and March 6, 1859, Hyatt Collection.

38. Gates, *Fifty Million Acres,* 78–79, 94.

39. Robinson to Sara, September 13, 1857, Robinson Collection.

40. Pomeroy to Hyatt, March 6, 1859, Hyatt Collection.

41. Pomeroy to Hyatt, February 17 and March 6, 1859, Hyatt Collection; Anderson, *The Widening Stream*, 10.

42. Gates, *Fifty Million Acres*, 114–16.

43. Samuel C. Smith to Robinson, December 19, 1858, Robinson to Hutchinson, December 31, 1858, both in Robinson Collection. On the attempt of Lawrence leaders to make their town a railroad hub, see I. E. Quastler, *The Railroads of Lawrence, Kansas, 1854–1900: A Case Study in the Causes and Consequences of an Unsuccessful American Urban Railroad Program* (Lawrence, 1979).

44. Robinson to Sara Robinson, January 6, 1859, Robinson Collection.

45. Gates, *Fifty Million Acres*, 113–118, 122, 125–127; Zornow, *Kansas*, 97–98.

46. Foner, *Politics and Ideology*, 97–127; C. Vann Woodward, *Origins of the New South, 1877–1913* (Baton Rouge, 1951). On the Woodward thesis and its critics, see note 53 below.

47. Foner, *Politics and Ideology*, 127; *Reconstruction: America's Unfinished Revolution* (New York, 1988), 29; Powell, *New Masters*, 73, 78–80, 117–18.

48. Smith, *Virgin Land*, 159.

49. Rawley, *Race and Politics*, 85.

50. *Thirteenth Annual Report of the AMA* (1859), AMA Archives.

51. Potter, *Impending Crisis*, 217–19.

52. Powell, *New Masters*.

53. C. Vann Woodward, *Reunion and Reaction: The Compromise of 1877 and the End of Reconstruction* (Boston, 1951), and *Origins of the New South*. To the query posed in Allen Peskin's article, "Was There a Compromise of 1877?" *Journal of American History* 60 (June 1973): 63–73, Woodward responded with an article entitled "Yes, There Was a Compromise of 1877," 215–23. Other challenges to Woodward's version of the 1877 Compromise include Carl V. Harris, "Right Fork or Left Fork? The Section-Party Alignments of Southern Democrats in Congress, 1873–1877," *Journal of Southern History* 42 (November 1976): 471–506; Michael Les Benedict, "Southern Democrats in the Crisis of 1876–1877: A Reconsideration of *Reunion and Reaction*," *Journal of Southern History* 46 (November 1980): 489–524; Keith Ian Polakoff, *The Politics of Inertia: The Election of 1876 and the End of Reconstruction* (Baton Rouge, 1973).

Woodward's thesis that the postbellum ascendancy of a new class of business-oriented bourgeoisie in the South marked a sharp departure from that section's pre–Civil War historical experience has also been called into question. Detractors have emphasized the continuity of Southern history—whether in terms of the persistence of racism, of economic themes and bourgeois relations, or the survival of the prewar agrarian elite. Nevertheless, Woodward's essential point still stands: namely that the New South's leadership included a relatively large proportion of Whiggish types, who—whatever their genealogies or social origins—shared the bourgeois outlook of Northern capitalists and sought to bring their section's economic profile in line with that of the North, although they may not have been prepared to embrace the social changes linked with modernization, any more than their alleged planter-foes were. Two excellent perspectives on the debate between Woodward and his critics include Harold D. Woodman, "Economic Reconstruction and the Rise of the New South, 1865–1900," in *Interpreting Southern History*, 254–307; and James C. Cobb, "Beyond Planters and Industrialists: A New Perspective on the New South," *Journal of Southern History* 54 (February 1988): 45–68. See also Woodward's response to his critics in *Thinking Back: The Perils of Writing History* (Baton Rouge, 1986).

Index

Abbott, J. B., 95, 77, 101, 124; and Wakarusa War, 103–4; and UGRR, 126

Abell, Peter T., 8, 33, 144, 152; founds Atchison, 31; slave of, 125; and the courts free-state business, 139, 149; and railroads, 151

Abolitionism and abolitionists, 82, 89, 103, 109, 112, 114; Garrisonian, 3, 18–19, 21, 113; evangelical, 10–11, 21; and NEEAC, 17–19; opposition to, in Missouri, 33; persecution of, in Kansas, 63–64; in proslavery rhetoric, 93, 107; and Big Springs convention, 99; and violent means, 111–15; size of average congregation, 156; defined, 161 (n. 4). *See also* Antislavery; American Missionary Association (AMA)

Adair, Florella, 25–26, 56; relationship with John Brown, 65; and UGRR, 66

Adair, Samuel L.: receives AMA appointment, 25; joins NEEAC colony, 25–26; and pioneer life, 47, 56–57, 59; and Ottawa Indians, 57; on free-soil racism, 64; and UGRR, 66; on Southern and western emigrants, 89; in territorial politics, 97; on "bogus" authorities, 98; on Wakarusa War, 106–7; on sack of Lawrence, 110; and John Brown, 111; on Pottawatomie massacre, 112–13; on Kansas slaves, 124; and sack of Osawatomie, 130; on Governor Walker, 134; on Lecompton constitution, 135

Adams, Charles Francis, 15

Adkins, Jim, 142

African Americans: sectional truce at expense of, 5, 138, 154–55, 157; and NEEAC, 18–19, 87, 88–89; and AMA, 21, 65–67, 87–88; Missourian attitudes toward, 32, 37, 42; as free women pioneers, 47; and free-soil racism, 64; and UGRR, 65–67, 124, 125–26; education of, in Kansas, 70, 88; and free labor ideology, 88, 154–55, 156–57; exclusion of, from Kansas, 99–100; and proslavery organized emigration to Kansas, 117. *See also* Slaves, in Kansas

Alabama and Alabamians, 110, 112, 116–17, 128, 141. *See also* South and Southerners